WORLD FOOTBALL RECORDS

Published in 2020 by Welbeck

An Imprint of Welbeck Non-Fiction Limited, part of Welbeck Publishing Group.

20 Mortimer Street London W1T 3JW

ISBN: 978-1-78739-439-1

Project Editor: Ross Hamilton
Design: Amazing 15, Stephen Cary, Luke Griffin
Picture research: Paul Langan
Production: Rachel Burgess

Printed in Slovenia

WORLD FOOTBALL RECORDS

FIFA OFFICIAL LICENSED PUBLICATION

TWELFTH EDITION

KEIR RADNEDGE

WELBECK

CONTENTS

INTRODUCTION 6

THE COUNTRIES 8

EUROPE 10

SOUTH AMERICA 84

AFRICA 102

ASIA & OCEANIA 112

CONCACAF 126

FIFA WORLD CUP™ 134

INTRODUCTION

Football's astonishing power has been built on simplicity, popularity and an ability to lift fans around the world out of the pressures and problems of their everyday lives. The superstar players are heroes, role models and inspirations to millions. That magic was more important than ever as the world's number-one sport shouldered its responsibilities in the midst of the COVID-19 pandemic.

The next pinnacle for the unified global game will be the FIFA World Cup finals in Qatar in 2022. Before then comes the rescheduled UEFA European Championship in 12 venues around Europe, as well as the *Copa América* plus a host of other continental events built on the foundation of the multitude of regional and national leagues and cups.

Football boasts a unique, mesmeric power in its matrix of team tradition and individual brilliance. Personification has been evident over the past decade in the goalscoring and trophy-winning achievements of Portugal's Cristiano Ronaldo and Argentina's Lionel Messi. One of the great fascinations of the year to come will be analysing the potential successors to their crowns. Will French 2018 World Cup-winner Kylian Mbappé lead the way, or are there other teenage talents about to explode on the game?

The age-group tournaments organised by world football's governing body provide a high-profile ladder for the finest young players from all six confederations. The men now also find themselves having to compete for media attention with the stars of the women's game, whose worldwide development is growing ever more significant.

All these many aspects of the grand football landscape feature in this latest, 12th edition of *World Football Records*. Here are the achievements and stars, old and new, from all of football's major international tournaments for men and women at senior and junior levels... and maybe those superstars of tomorrow as well.

Keir Radnedge
London, July 2020

THE COUNTRIES

The history of football is a long and illustrious journey, which has seen the beautiful game reach every corner of the planet.

Football is known as the global game. It knows no boundaries of politics or religion or race, and at its heart is a simple structure that has worked effectively for around 120 years.

At the head of the global football pyramid is FIFA, the world governing body. Supporting FIFA's work are national associations in 211 countries, across the six regional geographical confederations: Africa, Asia, Europe, Oceania, South America, and the Caribbean, Central and North America. These associations not only field the national teams who have built sporting history, but they also oversee the growth of football in their countries, from professional leagues to grassroots.

It was England and Scotland that played the first international football in the late 19th century; the British Home Championship followed, laying the foundations for international tournaments to come, with the *Copa América* of South America and FIFA World Cup following in 1916 and 1930 respectively.

Football's popularity has created an intense appetite for new competitions such as the Nations League and an expanded FIFA Club World Cup. Events of the past year have increased the focus on the development of the international calendar, particularly with an awareness of the adjustments needed ahead of the winter FIFA World Cup in Qatar in 2022.

CONCACAF
Founded: 1961
Associations: 35 (+6 non-FIFA members)
Headquarters: Miami, United States

CONMEBOL
Founded: 1916
Associations: 10
Headquarters: Luque, Paraguay

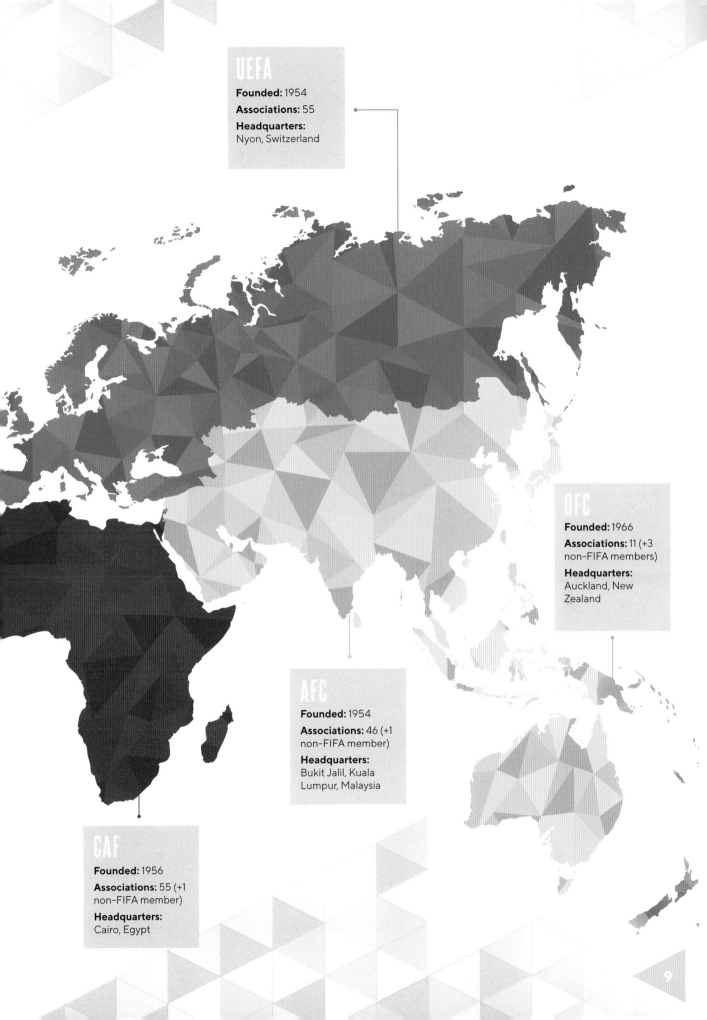

UEFA
Founded: 1954
Associations: 55
Headquarters:
Nyon, Switzerland

OFC
Founded: 1966
Associations: 11 (+3
non-FIFA members)
Headquarters:
Auckland, New
Zealand

AFC
Founded: 1954
Associations: 46 (+1
non-FIFA member)
Headquarters:
Bukit Jalil, Kuala
Lumpur, Malaysia

CAF
Founded: 1956
Associations: 55 (+1
non-FIFA member)
Headquarters:
Cairo, Egypt

EUROPE

European teams have dominated the world game at both national team and club levels over the past decade.

UEFA

Confederation founded: 1954

Number of associations: 55

Headquarters: Nyon, Switzerland

Most continental championship wins: Germany, Spain (three)

55

There are **55 full member associations** of UEFA, the governing body of European football.

The 1968 UEFA European Championship semi-final between Italy and the USSR was decided by a **coin toss**. The Italian captain, Giacinto Facchetti, guessed correctly to seal his side's progress to the final.

99

Cristiano Ronaldo has scored more international goals, 99, than any other European player.

RONALDO

The finals of the 2020 UEFA European Championship were deferred until the summer of 2021 because of the COVID-19 pandemic. The competition has retained the same name and will be played in a one-off system with 12 venues to mark the 60th anniversary of the first UEFA European Championship (then the European Nations Cup). **Wembley** will host the semi-finals and final as well as four other matches.

Despite not qualifying for the 1992 UEFA European Championship, Denmark won the tournament. Group runners-up in qualifying, the Danes were drafted into the tournament after the team that pipped them to qualification, Yugoslavia, were excluded.

ENGLAND

England is where football began; the country where the game was first developed, which saw the creation of the game's first football association and the first organised league, and which now plays host to the richest domestic league in the world.

Joined FIFA: 1905
Biggest win:
13-0 v. Ireland, 1882
Highest FIFA ranking: 3rd
Home stadium: Wembley Stadium, London
Honours: 1 FIFA World Cup (1966)

NATIONAL LEGEND
NEW SOUTHGATE, NEW HOPE

England enjoyed their best FIFA World Cup performance since 1990 at Russia 2018. Their manager was **Gareth Southgate**, the former England defender who missed the decisive penalty in the 1996 UEFA European Championship semi-final against Germany. In 2018, however, he guided England to their biggest victory at a FIFA World Cup, a 6-1 cruise past Panama in the group stage. They went on to finish fourth, losing 2-1 to Croatia after extra-time in their semi-final and then 2-0 to Belgium in the play-off for third place. Southgate's squad was the second-youngest in Russia and became the first England team to win a FIFA World Cup penalty shoot-out, at the fourth time of asking.

SOUTHGATE

201
Peter Crouch is England's tallest ever player at 201cm, or 6 foot 7 inches.

NATIONAL LEGEND
CAPTAINS COURAGEOUS

The international careers of Billy Wright and **Bobby Moore**, who both captained England a record 90 times, very nearly overlapped. Wright, of Wolverhampton Wanderers, played for England between 1946 and 1959, and West Ham United's Moore from 1962 to 1973. Moore remains England's youngest captain, having been 22 years and 47 days old when appointed against Czechoslovakia on 29 May 1963. He also remains the only man to have lifted the FIFA World Cup for England, after West Germany were beaten 4-2 at Wembley on 30 July 1966.

41
The oldest player to make his debut for England remains Alexander Morten, who was 41 years and 114 days old when he captained England against Scotland on 8 March 1873 in their first home game.

MOORE

HISTORIC MOMENT
IN THE BEGINNING

The day it all began... 30 November 1872, when England played their first official international, against Scotland, at Hamilton Crescent, Partick. The result was a 0-0 draw in front of a then-massive crowd of 4,000, who each paid an admission fee of one shilling (5p). Teams representing England and Scotland had actually played five times before, but most of the Scottish players had been based in England and the matches are considered unofficial. England's team for the first official game was selected by Charles Alcock, the secretary of The Football Association. His one regret was that, because of injury, he could not pick himself to play.

5

Five sons of former England internationals have earned caps for their country. The last was Alex Oxlade-Chamberlain, 28 years after the last of his father Mark Chamberlain's eight appearances.

BECKHAM

DISCIPLINARY
NAUGHTY BOYS

Raheem Sterling's red card against Ecuador in June 2014 was the 15th for an England player in a full international. Alan Mullery was the first England player to be dismissed, against Yugoslavia in June 1968. **David Beckham** and Wayne Rooney were both been sent off – both picked up red cards in FIFA World Cup knockout matches – and Paul Scholes was the only England player to be sent off at the old Wembley Stadium, against Sweden in June 1999. Sterling was dropped for England's UEFA EURO 2020 qualifier against Montenegro in November 2019 after a training-camp clash with Joe Gomez following a fiery match between their clubs Manchester City and Liverpool. It came after Sterling had scored eight goals in his last eight internationals – having scored only twice in his first 45 England appearances.

MOST APPEARANCES:
1 **Peter Shilton**, 125
2 **Wayne Rooney**, 120
3 **David Beckham**, 115
4 **Steven Gerrard**, 114
5 **Bobby Moore**, 108

6-3
Hungary's 6-3 win at Wembley in 1953 was the first time England had lost at home to continental opposition.

SCORING RECORD
SPURRED ON TO GLORY

Many England fans felt their team was cursed when it came to penalty shoot-outs, following spot-kick defeats to Germany in the 1990 FIFA World Cup and 1996 UEFA European Championship semi-finals, and to Portugal in the 2004 UEFA European Championship and 2006 FIFA World Cup quarter-finals. Yet they turned the tide by beating Colombia on penalties in the round of 16 at Russia 2018, en route to finishing fourth – they then repeated the trick against Switzerland to clinch third place in the following summer's inaugural UEFA Nations League. Everton goalkeeper Jordan Pickford was among the heroes on each occasion, not only saving a penalty each time but also scoring one against the Swiss. Midfielder Eric Dier struck England's decisive final spot kick on both occasions. Dier's club Tottenham Hotspur have provided England with more players than any other side, with fellow midfielder Harry Winks becoming the 78th in October 2017. England's third, fourth and sixth top scorers – Gary Lineker, **Jimmy Greaves** and current captain Harry Kane – are all Spurs legends, with Greaves (44 goals in 57 games) holding the England record for hat-tricks (six) while Lineker is the country's leading FIFA World Cup goalscorer, with ten across the 1986 and 1990 finals.

GREAVES

STAR PLAYER
FAST STARTS

Bryan Robson holds records for England's fastest goal in the FIFA World Cup – after 27 seconds in a 3-1 win against France in 1982 – and at the old Wembley Stadium, netting after 38 seconds in a 2-1 friendly victory over Yugoslavia in 1989. Robson scored three of England's 12 quickest goals. Tottenham Hotspur striker Teddy Sheringham scored England's quickest goal after coming on as a substitute. His first touch, a header 15 seconds into a substitute appearance, brought England level with Greece in a 2002 FIFA World Cup qualifier at Old Trafford, in October 2001.

STONES

MAGUIRE

SCORING RECORD
GAME OF STONES

No England defender had ever scored more than one FIFA World Cup goal until Manchester City centre-back **John Stones** managed two in 32 first-half minutes against Panama in Nizhny Novgorod in 2018. Three games later, in the quarter-final against Sweden, fellow centre-back **Harry Maguire** also got on the scoresheet, netting the first in a 2-0 win. Neither man had scored for England before Russia 2018. Maguire had only received his first international call-up in August 2017, having gone to UEFA EURO 2016 in France as an England fan with friends. Maguire later became the world's most expensive defender when he joined Manchester United for GBP 80 million in 2019.

NATIONAL LEGEND
GRAND OLD MAN

Stanley Matthews became England's oldest-ever player when he lined up at outside-right against Denmark on 15 May 1957 at the age of 42 years 104 days. That was 22 years and 229 days after his first appearance. Matthews was also England's oldest marksman. He was 41 years eight months old when he scored against Northern Ireland on 10 October 1956. In stark contrast to Matthews's longest England career, full-back Martin Kelly holds the record for the shortest – a two-minute substitute appearance in a 1-0 friendly win over Norway in 2012.

STAR PLAYERS
THE KIDS ARE ALRIGHT

England's youngest debutant remains then-Arsenal winger Theo Walcott, who was just 17 years and 75 days old when he faced Hungary on 30 May 2006. Chelsea forward Callum Hudson-Odoi became the youngest man to make his debut in a competitive match for England, coming on as a substitute in a 5-0 victory over the Czech Republic in a March 2019 qualifier for the 2020 UEFA European Championship – aged just 18 years and 135 days. This made him 40 days younger than Duncan Edwards had been when he debuted against Scotland in the British Home Championship on 2 April 1955.

England have hit double figures five times: beating Ireland 13-0 and 13-2 in 1882 and 1899, thrashing Austria 11-1 in 1908, crushing Portugal 10-0 in 1947, and then routing the United States 10-0 in 1964.

TOP SCORERS:

1 Wayne Rooney, 53
2 Bobby Charlton, 49
3 Gary Lineker, 48
4 Jimmy Greaves, 44
5 Michael Owen, 40

ROONEY

TOURNAMENT TRIVIA
ROON AT THE TOP

When **Wayne Rooney** scored against Macedonia in September 2003, he became England's youngest goalscorer at the age of 17 years and 317 days – and it long seemed only a matter of time before he broke Sir Bobby Charlton's record 49-goal haul. He drew level thanks to a penalty against San Marino in September 2015, and then reached his half-century with another spot kick, against Switzerland, three days later. Rooney's 100th cap in November 2014, at the age of 29 years and 22 days, made him the youngest man to rack up a century of appearances for England. He retired from international football in August 2017 but made a brief return as a substitute on 15 November 2018, against the United States, for a farewell 120th appearance.

SCORING RECORD
SHARED RESPONSIBILITY

Substitutions meant the captain's armband passed between four different players during England's 2-1 friendly win over Serbia and Montenegro on 3 June 2003. Regular captain David Beckham was missing, so Michael Owen led the team out, but was substituted at half-time. England's second-half skippers were Owen's then-Liverpool team-mates Emile Heskey and Jamie Carragher, and Manchester United's Phil Neville. The first time three different players captained England in one FIFA World Cup finals match was a goalless draw against Morocco in 1986, when first-choice skipper Bryan Robson went off injured, his vice-captain Ray Wilkins was then sent off, and goalkeeper Peter Shilton took over leadership duties.

1

Claude Ashton equalled a record when he captained England on his only international appearance – a 0-0 draw against Northern Ireland in Belfast on 24 October 1925. It had previously been done by Arthur Knight, Max Woosnam and Graham Doggart

35

Striker Jermain Defoe came on as a substitute 35 times for England – more often than any other player in England's history – between his debut in 2004 and his final appearance in 2017.

TOURNAMENT TRIVIA
ROLL UP, ROLL UP

The highest attendance for an England game came at Hampden Park in Glasgow on 17 April 1937, when 149,547 spectators saw Scotland win 3-1 in the British Home Championship. By contrast, only 2,378 turned up in Bologna, Italy, to see San Marino stun England and take the lead after just seven seconds on 17 November 1993. A 7-1 victory for Graham Taylor's side was not enough to secure England a place at the 1994 FIFA World Cup.

7-1
England's biggest defeat came against Hungary in 1954. They lost 7-1.

STAR PLAYER
NEW KING KANE

Centre-forward **Harry Kane** – who scored 79 seconds into his international debut as a substitute against Lithuania in March 2015 – went into the 2018 FIFA World Cup as England's new permanent captain and ended it as the nation's first FIFA World Cup Golden Boot winner since Gary Lineker in 1986. His six goals included a hat-trick in a 6-1 first-round victory over Panama, making him only the third England player to score a FIFA World Cup treble after Sir Geoff Hurst in the 1966 final and Lineker in 1986. In November 2018, Kane's late winner secured a 2-1 victory over Croatia at Wembley and clinched England's place in the following summer's inaugural UEFA Nations League finals. In 2019, he scored 12 goals in ten England appearances to equal the calendar-year records of George Hilsdon in 1908 and Dixie Dean in 1927. Kane's strikes included the only back-to-back England hat-tricks at Wembley, against Bulgaria and Montenegro – the Montenegro game being England's 1,000th international, when he became the nation's highest-scoring captain.

KANE

NATIONAL LEGEND
WONDERFUL WALTER

Walter Winterbottom was England's first full-time manager and he remains both the longest-serving (with 138 games in charge) and the youngest, aged just 33 when he took the job in 1946. The former teacher and Manchester United player led his country to four FIFA World Cups, from their first appearance in 1950, to the 1962 tournament in Chile.

WINTERBOTTOM

FRANCE

With two world titles and a rich history of helping to develop the game, *Les Bleus* are footballing heavyweights and current FIFA World Cup holders

Joined FIFA: 1907

Biggest win:
10-0 v. Azerbaijan, 1995

Highest FIFA ranking: 1st

Home stadium:
Stade de France,
Saint Denis

Honours:
2 FIFA World Cups (1998, 2018), 2 UEFA European Championships (1984, 2000)

MBAPPÉ

FRANCE AND FIFA
Jules Rimet – FIFA president from 1921 to 1954 – was the driving force behind the creation of the FIFA World Cup and the first version of the trophy was named in his honour.

STAR PLAYER
IN FOR THE KYL
France won their second FIFA World Cup in July 2018, 20 years after their first. Nineteen-year-old **Kylian Mbappé** scored their last goal in the 4-2 final triumph over Croatia, and was named the best young player of the tournament. Mbappé also became the second teenager to score in the final of the FIFA World Cup, following Pelé against Sweden in 1958, and with his strike against Peru in the group stage, he also became France's youngest scorer at a major tournament at the age of just 19 years and 183 days. Mbappé moved from AS Monaco to Paris Saint-Germain in the summer of 2017 in a deal worth EUR 180m.

7
Seven French players have won the FIFA World Cup, UEFA European Championship and UEFA Champions League: Didier Deschamps, Marcel Desailly, Christian Karembeu, Bixente Lizarazu, Fabien Barthez Thierry Henry and Zinédine Zidane.

STAR PLAYER
GRIEZ LIGHTNING
Striker **Antoine Griezmann** won the 2016 UEFA European Championship Golden Boot as the six-goal top scorer as well as the Golden Ball as the best player for good measure. France lost the final 1-0 to Portugal, but two years later Griezmann's four goals helped France win the 2018 FIFA World Cup. His tally included three penalties, with one in the final giving his team a 2-1 lead over Croatia. Griezmann's FIFA World Cup triumph came just weeks after he scored twice in Atlético's 3-0 defeat of Marseille in the UEFA Europa League final.

GRIEZMANN

MANAGER RECORD
WORLD CUP COMEDOWN
France have enjoyed mixed fortunes since winning their second FIFA World Cup in 2018. They became the sixth consecutive world champions to fail to win their first game since lifting the trophy when they were held to a goalless draw by Germany in their opening UEFA Nations League clash in September 2018. France did at least go four matches without defeat though, the best record of any world champions since the French team of 20 years earlier. This run included 2-1 victories in the UEFA Nations League over both the Netherlands and Germany. The Dutch won 2-0 in the return game in Rotterdam to clinch a place at the UEFA Nations League finals, but France ended 2019 on a high, finishing top of their UEFA EURO 2020 qualifying group.

NATIONAL LEGEND
KOPA – FRANCE'S FIRST SUPERSTAR

Raymond Kopa was France's first international superstar. Born into a family of Polish immigrants (his family name was Kopaszewski) on 13 October 1931, he was instrumental in Reims's championship successes of the mid-1950s. He later joined Real Madrid and, in 1956, became the first French player to claim a European Cup winner's medal. He was also the playmaker of the France team that finished third at the 1958 FIFA World Cup, his performances for his country that year earning him the European Footballer of the Year award. Kopa's death, aged 85, on 3 March 2017 was met with sadness around the world.

KOPA

UMTITI BOOM

In 2016, Samuel Umtiti became the first outfield player to make his French international debut at a major tournament since Gabriel De Michèle at the 1966 FIFA World Cup. Umtiti came on in *Les Bleus*' 5-2 victory against Iceland.

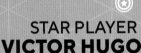

STAR PLAYER
VICTOR HUGO

Hugo Lloris has worn the captain's armband more than any other Frenchman. He lifted the FIFA World Cup Trophy in June 2018 in his 104th appearance for his country and his 80th as skipper. Yet it took some time for Lloris to be given the honour. After Patrice Evra lost the captaincy in 2010, new coach Laurent Blanc tried three captains during qualification for UEFA EURO 2012 before turning to Lloris, who was given the job permanently in February 2012.

LLORIS

PLATINI

HIDALGO

MANAGER RECORD
MICHEL, MICHEL

Michel Hidalgo, who died aged 87 in March 2020, was the first coach to lead France to glory at a major tournament when the hosts won the UEFA European Championship in 1984, helped in no small part by captain **Michel Platini**'s haul of nine goals. Platini would later coach France at UEFA EURO 1992, help to organise the 1998 FIFA World Cup in his home country, and serve as UEFA President between 2007 and 2015. Hidalgo was the first man to reach 75 games in charge of France, although this was later surpassed by both Raymond Domenech, whose 79 games included a run to the 2006 FIFA World Cup final, and Didier Deschamps.

ZIDANE

17

NATIONAL LEGEND
DESAILLY: JE SUIS UN ROCK STAR

Despite having been born in the Ghanaian capital of Accra, **Marcel Desailly** always insisted he only ever wanted to play for France – the country he moved to as a four-year-old – and he duly became the nation's most-capped player in 2003. He retired the following year with a then-record of 116 international appearances, although this was later passed by frequent team-mate Lilian Thuram. Desailly, a commanding presence at either centre-back or in midfield that saw him dubbed "The Rock", not only won both the 1998 FIFA World Cup and 2000 UEFA European Championship with France, but he was also the first player to win the UEFA Champions League in successive seasons with different clubs – with Marseille in 1993, and then with AC Milan the following year.

DESCHAMPS

17

Fabien Barthez holds his country's record for the most FIFA World Cup finals appearances, 17 between 1998 and 2006.

NATIONAL LEGEND
DESCHAMPS THE MULTIPLE CHAMP

Didier Deschamps is one of only three men to have won the FIFA World Cup as a player and manager, together with Brazil's Mário Zagallo in 1958 and 1970 and Franz Beckenbauer with West Germany in 1974 and 1990. Defensive midfielder Deschamps captained France in 1998 and in 2000 for their UEFA European Championship triumph, and retired after winning 103 caps – 55 as captain. He became national team head coach in 2012, leading his side to the UEFA EURO 2016 final on home soil, where they lost 1–0 to Portugal, before lifting the 2018 FIFA World Cup with a 4–2 victory over Croatia in Moscow. He now holds the French record for most victories as a manager, with his 65th coming in a 2–0 win over Albania in November 2019. It was a double landmark for Deschamps as it came in his 100th international at the helm.

EARNING THEIR STRIPES

France are the only country to play at a FIFA World Cup while wearing another team's kit. At Argentina 1978, *Les Bleus* were forced to wear the green-and-white stripes of a local club side, Atlético Kimberley, after a colours mix-up with Hungary.

BARTHEZ

NATIONAL LEGEND
LILIAN IN THE PINK

Lilian Thuram made his 142nd and final appearance for France in their defeat by Italy at UEFA EURO 2008. The defender's international career had spanned nearly 14 years since his debut against the Czech Republic in August 1994. Thuram played his club football for Monaco, Parma, Juventus and Barcelona before retiring in the summer of 2008 because of a heart problem. He was also one of the stars of France's 1998 FIFA World Cup-winning side, scoring both goals in their semi-final victory over Croatia: the only international goals of his career.

100

STAR PLAYER
GIROUD AWAKENING

IIn June 2017 against Paraguay, Olivier Giroud became the first Frenchman to hit an international hat-trick since winger Dominique Rocheteau in a 6-0 win against Luxembourg 32 years earlier. Giroud joined Zinédine Zidane as France's joint-fourth top scorer after scoring against Colombia and the Republic of Ireland in early 2018. Giroud finished the 2016 UEFA European Championship as joint-second top scorer with three goals, but at the 2018 FIFA World Cup, Giroud was not credited with a single shot on target, despite featuring In all of France's seven games en route to picking up a winner's medal.

NATIONAL LEGEND
HENRY BENCHED

Thierry Henry did not play in the 1998 FIFA World Cup final because of Marcel Desailly's red card. Henry, France's leading goalscorer in the finals with three, was a substitute and coach Aimé Jacquet planned to use him late in the game. But Desailly's sending-off forced a re-think: Jacquet instead reinforced his midfield with future Arsenal team-mate Patrick Vieira going on instead, leaving Henry as an unused substitute. But Henry does have the distinction of being the only Frenchman to play at four different FIFA World Cups (1998, 2002, 2006 and 2010). He also passed Michel Platini's all-time goal-scoring record for France with a brace against Lithuania in October 2007.

HENRY

SO NEAR YET SO VAR

Antoine Griezmann became the first man to have an international goal disallowed by the intervention of a video assistant referee when he was judged to be offside after finding the net against Spain in March 2017, a match Spain won 2-0.

NATIONAL LEGEND
NO TIME FOR FONTAINE

Former striker **Just Fontaine** spent the shortest ever spell in charge of the French team. He took over on 22 March 1967 and left on 3 June after two defeats in friendlies. More happily, he still holds the record for the most goals at a single FIFA World Cup – 13 across the six games he played at the 1958 tournament, including four in France's 6-3 victory over West Germany to finish third. He remains the only Frenchman to score a FIFA World Cup hat-trick.

POGBA

STAR PLAYER
POGBA POWER

Dynamic midfielder and captain **Paul Pogba** spearheaded France to glory at the FIFA U-20 World Cup in Turkey in 2013, as they became the first country to complete a grand slam of FIFA 11-a-side international men's titles. This followed triumphs in the FIFA World Cup (1998), the FIFA U-17 World Cup (2001) and the Olympic Games (1984). In 2013, Pogba was among those who scored from the spot as Uruguay were beaten 4-1 on penalties in the final following a goalless draw. He was also on the scoresheet in the 4-2 win over Croatia in the 2018 FIFA World Cup final, two years after briefly becoming the world's most expensive footballer with a GBP 90m move from Juventus to Manchester United – whom he had left on a free transfer in 2012.

GERMANY

1993
Germany ended 2014 at the top of the FIFA/Coca-Cola World Ranking – the first time they had occupied this position in December since 1993, when the ranking was originally introduced.

Germany are almost ever-presents in the closing stages of major tournaments. Their 2014 success ended an 18-year trophy drought and was their first FIFA World Cup success as a reunified nation after winning in 1954, 1974 and 1990 as West Germany.

Joined FIFA: 1908
Biggest win:
16-0 v. Russia, 1912
Highest FIFA ranking: 1st
Home stadium:
(rotation)
Honours:
4 FIFA World Cups (1954, 1974, 1990, 2014),
3 UEFA European Championships (1972, 1980, 1996)

30

Philipp Lahm shocked the international football world when he retired aged just 30 after winning the FIFA World Cup in 2014.

SCORING RECORD
KLOSE ENCOUNTERS

In 2014, **Miroslav Klose** became the third player, after Uwe Seeler and Pelé, to score in four FIFA World Cup final competitions. After strikes in 2002, 2006 and 2010, his first goal in 2014 – an equaliser against Ghana – put him alongside former Brazil star Ronaldo at the top of the all-time FIFA World Cup scoring charts. And it was against the Brazilians that Klose would later push out ahead on his own. His 24 appearances left him behind only compatriot Lothar Matthäus (25), but Klose's 17 wins were one more than previous record-holder Cafu, of Brazil. Klose retired in 2014 as Germany's all-time leading scorer, with 71 goals in 137 matches – and his team-mates never lost an international in which he found the net.

KLOSE

TOP SCORERS:
1 Miroslav Klose, 71
2 Gerd Müller, 68
3 Lukas Podolski, 49
4 Jürgen Klinsmann, 47
= Rudi Völler, 47

BECKENBAUER

NATIONAL LEGEND
DER KAISER

Franz Beckenbauer is widely regarded as the greatest player in German football history. He defined the role of attacking sweeper, first in the 1970 FIFA World Cup finals, and then as West Germany won the 1972 UEFA European Championship and the 1974 FIFA World Cup. Beckenbauer later delivered a FIFA World Cup final appearance in 1986 as an inexperienced coach, and the 1990 trophy in his final game in charge. He later became President of Bayern Munich, the club he captained to three consecutive European Cup victories between 1974 and 1976. He also led Germany's successful bid for the 2006 FIFA World Cup finals and headed the organising committee.

TOURNAMENT TRIVIA
SAMBA SILENCED

Germany's 1-0 win over Argentina in 2014 came in their record eighth FIFA World Cup Final, this coming after they were the first side to reach four consecutive semi-finals. But their 7-1 semi-final humiliation of Brazil may well live longest in the memory – and the record books. Germany led 5-0 at half-time in what became the biggest FIFA World Cup semi-final win and the hosts' heaviest defeat. Other FIFA World Cup finals records include: Germany were the first team to score four goals in six minutes, and Toni Kroos, whose two goals in 69 seconds is the fastest brace, is the only FIFA World Cup winner born in East Germany. Thomas Müller's opening goal was also Germany's 2,000th in full internationals.

NATIONAL LEGEND
KEEPING A LÖW PROFILE

In 2014, **Joachim Löw** became the 19th coach to win the FIFA World Cup, but the first German coach to do so without having played for his country. After a respectable career as a midfielder for a number of clubs, including SC Freiburg, and following coaching spells in Germany, Austria, Switzerland and Turkey, Löw was appointed as Jürgen Klinsmann's assistant in 2004 before taking the top job after the 2006 FIFA World Cup. He led Germany to the 2008 UEFA European Championship final and the semi-finals of EURO 2012, as well as to third place at the 2010 FIFA World Cup.

LÖW

NATIONAL LEGEND
GIFT OF THE GNABRY

Serge Gnabry's hat-trick against Northern Ireland in November 2019 made him the first man to score 13 goals in his first 13 Germany internationals since Gerd Müller hit 16 in 13 in 1969 – both men also netted ten in their first ten. Gnabry, who scored a debut hat-trick in an 8-0 victory against San Marino in 2016, made his club debut for Arsenal aged 17 before joining Werder Bremen and then Bayern Munich. In the 2019-20 UEFA Champions League, Gnabry enjoyed two returns to London, scoring four as Tottenham Hotspur were trounced 7-2 and another two in a 3-0 defeat of Chelsea.

11 HOURS AND 19 MINUTES
Germany went a national record of 11 hours and 19 minutes without conceding a goal, between Antoine Griezmann scoring for France in the 2016 UEFA European Championship semi-final and a 31st-minute equaliser by Azerbaijan's Dimitrij Nazarov in a 2018 FIFA World Cup qualifier on 26 March 2017, a match Germany went on to win 4-1.

100

Ulf Kirsten is one of eight players who played for both the old East Germany and the reunified Germany after 1990. He managed 100 appearances: 49 for East Germany and 51 for Germany.

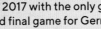

GNABRY

NATIONAL LEGEND
YOUNGEST CENTURION LUKAS

Lukas Podolski was briefly the youngest European footballer to reach 100 caps when, aged 27 years and 13 days old, he appeared in Germany's third first-round game of the 2012 UEFA European Championship, against Denmark. He marked the occasion by scoring the opener in a 2-1 win. He was voted best young player of the tournament when Germany hosted and finished third at the 2006 FIFA World Cup. He bowed out of international football in March 2017 with the only goal – his 49th – of what he said in advance would be his 130th and final game for Germany, a 1-0 friendly win over England in Dortmund.

NEUER

Germany went into the 2018 FIFA World Cup as defending champions – and FIFA Confederations Cup holders, which they had won in Russia a year earlier. Yet Joachim Löw's side finished bottom of Group F, ensuring their first first-round exit for 80 years – they did not compete in 1950 – and only their second ever. Germany were eliminated in 1938, a straight knock-out tournament, after losing 4–2 to Switzerland in a first-round replay following a 1–1 draw. That German team featured several Austrian players following the *Anschluss* (German annexation of Austria) earlier in the year.

1-0

East and West Germany met only once at senior national team level, in the FIFA World Cup finals on 22 June 1974. After the teams were drawn into the same group, East Germany produced a shock 1-0 win in Hamburg, but both teams advanced.

STAR PLAYER
NEUER RECORD

Manuel Neuer holds the German record for the longest run between conceding international tournament goals. There were 557 minutes between Brazil's late consolation in the 7-1 2014 FIFA World Cup semi-final rout and a goal from Italy's Leonardo Bonucci in the 2016 UEFA European Championship quarter-final. Germany won that game 6-5 on penalties, helped by two spot-kick saves by Neuer. The previous best run had been Sepp Maier's 481-minute shutout in the 1970s. Neuer – renowned for his ease with the ball at his feet as a "sweeper keeper" – was appointed Germany captain in September 2016 after Bastian Schweinsteiger retired.

GÖTZE

SCHÜRRLE

NATIONAL LEGEND
FABULOUS PHIL

Four German men have lifted the FIFA World Cup as captain: Fritz Walter in 1954, Franz Beckenbauer in 1974, Lothar Matthäus in 1990, and **Philipp Lahm** in 2014. Lahm, a full-back comfortable on either flank, was Germany's youngest FIFA World Cup captain when they finished third in 2010, and he later retired from international football aged just 30 after the Germans defeated Argentina in the 2014 final. A Bayern Munich ballboy as a teenager, Lahm also wore the armband as they won the UEFA Champions League in 2013. Lahm's only other club was VfB Stuttgart, for a brief loan spell.

Bayern Munich's **Mario Götze** was the hero when Germany finally overcame Argentina's resistance in the 2014 FIFA World Cup final. His 113th-minute volley was the first winner hit by a substitute. It seemed apt that Germany's first FIFA World Cup triumph since the reunification of East and West Germany in 1990 was secured by Götze, set up by **André Schürrle**. They had jointly become the first German football internationals born post-reunification, when making their debuts as 79th-minute substitutes against Sweden in November 2010.

LAHM

5

Lothar Matthäus is Germany's most-capped player. He appeared in five FIFA World Cup finals – 1982, 1986, 1990, 1994 and 1998 – a record for an outfield player that he shares with Mexico's Rafael Márquez.

V STAR PLAYER
⊙ GOLDEN BOY JULIAN

World champions Germany won their first FIFA Confederations Cup title in Russia in 2017, despite coach Joachim Löw resting many of his senior stars, including Thomas Müller, Mesut Özil and Toni Kroos. Lars Stindl scored the only goal of the final, against Chile, while goalkeeper Marc-André ter Stegen was named man of the match. The Golden Ball for the tournament's best player went to 23-year-old captain **Julian Draxler** – Germany's youngest skipper at a tournament since Max Breunig at the 1912 Summer Olympics – and the Golden Boot went to three-goal team-mate Timo Werner. Germany also had the youngest average age of any FIFA Confederations Cup-winning squad: 24 years and four months.

DRAXLER

22

Sepp Herberger (1897-1977) was Germany's longest-serving coach (22 years at the helm) and his legendary status was assured after West Germany surprised odds-on favourites Hungary to win the 1954 FIFA World Cup final – a result credited with dragging the country out of a post-war slump.

NATIONAL LEGEND
BASTIAN THE BASTION

No-one has played more matches at the FIFA World Cup and UEFA European Championship than Germany's **Bastian Schweinsteiger** and Portugal's Cristiano Ronaldo, who both sit on 38 appearances. "Schweini" reached the mark at EURO 2016. However, the occasion – a semi-final against France – was not a happy one. A handball by German captain Schweinsteiger conceded an opening penalty in a 2-0 defeat. Happier times followed, however. A week later, he married Serbian tennis star Ana Ivanović.

0

Germany are renowned as penalty specialists, but they needed no shoot-outs to win the 2014 FIFA World Cup, unlike their previous two titles, the 1990 FIFA World Cup and the 1996 UEFA European Championship, which both involved semi-final victories on penalties against England.

SCHWEINSTEIGER

NATIONAL LEGEND
DER BOMBER

Gerd Müller was the most prolific scorer of Germany's modern era. Though not particularly tall, he was quick, strong and had a predator's eye for the net. He also had the temperament to score decisive goals in big games, including the winner in the 1974 FIFA World Cup final, the winner in the semi-final against Poland and two goals in West Germany's 1972 UEFA European Championship final victory over the USSR. He netted 68 goals in 62 appearances for West Germany and remains the leading scorer in the *Bundesliga* and the all-time top scorer for Bayern Munich.

NATIONAL LEGEND
GRAND SAMMER

Matthias Sammer is not only one of eight men to play for both East Germany and the reunified Germany, but he also holds the honour of captaining the side and scoring both goals in East Germany's final game, a 2-0 away win over Belgium on 12 September 1990, 21 days before the official reunification. His powerhouse midfield performances later drove Germany to glory at the 1996 UEFA European Championship, where he was voted the player of the tournament.

ITALY

Only Brazil (with five victories) have won the FIFA World Cup more times than Italy. The *Azzurri*, however, were the first nation to retain the trophy (winning in 1934 and 1938), were surprise champions in Spain in 1982, and collected football's most coveted trophy for a fourth time in 2006.

Joined FIFA: 1910

Biggest win:
9-0 v. USA, 1948

Highest FIFA ranking: 1st

Home stadium:
Stadio Olimpico, Rome

Honours:
4 FIFA World Cups (1934, 1938, 1982, 2006), 1 UEFA European Championship (1968)

MANCINI

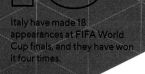

18
Italy have made 18 appearances at FIFA World Cup finals, and they have won it four times.

NATIONAL LEGEND
ON THE REBOUND

The 2018 FIFA World Cup in Russia was the first since 1958 not to feature Italy. Their 1-0 aggregate defeat by Sweden in a qualifying play-off saw manager Gian Piero Ventura and Italian FA President Carlo Tavecchio depart. New coach **Roberto Mancini** – a former classy forward who had been in the squad for the third-placed 1990 FIFA World Cup hosts – has overseen a superb resurgence. His *Azzurri* coasted to qualification for the postponed 2020 UEFA European Championship finals with ten wins in ten matches. They also set a new national record of 11 consecutive victories when they beat Armenia 9-1 in November 2019.

TOURNAMENT TRIVIA
SHARE AND SHARE ALIKE

Manager Marcello Lippi used all of his outfield squad members to lead Italy to their fourth FIFA World Cup title in Germany in 2006 – and all six of his named strikers found the net once apiece, apart from Luca Toni who scored twice. He might have had a third, but his 61st-minute header against France in the final was disallowed for a marginal offside. The other forwards to score were Alessandro Del Piero, Francesco Totti, Alberto Gilardino, Vincenzo Iaquinta and Filippo Inzaghi. Toni retired from football at the end of the 2015-16 season at the age of 39, having a year earlier become the oldest man to finish as *Serie A*'s top scorer.

NATIONAL LEGEND
ZOFF THE SCALE

Goalkeeper **Dino Zoff** set an international record by going 1,142 minutes without conceding a goal between September 1972 and June 1974. Zoff was Italy's captain when they won the 1982 FIFA World Cup – emulating the feat of another Juventus goalkeeper, Gianpiero Combi, who had been the victorious skipper in 1934. Zoff later coached Italy to the final of the 2000 UEFA European Championship, which they lost 2-1 to France thanks to an extra-time "golden goal" – then quit a few days later, unhappy following the criticism levelled at him by Italy's then Prime Minister, Silvio Berlusconi.

ZOFF

2

Vittorio Pozzo is the only man to have won the FIFA World Cup twice as manager – both times with Italy, in 1934 and 1938. Only two players, Giuseppe Meazza and Giovanni Ferrari, played in both finals.

STAR PLAYER
THE YOUNG ONES

Striker **Moise Kean** marked his first senior start for Italy by becoming his country's youngest scorer for 60 years and the second youngest ever, finding the net in March 2019 in a 2-0 UEFA European Championship qualifier win over Finland. He was just 19 years and 23 days old. The other goal was scored by Fabio Quagliarella, who – at 36 years and 54 days – became Italy's oldest-ever scorer. The youngest, albeit in a non-competitive match, remains Bruno Nicole, who was 18 years and 258 days when he bagged a brace in a 2-2 draw against France on 9 November 1958. Nicole later became Italy's youngest captain, aged 21 years and 61 days, in April 1961.

KEAN

19 SECONDS

Emanuele Giaccherini holds the record for Italy's fastest goal, which came just 19 seconds into a June 2013 friendly against Haiti – one second quicker than Salvatore Bagni's strike against Mexico 29 years earlier.

NATIONAL LEGEND
HAPPY CENTENARY

After captaining Italy to the 2006 FIFA World Cup title, **Fabio Cannavaro** was named FIFA World Player of the Year – at 33, the oldest winner of the prize, as well as the first defender. Cannavaro, born in Naples in 1973, played every minute of the 2006 tournament, and the final triumph against France was the ideal way to celebrate his 100th international appearance. Cannavaro is widely considered to be one of the greatest defenders of the modern-day game and played for clubs including Juventus, Internazionale and Real Madrid.

NATIONAL LEGEND
APPETITE FOR SUCCESS

The stadium shared by AC Milan and Internazionale is popularly known as the San Siro, after the district in which it is located. Its official title is the Stadio Giuseppe Meazza, named after the star inside-forward who played for both clubs, as well as Italy's 1934 and 1938 FIFA World Cup-winning sides. Meazza, born in Milan on 23 August 1910, was spotted by an Inter scout while playing keepy-uppy in the street with a ball made of rags. He was so thin he had to be fattened up with a diet of steaks. His last goal for Italy was a penalty in the 1938 FIFA World Cup semi-final against Brazil – taken while using one hand to hold up his shorts, whose elastic had broken.

CANNAVARO

1925

Italy extended their unbeaten run in Milan to 47 games when they drew 0-0 with Portugal at the San Siro in a UEFA Nations League game in November 2018. Their last loss in the city dates back to 1925.

MOST APPEARANCES:

1 Gianluigi Buffon, 176
2 Fabio Cannavaro, 136
3 Paolo Maldini, 126
4 Daniele De Rossi, 117
5 Andrea Pirlo, 116

NATIONAL LEGEND
KEEPING IT IN THE FAMILY

Cesare and **Paolo Maldini** are the only father and son to have hoisted the European Cup/Champions League as captains – both with AC Milan and both for the first time in England. Cesare lifted the trophy after his team beat Benfica at Wembley Stadium in 1963. Paolo repeated the feat 40 years later when Milan defeated Juventus at Old Trafford, Manchester. Although he retired as Italy's second most-capped player, Paolo never managed to win an international tournament – he played for Italy sides that finished third and runners-up at the FIFA World Cup and runners-up in the UEFA European Championship. Paolo's son, 18-year-old midfielder Daniel, became the third Maldini to play for AC Milan when he came on as a stoppage-time substitute against Verona in February 2020.

MALDINI

TOURNAMENT TRIVIA
IN SAFE KEEPING

During World War Two, the Jules Rimet Trophy – won by Italy at the 1938 FIFA World Cup – was hidden in a shoebox under the bed of football official Ottorino Barassi. He preferred to keep it there, rather than at its previous home – a bank in Rome. The trophy was only handed back to FIFA, safe and untouched, when the FIFA World Cup resumed in 1950. Barassi also helped to organise the 1934 FIFA World Cup, which was played in his native Italy.

NATIONAL LEGEND
WHEN THE GOING GETS BUFF

Gianluigi Buffon has not only been one of the finest modern-day goalkeepers in the world but he has also even surpassed some of the achievements of legendary Italian predecessor Dino Zoff. Buffon emulated 1982 world champion Zoff by being part of Italy's 2006 FIFA World Cup-winning side – only conceding two goals during the tournament, one an own goal and the other a penalty. Buffon also became only the third player to be selected for five different FIFA World Cups when he made two appearances in Brazil in 2014, only missing one of Italy's three matches – their opener against England – due to a late ankle injury.

BUFFON

26

21

No team has drawn more FIFA World Cup matches than Italy, who took their tally to 21 with 1–1 draws against Paraguay and New Zealand at South Africa 2010.

NATIONAL LEGEND
COMEBACK KID

Paolo Rossi was the unlikely hero of Italy's 1982 FIFA World Cup triumph, winning the Golden Boot with six goals – including a memorable hat-trick against Brazil in the second round, and the first of Italy's three goals in their final win over West Germany. But he only just made it to the tournament at all, having completed a two-year ban for his alleged involvement in a betting scandal only six weeks before the start of the tournament.

3

Only England and Spain have lost as many FIFA World Cup penalty shoot-outs as Italy – three apiece. Roberto Baggio, nicknamed "The Divine Ponytail", was involved in all three of Italy's spot-kick defeats, in 1990, 1994 and 1998.

NO. 3
No Internazionale footballer will ever wear the No. 3 shirt again after it was retired in tribute to legendary full-back Giacinto Facchetti following his death in 2006 at the age of 64.

ROSSI

NATIONAL LEGEND
MEDAL COLLECTORS

Giovanni Ferrari not only won both the 1934 and 1938 FIFA World Cup with Italy, he also held the record for the most *Serie A* titles until 2018. He won it eight times, five with Juventus, two with Internazionale and one with Bologna. Five other players have won eight *Serie A* titles: Virginio Rosetti, Giuseppe Furino, Andrea Barzagli, Giorgio Chiellini and Leonardo Bonucci. Gianluigi Buffon now holds the record, with nine. Buffon has in fact won 11 titles, but the ones in 2004-05 and 2005¬-06 were rescinded in light of the *Calciopoli* scandal.

NATIONAL LEGEND
BOSSI DE ROSSI

Central midfielder Daniele de Rossi was roundly condemned when he was sent off for elbowing Brian McBride of the USA in a 2006 FIFA World Cup group match. His suspension finished just in time for him to be a substitute in the final, which Italy won against France. However, three months earlier, in March 2006, De Rossi had won widespread praise for his honesty. During a *Serie A* match, his club AS Roma were awarded a goal against Messina when he diverted the ball into the net with his hand and he persuaded the referee to disallow it (Roma still won 2–1).

NATIONAL LEGEND
KEEPING CHIELLINI

Versatile defender **Giorgio Chiellini** was one of the big names who announced their retirement from international football after Italy's failure to qualify for the 2018 FIFA World Cup, but caretaker manager Luigi Di Biagio nevertheless insisted on calling him and goalkeeper Gianluigi Buffon up for friendlies in March 2018. New permanent boss Roberto Mancini then appointed Chiellini as Buffon's successor as captain, and the defender went on to become the seventh Italian man to reach a century of caps in a goalless draw with Portugal in November 2018.

CHIELLINI

1000

Christian Vieri's first goal for Italy in 1997 not only came on his debut, it also marked the *Azzurri*'s 1,000th goal scored in all internationals.

NETHERLANDS

Patrick Kluivert's son Justin made his international debut as a 78th-minute substitute against Portugal in March 2018, aged 18 – the same age at which Patrick first appeared for his country.

Banks of orange-shirted Dutch fans have become a regular sight at the world's major football tournaments, not least thanks to Johan Cruijff and his team's spectacular brand of "Total Football".

Joined FIFA: 1905

Biggest win:
11-0 v. San Marino, 2011

Highest FIFA ranking: 1st

Home stadium: Johann Cruijff Arena, Amsterdam

Honours: 1 UEFA European Championship (1988)

CRUIJFF

NATIONAL LEGEND
CRUIJFF THE MAGICIAN

Johan Cruijff was not only a genius with the ball at his feet but also an inspirational football philosopher, who spread the concept of "Total Football" not only with Ajax and the Netherlands in the 1970s but also in Spain where he played for and managed FC Barcelona and acted as a mentor to those who followed him there, such as Pep Guardiola and Xavi Hernández. He also gave the world the much-imitated "Cruijff turn", after pushing the ball with the inside of his foot behind his standing leg before swivelling and surging past bemused Swedish defender Jan Olsson.

100
Midfielder Davy Klaassen's first international appearance, a 2-0 defeat to France in March 2014, meant he was the 100th player to make his Netherlands debut as an Ajax player, having been brought up in the club's famed youth academy.

NATIONAL LEGEND
THE WINNING CAPTAIN

With his distinctive dreadlocks, Ruud Gullit cut a swathe through world football through the 1980s and '90s. Twice a European Cup winner with AC Milan and a European Footballer of the Year, he will always be remembered fondly by Dutch fans for being the first man in a Netherlands shirt to lift a major trophy – the 1988 UEFA European Championship. In 1996, Gullit signed for Chelsea and a year later was appointed the club's player-manager.

NATIONAL LEGEND
MICHELS THE MASTER

Rinus Michels (1928-2005) was named FIFA's Coach of the Century in 1999 for his achievements with the Netherlands and Ajax. The former Ajax and Netherlands striker took over the manager's job at his old club in 1965 and built the team around Johan Cruijff – as he later did with the national side, introducing "Total Football". He moved to Barcelona after Ajax's 1971 European Cup victory, but was called back home to mastermind the Netherlands' 1974 FIFA World Cup bid. Nicknamed "The General", he was known as a disciplinarian who took over the national team again for their victorious 1988 UEFA European Championship campaign.

MICHELS

NATIONAL LEGEND
DIFFERENT SIDES OF SNEIJDER

In 2017, **Wesley Sneijder** not only became his country's most-capped footballer but also marked his 131st international appearance with his 31st goal. He enjoyed an almost perfect 2010 as he won the treble with Italy's Internazionale – a domestic league and cup double and the UEFA Champions League – but just missed out on adding the FIFA World Cup as the Netherlands lost 1-0 to Spain in the final. Sneijder almost won the tournament's Golden Boot too – his five goals left him level with Diego Forlán, Thomas Müller and David Villa, but it was Müller who claimed the award by virtue of registering more assists.

MOST APPEARANCES:

1 **Wesley Sneijder**, 134
2 **Edwin van der Sar**, 130
3 **Frank de Boer**, 112
4 **Rafael van der Vaart**, 109
5 **Giovanni van Bronckhorst**, 106

38

Abe Lenstra is still the Netherlands' oldest goalscorer. He was 38 years and 144 days old when he netted in his final game, a 2-2 draw with Belgium, on 19 April 1959.

STAR PLAYER
VIRGIL RECORD

Virgil van Dijk became the world's most expensive defender in January 2018 after joining Liverpool from Premier League rivals Southampton for a reported GBP 75 million. Two months later, he was named as the Netherlands' new captain, replacing Arjen Robben who had retired from international football the previous October. Van Dijk's first international goal came in his 18th international appearance – his second as skipper – in a 3-0 friendly win over European champions Portugal in March 2018. Van Dijk helped Liverpool to the 2019 UEFA Champions League and finished runner-up to Lionel Messi In the voting for The Best FIFA Men's Player.

SNEIJDER

WIJNALDUM

NATIONAL LEGEND
THE NON-FLYING DUTCHMAN

Dennis Bergkamp would have won many more than 79 caps but for his fear of flying. Bergkamp refused to board aircraft after developing a flying phobia during his time with Internazionale in Italy. He missed every away game for the Netherlands and his clubs unless he could reach the venue by road, rail or boat. His intricately skilful last-minute winner against Argentina in the quarter-finals of the 1998 FIFA World Cup is seen by many as one of the tournament's finest and most elegant goals.

BERGKAMP

STAR PLAYER
DUTCH DOUBLE

Substitute **Memphis Depay** – aged 20 years and 125 days – became the Netherlands' youngest FIFA World Cup goalscorer with a goal in the 3-2 Group B victory over Australia in Porto Alegre in 2014. He also scored as a substitute against Chile five days later. He and midfielder **Georginio Wijnaldum** combined in a remarkable double act in 2019 as the pair scored or assisted 23 of the Netherlands' 27 goals. Wijnaldum scored nine goals in eight appearances, including a hat-trick in his first match as captain in a 5-0 defeat of Estonia in November 2019.

DEPAY

NATIONAL LEGEND
WORK OF VAART

Rafael van der Vaart became the fifth player to make 100 appearances for the Netherlands, yet for a while it looked as if he might just miss out on the milestone: he ended UEFA EURO 2012 on 99 caps and coach Bert van Marwijk said he may be left out of future squads. But Van Marwijk's departure after the tournament was a boost for Van der Vaart, who duly made his 100th appearance in a 4-2 friendly loss to Belgium in August 2012. Sadly for him, a calf injury ruled him out of the 2014 FIFA World Cup three days before Louis van Gaal announced his 23-man squad.

NATIONAL LEGEND
DE BOER BOYS SET RECORD

Twins **Frank** and **Ronald de Boer** hold the record for the most games played by brothers for the Netherlands. Frank won 112 caps, while Ronald won 67. Ronald missed a crucial spot-kick as the Dutch lost to Brazil in the semi-finals of the 1998 FIFA World Cup, while Frank suffered a similar unfortunate fate at the same stage of the UEFA European Championship two years later. Frank took over as Ajax manager in December 2010, having earlier that year been assistant to Bert van Marwijk as the Netherlands reached the FIFA World Cup final.

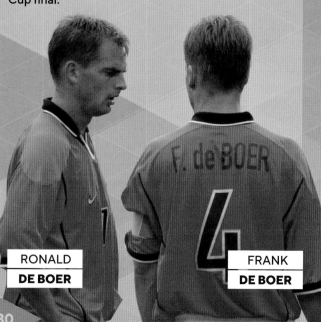

RONALD
DE BOER

FRANK
DE BOER

KOEMAN

NATIONAL LEGENDS
KOEMAN PEOPLE

Brothers **Ronald** and Erwin **Koeman** were Netherlands team-mates when they won the 1988 UEFA European Championship and they later teamed up in management. Elder brother Erwin served as Ronald's assistant at English clubs Everton and Southampton, but when Ronald was appointed the Netherlands' head coach in February 2018, Erwin opted not to join him. The Dutch missed out on both UEFA EURO 2016 and the 2018 FIFA World Cup, but Koeman's reign started encouragingly with his team topping their UEFA Nations League group above France and Germany. New captain Virgil van Dijk scored in both games against Germany, the opener in a 3-0 home win and a stoppage-time equaliser in a 2-2 away draw.

TOURNAMENT TRIVIA
KRUL TO BE KIND

Louis van Gaal pulled off a masterstroke when he replaced goalkeeper Jasper Cillessen with Tim Krul in the 119th minute of the Netherlands' quarter-final against Costa Rica at the 2014 FIFA World Cup. He reasoned that the Dutch stood a better chance of winning the resulting shoot-out with Krul as he was two inches taller than Cillessen. Sure enough, Krul saved two penalties and the Dutch went through. Van Gaal could not repeat the trick against Argentina in the semi-final though, but third-choice goalkeeper Michel Vorm also replaced Cillessen during stoppage time of the third-place play-off against Brazil, making the Netherlands the first country to field all 23 squad members at a FIFA World Cup.

9 Nine Netherlands players were on the losing side in both the 1974 (2-1 to West Germany) and 1978 (3-1 to Argentina) FIFA World Cup finals.

VAN PERSIE

5

Four players have scored five goals in a game for the Netherlands: Jan Vos, Leen Vente, John Bosman and Marco van Basten.

STAR PLAYER
MATT START

At 17 years and 225 days, centre-back **Matthijs de Ligt** became the Netherlands' youngest player since Mauk Weber in 1931 (17 years and 92 days) when he made his international bow against Bulgaria in March 2017. Sixty days later, De Ligt became the youngest player to feature in a UEFA final as his Ajax side lost to Manchester United in the Europa League final in Stockholm. Another Dutch defender, left-back Jetro Willems, is the youngest player in UEFA European Championship finals history. In the Netherlands' UEFA EURO 2012 opener against Denmark on 9 June, Willems, aged 18 years and 71 days, was 44 days younger than Belgium's Enzo Scifo had been in 1984.

NATIONAL LEGEND
ROCKIN' ROBIN

In 2014, **Robin van Persie** became the first Dutchman to score at three different FIFA World Cups when he planted a spectacular looping header over Iker Casillas in the Dutchmen's 5-1 victory over holders Spain. The Netherlands eventually finished third, beating hosts Brazil in the third-place play-off, making them the first country to enjoy three World Cup wins over Brazil. Van Persie had become his country's leading scorer in a pre-tournament friendly against Ghana, but his final international goals came in a 3-2 defeat to the Czech Republic that denied the Dutch a 2016 UEFA European Championship slot. Unfortunately for him, goal no. 50 came after his own goal had put the Czechs 3-1 up.

TOP SCORERS:

1 **Robin van Persie**, 50

2 **Klass-Jan Huntelaar**, 42

3 **Patrick Kluivert**, 40

4 **Dennis Bergkamp**, 37
= **Arjen Robben**, 37

4

Rinus Michels managed the Netherlands in four separate spells between 1974 and 1992, more than any other manager.

DE LIGT

NATIONAL LEGEND
SENIOR ADVOCAAT

Dick Advocaat holds two records as Dutch national team coach. When he was re-appointed for his third spell in May 2017, he became, at 69, his country's oldest national coach – one year older than Guus Hiddick had been when he was fired in 2015. Advocaat also boasts the most wins as national coach, victories in November 2017 friendlies over Scotland and Romania taking him to 37, one more than Englishman Bob Glendenning, who was in charge between 1925 and his death in 1940. After the Romania victory, however, Advocaat stood down as national coach and former player Ronald Koeman was appointed to replace him.

ADVOCAAT

SPAIN

Spanish clubs have won a record number of European Cup/UEFA Champions League titles between them and the country has produced some of world football's finest players. Spain won their first FIFA World Cup in 2010.

Joined FIFA: 1920

Biggest win:
13-0 v. Bulgaria, 1933

Highest FIFA ranking: 1st

Home stadium:
(rotation)

Honours:
1 FIFA World Cup (2010),
3 UEFA European
Championships (1964,
2008, 2012)

NATIONAL PLAYER
ANDRÉS THE GIANT

Andrés Iniesta left Barcelona in 2018, having won nine *La Liga* titles, six *Copa del Rey* trophies and four UEFA Champions League titles in his 17 years at the club. He also bade farewell to international football after the 2018 FIFA World Cup, aged 34, having played 131 times for Spain and scored 13 goals – the most important of which won the 2010 FIFA World Cup. Uniquely, Iniesta picked up man-of-the-match awards in a UEFA Champions League final (2015), a UEFA European Championship final (2012) and a FIFA World Cup final (2010).

INIESTA

4-3
When Spain came back from 2-0 and then 3-2 down to win 4-3 in Madrid in May 1929, they became the first non-British team to beat England.

70
In 2008, a month short of his 70th birthday, Spain's Luis Aragonés became the oldest coach to win the UEFA European Championship.

TOURNAMENT TRIVIA
DOUBLING UP

Spain's 2010 FIFA World Cup triumph made them the first country since West Germany in 1974 to lift the trophy as the reigning European champions. When France combined the two titles, they did it the other way around, winning the 1998 FIFA World Cup and then the UEFA European Championship two years later. No country had ever won three major tournaments in a row until Spain won UEFA EURO 2012, trouncing Italy 4–0 in the final. This also made Spain the first team to make a successful defence of their UEFA European Championship title.

🌐 NATIONAL LEGEND
HAPPY XAVI

When Spain's second most-capped outfield player, with 133, retired from international football after the 2014 FIFA World Cup – and when he left Spanish club football a year later – he was recognised as his country's most-decorated player. Curiously, both the first and final appearances of **Xavi Hernández**'s international career were defeats to Netherlands sides coached by Louis van Gaal, 2-1 in 2000 and 5-1 in 2014. Triumph was far more familiar to the midfield playmaker, a mainstay of Spain's 2010 FIFA World Cup-winning side as well as the teams that lifted the UEFA European Championship trophy in 2008 and 2012.

XAVI

🏆 TOURNEMENT TRIVIA
RED ALERT

Spain refused to play in the first UEFA European Championship in 1960, in protest at having to travel to the Soviet Union, a Communist country. But they changed their minds four years later, not only hosting the tournament but also winning it – beating the visiting Soviets 2-1 in the final for good measure. Spain were captained by Fernando Olivella and managed by José Villalonga, who had been the first coach to win the European Cup, with Real Madrid in 1956.

TORRES

⬥ STAR PLAYER
PAU POWER

Villarreal centre-back **Pau Torres** needed just 58 seconds to score his first goal for Spain, finding the net almost instantly after being introduced as a substitute for Sergio Ramos in a 7-0 victory over Malta in a UEFA EURO 2020 qualifier in November 2019. Also on the scoresheet that day was RB Leipzig winger Dani Olmo, three minutes after coming on for his first international appearance. That meant two Spain debutants found the net in the same game for the first time since Juanito and Fernando Gómez against Hungary – 30 years to the day earlier.

🌐 NATIONAL LEGEND
BEST CAS SCENARIO

Goalkeeper **Iker Casillas** has long been known to devotees back home as "Saint Iker" – an anointment richly supported by his haul of trophies and medals, both for team and individual. He is one of only three men to lift the FIFA World Cup, the UEFA European Championship and the UEFA Champions League/European Cup trophies as captain, emulating Germany's Franz Beckenbauer and France's Didier Deschamps. As well as winning the 2008 and 2012 UEFA European Championships and the 2010 FIFA World Cup, Casillas also became the first goalkeeper to reach 100 international clean sheets in a 2-0 friendly win over England in November 2015.

CASILLAS

3
David Villa and Fernando Torres share Spain's record for most hat-tricks, with three. They even managed one apiece in the same match, the 10-0 crushing of Tahiti at the FIFA Confederations Cup in 2013.

MOST APPEARANCES:
1 **Sergio Ramos**, 170
2 **Iker Casillas**, 167
3 **Xavi Hernández**, 133
4 **Andrés Iniesta**, 131
5 **Andoni Zubizarreta**, 126

1 Luis Suárez was named European Footballer of the Year in 1960 – and he is still the only Spanish-born player to have taken the prize.

7 Seven players played in Spain's three UEFA European Championship and FIFA World Cup finals from 2008 to 2012.

SCORING RECORD
VILLA FILLS HIS BOOTS

David Villa became Spain's all-time FIFA World Cup top scorer with his first-round goal against Chile in 2010, his sixth across the 2006 and 2010 tournaments. Villa became Spain's all-time leading scorer with a brace against the Czech Republic in March 2011, but a broken leg ruled him out of the 2012 UEFA European Championship, so he missed out on adding to his UEFA EURO 2008 and 2010 FIFA World Cup winner's medals.

1 Only one Spanish club – Real Madrid – was formally represented at FIFA's first meeting in Paris in 1904, known then as Madrid FC. The word "Real" is Spanish for "Royal".

TOP SCORERS:

1 David Villa, 59

2 Raúl, 44

3 Fernando Torres, 38

4 David Silva, 35

5 Fernando Hierro, 29

VILLA

TOURNAMENT TRIVIA
HARD TO BEAT

Spain share with Brazil the record for the longest international unbeaten run – the Brazilians went 35 games without defeat between 1993 and 1996, a tally matched by the Spanish between 2007 and 2009, when they lost 2-0 to the United States in the semi-finals of the FIFA Confederations Cup. That vintage Spain side also became the first country to take maximum points, 30 out of 30, in a FIFA World Cup qualification campaign, and they duly went on to lift the trophy in South Africa in 2010.

STAR PLAYER
SILVA SERVICE

Spain entered the 2018 FIFA World Cup finals on an unbeaten qualifying run of 63 matches, their last defeat having been to Denmark in 1993. **David Silva** scored in his fourth consecutive international in a June 2017 qualifying victory over Macedonia and he was also on target in the 8-0 rout of Liechtenstein in September 2017. Other important Silva goals include the last in a 3-0 defeat of Russia in the 2008 UEFA European Championship semi-final, and the opener as Spain defeated Italy 4-0 in the UEFA EURO 2012 final to retain their crown. Silva called time on his international career after the 2018 FIFA World Cup with 35 goals in 125 appearances for his country.

SILVA

STAR PLAYER
SURGING SERGIO

In March 2013, Sergio Ramos became the youngest-ever European player to reach 100 international caps at the age of 26 years and 358 days – and he marked the occasion by scoring Spain's goal in a 1-1 draw with Finland. Germany's Lukas Podolski had been 21 days older when he won his 100th cap. Korea Republic's Cha Bum-kun, who was 24 years and 139 days old when he achieved the landmark, holds the global record. Ramos, a right-back or central defender who has 2010 FIFA World Cup and 2008 and 2012 UEFA European Championships to his name, not only became Spain's most-capped player when he won his 168th cap in October 2019 but also the most-capped outfield player in European men's football.

NATIONAL LEGEND
TORRES! TORRES!

As a child, **Fernando Torres** wanted to be a goalkeeper, but he made the wise decision to become a striker instead. He had a penchant for scoring the only goal in the final of a tournament, doing so for Spain in the 2008 UEFA European Championship against Germany in Vienna, having done the same in the U-16 UEFA European Championship in 2001 and for the Under-19s the following year. Torres became the most expensive Spanish footballer ever when Chelsea paid GBP 50 million to sign him from fellow English club Liverpool in January 2011. After stints in Italy and back home in Spain, he moved to play in Japan in July 2018 and retired 11 months later.

TORRES

STAR PLAYER
SUPER PED

Spanish winger Pedro is the only player to have scored in six separate official club tournaments in one calendar year, managing to hit the net for Barcelona in Spain's *Primera Liga*, *Copa del Rey* and Super Cup in 2009, as well as in the UEFA Champions League, UEFA European Super Cup and FIFA Club World Cup. He was also in the starting line-up for the 2010 FIFA World Cup final – less than two years after being a member of the Barcelona reserve team in Spain's third division and needing new club manager Pep Guardiola's intervention to prevent him being sent home to Tenerife.

NATIONAL LEGEND
THE RAÚL THING

Raúl González Blanco – known as Raúl – remains a Spain and Real Madrid icon, despite his record goal tallies being passed, respectively, by David Villa and Cristiano Ronaldo. He was an Atlético Madrid youth-teamer before signing for city rivals Real, where he scored 228 goals in 550 games and captained them from 2003 to 2010. But despite playing for Spain at five tournaments between the 1998 and 2006 FIFA World Cups, he was left out of Spain's UEFA EURO 2008 squad – and they promptly won the trophy. After leaving Real, Raúl enjoyed further success at Schalke 04 in Germany, Al Sadd in Qatar and New York Cosmos in the United States.

RAÚL

50

Centre-back Carlos Marchena became the first footballer to go 50 internationals in a row unbeaten when he played in Spain's 3-2 victory over Saudi Arabia in May 2009.

NATIONAL LEGENDS
SPANIARDS IN THE WORKS

After the glory years of Luis Aragones and **Vicente Del Bosque** between 2008 and 2016, Spain's coaching role has been more volatile. Julen Lopetegui was sacked a day before the start of the 2018 FIFA World Cup, having agreed to join Real Madrid. Sporting director Fernando Hierro stepped in for the tournament, but Spain reached only the second round. Former Barcelona coach Luis Enrique took over in July 2018, resigned for personal reasons the following June, but returned to the role in November – after Robert Moreno had overseen Spain's qualification for the next UEFA European Championship.

35

Aritz Aduriz became Spain's oldest goalscorer when he found the net in a 4-0 win over FYR Macedonia on 13 November 2016 in a 2018 FIFA World Cup qualifier. He was 35 years and 275 days old – 50 days older than the previous record-holder José Maria Peña, who scored the only goal in 30 November 1930 friendly against Portugal.

DEL BOSQUE

BELGIUM

Belgium's golden generation has risen: they reached the 2014 FIFA World Cup quarter-finals, and the *Red Devils* surpassed any previous achievements by finishing third at the 2018 FIFA World Cup.

Joined FIFA: 1904

Biggest win: 10-1 v. San Marino, 2001

Highest FIFA ranking: 1st

Home stadium: (rotation)

Honours: -

HAZARD

LUK'S GOOD

Romelu Lukaku, Belgium's all-time leading scorer, had to wait a national record of 24 internationals before completing 90 minutes for his country. Even so, Lukaku has made the most of his time on the field. His 52 goals by the end of 2019 put him 20 ahead of his nearest compatriots, and no man anywhere in the world scored more international goals in 2018 than his tally of 14 in 14 games. Among them were four at the 2018 FIFA World Cup – braces against Panama and Tunisia in successive first-round games – that helped him clinch the Bronze Ball for third top scorer at the tournament.

STAR PLAYER
BELGIUM'S PERSONAL BEST

Belgium, under Spanish manager Roberto Martínez, enjoyed their most successful FIFA World Cup in Russia in 2018, finishing third. They were the tournament's top scorers with 16 goals and won widespread admiration with centre-backs Jan Vertonghen and Toby Alderweireld, playmaker Kevin De Bruyne and attacking right-back Thomas Meunier all standing out. There were also individual prizes for goalkeeper Thibaut Courtois, who took the tournament's Golden Glove award for best goalkeeper, and captain Eden Hazard who won the Silver Ball as second best player, behind Croatia's Luka Modrić.

2

Striker Romelu Lukaku's two goals against the Republic of Ireland at UEFA EURO 2016 made him the first Belgian player to score a brace at a tournament since his international manager Marc Wilmots did the same against Mexico at the 1998 FIFA World Cup.

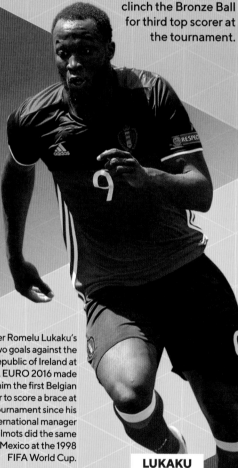

LUKAKU

STAR PLAYER
HAZ A GO HERO

Eden Hazard is the son of not just one former footballer but two – his mother Carine only retired from the women's game when she was pregnant with him. His father Thierry spent a lot of his career at semi-professional level with La Louvière in the Belgian second division, playing mainly as a defensive midfielder. Eden Hazard – and brothers Thorgan, Kylian and Ethan, were all born in La Louvière, so they share a same birthplace with former star Enzo Scifo – once the youngest player at a UEFA European Championship, aged 18 years and 115 days when Belgium beat Yugoslavia in their opening game at the 1984 tournament.

TOP SCORERS:

1 Romelu Lukaku, 52

2 Eden Hazard, 32

3 Paul Van Himst, 30
= Bernard Voorhoof, 30

5 Marc Wilmots, 29

TOURNAMENT TRIVIA
COMEBACK KINGS

Belgium's 3-2 victory over Japan in Rostov-on-Don at the 2018 FIFA World Cup was the first time since 1970 that a team had come back from two goals down to win a knockout game – when West Germany had needed extra time to beat England 3-2 in a quarter-final tie. Jan Vertonghen scored Belgium's first goal after 69 minutes, followed by Marouane Fellaini's equaliser five minutes later. Fellow substitute Nacer Chadli got the winner four minutes into stoppage time. Belgium's ten different goalscorers in Russia equalled the FIFA World Cup record held by France (1982) and Italy (2006).

MOST APPEARANCES:

1. Jan Vertonghen, 118
2. Eden Hazard, 106
3. Axel Witsel, 105
4. Toby Alderweireld, 98
5. Jan Ceulemans, 96

11

Belgium's most-capped footballer, defender **Jan Vertonghen** made his 100th appearance on 2 June 2018 against Portugal – 11 years to the day after his first cap, against the same country. His mother Ria Mattheeuws handed over a commemorative cap to celebrate the 100-match landmark.

VERTONGHEN

THYS

3

Major European competition finals hosted by the Heysel/King Baudouin stadium are: the 1976 UEFA European Championship, four UEFA European Champions Cups and three UEFA European Cup Winners' Cups.

ALDERWEIRELD

NATIONAL LEGEND
HE'S OUR GUY

Unquestionably Belgium's greatest manager – as well as their longest-serving – was **Guy Thys**. He led them to the final of the 1980 UEFA European Championship and – with a team featuring the likes of Enzo Scifo and Nico Claesen – the semi-finals of the FIFA World Cup six years later. He spent 13 years in the job from 1976 to 1989, then returned for a second spell just eight months after quitting. He stepped down again after managing Belgium at the 1990 FIFA World Cup. During his playing days in the 1940s and 1950s, he was a striker and won two caps for Belgium.

39

Belgium's sixth most-capped player, Timmy Simons, became his country's oldest international when he faced Estonia in a 2018 FIFA World Cup qualifier in November 2016, aged 39 years and 338 days.

SCORING RECORD
FINE NINE

Belgium have won an international by nine goals on four occasions – most recently on 10 October 2019, when they also set a national record by getting seven of their own men plus an opponent on the scoresheet. Romelu Lukaku struck twice as San Marino were beaten 9-0 at the King Baudouin Stadium in Brussels, while the other goals came from Nacer Chadli, **Toby Alderweireld**, Youri Tielemans, Christian Benteke, Yari Verschaeren and Timothy Castagne, and also there was an own goal by the visitors' Cristian Brolli. Belgium also beat San Marino 10-1 in February 2001, and they enjoyed 9-0 victories over Zambia in June 1994 and Gibraltar in August 2017.

BULGARIA

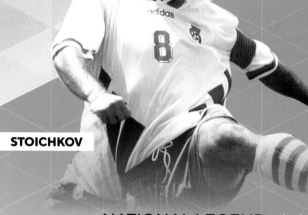
STOICHKOV

Regular qualifiers for the game's major competitions, and the birthplace of some of the sport's biggest names, Bulgaria have too often failed to deliver on the big occasions and make a mark on world football.

Joined FIFA: 1922

Biggest win: 15-0 v. Ghana, 1968

Highest FIFA ranking: 3rd

Home stadium: Vasil Levski National Stadium, Sofia

Honours: -

6

Defender Aleksandar Shalamanov played for Bulgaria at the 1966 FIFA World Cup, just six years after representing his country as an alpine skier at the Winter Olympics at Lake Placid.

NATIONAL LEGEND
HRISTO'S HISTORY

Hristo Stoichkov, born in Plovdiv, Bulgaria, on 8 February 1968, shared the 1994 FIFA World Cup Golden Boot, awarded to the tournament's top scorer, with Russia's Oleg Salenko. Both scored six times, though Stoichkov became the sole winner of that year's European Footballer of the Year award. Earlier the same year, he had combined up-front with Brazilian Romario to help Barcelona reach the final of the UEFA Champions League.

1994

Yordan Letchkov headed the winning goal against holders and defending champions Germany in the 1994 FIFA World Cup quarter-final in the United States. At the time, he played for German club Hamburg. He later became mayor of Sliven, the Bulgarian town he was born in.

BERBATOV

NATIONAL LEGEND
MOB RULES

Much-travelled Bulgaria centre-forward **Dimitar Berbatov** claims to have learned English by watching the *Godfather* movies. Berbatov joined Manchester United from Tottenham in 2008 for a club and Bulgarian record fee of GBP 30.75m. Before joining Spurs, he had been a member of the Bayer Leverkusen side who narrowly missed out on a treble in 2002. They lost in the final of both the UEFA Champions League and the German cup and finished runners-up in the German *Bundesliga*. Berbatov surprised and disappointed fans back home when he announced his international retirement aged just 29, in May 2010, having scored a national-record 48 goals in his 78 appearances for Bulgaria.

TOP SCORERS:

1. **Dimitar Berbatov**, 48
   = **Hristo Bonev**, 48
3. **Hristo Stoichkov**, 37
4. **Liubomir Angelov**, 26
   = **Emil Kostadinov**, 26

NATIONAL LEGEND
BOSSMAN BONEV

Hristo Bonev was out on his own as Bulgaria's leading man both for appearances and goals – and a national hero for his stylish flair on the field. A mainstay of the side at the 1970 and 1974 FIFA World Cups, Bonev scored in Bulgaria's opening game at the 1970 tournament, a 3-2 defeat to Peru, and again four years later in a 1-1 draw against Uruguay. His 48th and final goal came on his last game (his 96th) for his country, a 2-1 loss to Argentina in April 1979. Bonev coached Bulgaria at the 1998 FIFA World Cup in France, the last manager to lead them at the finals, but they were knocked out in the first round.

BONEV

3

Three of Bulgaria's 1994 FIFA World Cup semi-finalists later coached the national team: Hristo Stoichkov between 2004 and 2007, Petar Hubchev, 2016–19, followed immediately by Krasimir Balakov, but only for six games.

NATIONAL HERO
STAN THE BURGER VAN MAN

Stiliyan Petrov – "Stan" to fans of his English club Aston Villa – was applauded onto the field when he became Bulgaria's first outfield player to reach 100 caps, against Switzerland in March 2011. The elegant midfielder received far more acclaim after recovering from a March 2012 diagnosis of acute leukaemia – Villa fans stood and clapped for 60 seconds in the 19th-minute of every game for the rest of the season, 19 being his squad number. He previously fought homesickness when playing for Scottish club Celtic but improved his English skills by working behind the counter of a friend's burger van. Petrov became Bulgaria's most-capped player in a 3-1 defeat to Switzerland in September 2011 and bowed out of international football a month later.

DISCIPLINARY-RELATED
POP OF HORRORS

Bulgaria captain Ivelin Popov has experienced a chequered career with the national side – including several scandals and banishments. He scored twice from the penalty spot in February 2011 in a 2-2 friendly draw with Estonia that was later officially expunged from the records by FIFA amid allegations of match-fixing involving the officials. Popov announced his international retirement in November 2019 aged 32, claiming satisfaction on Bulgaria reaching the (later suspended) play-offs for the 2020 UEFA European Championship.

NATIONAL LEGEND
A NATION MOURNS

Bulgaria lost two of its most popular footballing talents when a June 1971 car crash claimed the lives of strikers Georgi Asparukhov and Nikola Kotkov; Asparukhov was only 28 years old at the time, while Kotkov was 32. Asparukhov scored 19 goals in 50 internationals, including Bulgaria's only goal of the 1966 FIFA World Cup finals in a 3-1 defeat to Hungary. Asparuhov was nominated for the 1965 Ballon d'Or award and finished eighth: over 500,000 people attended his funeral in Sofia.

MIHAILOV

PETROV

8

Martin Petrov suffered a terrible start to his international career when he was sent off for two yellow cards just eight minutes into his debut as a substitute in a UEFA EURO 2000 qualifier. He went on to win 89 caps, 1999–2013.

MOST APPEARANCES:

1. **Stiliyan Petrov**, 106
2. **Borislav Mihailov**, 102
3. **Hristo Bonev**, 96
4. **Krasimir Balakov**, 92
5. **Dimitar Penev**, 90
   = **Martin Petrov**, 90
   = **Ivelin Popov**, 90

39

CROATIA

Croatia's distinctive red-and-white chequered jersey has become one of the most recognised in world football. They hit a new peak in 2018 when they reached their first FIFA World Cup final.

Joined FIFA: 1992
Biggest win: 10-0 v. San Marino, 2014
Highest FIFA Ranking: 3rd
Home stadium: (rotation)
Honours: -

NATIONAL LEGEND
SUPER ŠUKER

Striker **Davor Šuker** won the Golden Boot for top scorer at the FIFA World Cup in 1998, scoring six goals in seven games as Croatia finished third. His strikes included the opening goal in Croatia's 2-1 semi-final defeat to eventual champions France, and the winner in a 2-1 triumph over the Netherlands in the third-place play-off. Šuker, by far his country's leading scorer of all time, had hit three goals at the 1996 UEFA European Championship – including an audacious long-distance lob over Denmark goalkeeper Peter Schmeichel. Šuker was named president of the Croatian FA in July 2012.

ŠUKER

TOP SCORERS:

1. Davor Šuker, 45
2. Mario Mandžukić, 33
3. Eduardo da Silva, 29
4. Ivan Perišić, 26
5. Darijo Srna, 22

MODRIĆ

STAR PLAYER

MAGICAL MODRIĆ

Croatia made history by reaching their first FIFA World Cup final in 2018 – and star of the show was captain and playmaker **Luka Modrić**, who won the Golden Ball for the tournament's best player despite their 4-2 final defeat to France. Modrić began his career with Dinamo Zagreb before moving to Tottenham Hotspur in England and then winning four UEFA Champions League titles with Spain's Real Madrid. In Russia, Croatia became the first country since Argentina in 1990 to win two penalty shoot-outs at the same FIFA World Cup – beating Denmark in the round of 16 as well as hosts Russia in the quarter-finals.

SRNA

4-0

Croatia's second game at the 2014 FIFA World Cup, a 4-0 trouncing of Cameroon, was notable as it was the first time they had scored as many as four goals in a single FIFA World Cup finals match.

Darijo Srna is Croatia's fifth top scorer of all time, despite playing many games as a right-back or wing-back.

STAR PLAYER
RAK ATTACKS

Only three footballers have won Croatia's Sportsman of the Year award since Davor Šuker in 1998: Mario Mandžukić in 2013, Ivan Rakitić two years later, and Luka Modrić in 2018 – the year Rakitić made history at the 2018 FIFA World Cup. The Barcelona midfielder became the first man to convert the decisive penalty in two different shoot-outs at the same FIFA World Cup: against Denmark and Russia. Rakitić was born in Switzerland but opted to play senior football for Croatia, the land of both his parents. He was named Croatian Footballer of the Year in 2015, the only time since 2013 it has not gone to seven-time winner Luka Modrić.

STAR PLAYER
UNLUCKY MANDS

Striker **Mario Mandžukić** was Croatia's hero in their 2018 FIFA World Cup semi-final – only to unwittingly turn villain in the final four days later. In the semi, his goal, 19 minutes into extra time, beat England 2-1 and sent Croatia to their first-ever FIFA World Cup final. In the final, however, he headed an Antoine Griezmann free kick into his own net after 18 minutes to give France the lead. Mandžukić did pull a goal back to make the score 4-2 to France with 21 minutes left. He thus became the first man to score for both sides in a FIFA World Cup final – only Dutch defender Ernie Brandts, against Italy in 1978 – had done it any FIFA World Cup finals match.

MANDŽUKIĆ

22

Croatia competed in the 2018 FIFA World Cup with only 22 squad players for the majority of the tournament. Coach Zlatko Dalić sent Nikola Kalinić home after the striker allegedly refused to come on as a substitute in their opening game against Nigeria.

NATIONAL LEGEND
PERIŠIĆ THE THOUGHT

Winger **Ivan Perišić** became the first Croat to score at the right end in a FIFA World Cup final, levelling up in first-half stoppage time after team-mate Mario Mandžukić had inadvertently given France the lead in the 2018 final. Perišić had previously equalised against England in the semi-final, while he and Mandžukić had also scored in a first-round 4-0 victory over Cameroon at the 2014 tournament. Perišić has scored or set up 11 goals for Croatia at major tournaments, a national record – his strikes also including a winner against Spain to clinch the Croats' place in the knock-out stages at the 2016 UEFA European Championship.

MOST APPEARANCES:

1 Darijo Srna, 134
2 Luka Modrić, 127
3 Stipe Pletikosa, 114
4 Ivan Rakitić, 106
5 Josip Šimunić, 105

2

Croatia's 4-0 victory over Cameroon in the 2014 FIFA World Cup saw striker Ivica Olić become the first player to score for Croatia at two separate FIFA World Cups, having previously found the net in 2002.

3

Three players – Darijo Srna, Stipe Pletikosa and defender Josip Šimunić – all reached 100 caps for Croatia in the same game – a 4-0 friendly win over Korea Republic in 2013.

PERIŠIĆ

TOURNAMENT TRIVIA
DOUBLE IDENTITY

Robert Jarni and Robert Prosinečki both have the rare distinction of playing for two different countries at different FIFA World Cup tournaments. They both represented Yugoslavia in Italy in 1990, and then newly independent Croatia in France eight years later. Full-back Jarni actually played for both Yugoslavia and Croatia in 1990, then only Yugoslavia in 1991, before switching back – and permanently – to Croat colours in 1992 after the country officially joined UEFA and FIFA. He retired with 81 caps for Croatia, seven for Yugoslavia.

JARNI

CZECH REPUBLIC

The most successful of the former Eastern Bloc countries, as Czechoslovakia, they finished as runners-up in the 1934 and 1962 FIFA World Cups. As Czech Republic, they have failed to qualify for the last three FIFA World Cups.

Joined FIFA: 1994

Biggest win: 11-0 v. Senegal, 1966

Highest FIFA ranking: 2nd

Home stadium: (rotation)

Honours: 1 UEFA European Championship (1976)

ČECH

30 MINUTES
Belgium's 1920 victory at the Olympic Games was overshadowed when Czechoslovakia walked off the pitch after only 30 minutes in protest at what they saw as biased refereeing. Czechoslovakia are still the only team in the history of Olympic football to have been disqualified.

NATIONAL LEGEND
ČECH CAP

Goalkeeper **Petr Čech** always wore a protective cap after suffering a fractured skull during an English Premier League match in October 2006. The young Čech had served notice of his talent when he was beaten by only one penalty in a shoot-out against France in the 2002 UEFA U-21 European Championship final, helping the Czechs win the trophy. He later claimed winner's medals as Chelsea won the UEFA Champions League in 2012 (he was named man of the match) and the UEFA Europa League a year later. He retired after the UEFA Europa League final in 2019, but just a few months later he was back between the posts as an ice hockey goalie in England. He even saved a penalty shot on his debut.

NATIONAL LEGEND
PLAŠIL'S PLACE

Midfielder **Jaroslav Plašil** went into UEFA EURO 2016 as only the fourth Czech player to have reached a century of caps, hitting the landmark in a 2-1 friendly defeat to Korea Republic. He had been part of the side that reached the semi-finals of the 2004 UEFA European Championship, scored against Turkey at the tournament four years later, and also played every minute of his side's progress to the second round at EURO 2012. He was also a mainstay in helping the Czechs reach the 2016 UEFA European Championship.

NEDVĚD

NATIONAL LEGEND
THE CANNON COLLECTS

Pavel Nedvěd's election as European Footballer of the Year in 2003 ended a long wait for fans in the Czech Republic who had seen a string of outstanding players overlooked since Josef Masopust had been honoured back in 1962. Masopust, a midfield general, had scored the opening goal in the FIFA World Cup final that year before Brazil hit back to win 3-1 in the Chilean capital of Santiago. Years later, Masopust was remembered by Pelé and nominated as one of his 125 greatest living footballers. At club level, Masopust won eight Czechoslovak league titles with Dukla Prague, the army club.

MOST APPEARANCES:

1. **Petr Čech**, 124
2. **Karel Poborský**, 118
3. **Tomáš Rosický**, 105
4. **Jaroslav Plašil**, 103
5. **Milan Baroš**, 93

34

Antonín Puč was the country's top international scorer with 34 goals for Czechoslovakia when he retired in 1938 until he was passed, first by Jan Koller 67 years later, and, latterly, by Milan Baroš.

NATIONAL LEGEND
MOSTLY MOZART

The last Czech player to score at a FIFA World Cup was **Tomáš Rosický**, who bagged a double in a 3–0 victory over the United States in 2006. Despite an injury-plagued career, he became only the third Czech to reach a century of caps, in a 2–1 2016 European Championship qualifier defeat to Iceland in June 2015. The midfielder, nicknamed "The Little Mozart" for the way he orchestrated play, retired from international football after the Czech Republic were eliminated from EURO 2016 in the first round, during which he became the oldest Czech player to appear in a UEFA EURO finals, aged 35. He had also been their youngest, aged 19, in 2000.

ROSICKÝ

NATIONAL LEGEND
TEN OUT OF TEN

Jan Koller is Czech football's all-time leading international marksman with 55 goals in 91 appearances. Koller scored on his debut against Belgium and struck ten goals in ten successive internationals. He scored six goals in each of the 2000, 2004 and 2008 UEFA European Championship qualifying campaigns. He began his career with Sparta Prague, who converted him from goalkeeper to goalscorer. Then, in Belgium, he was top scorer with Lokeren, before scoring 42 goals in two league title-winning campaigns with Anderlecht. Later, with Borussia Dortmund in Germany, he once went in goal after Jens Lehmann had been sent off and kept a clean sheet – having scored in the first half.

1934
The final of the 1934 FIFA World Cup was the first to go into extra time, with Czechoslovakia ultimately losing 2-1 to hosts Italy.

TOP SCORERS:
1 Jan Koller, 55
2 Milan Baroš, 41
3 Vladimir Šmicer, 27
4 Tomáš Rosický, 23
5 Pavel Kuka, 22 (plus 7 for Czechoslovakia)

KOLLER

1976
In 1976, Antonín Panenka invented the calmly chipped penalty style that is still performed to this day. It is commonly known as "a Panenka".

NATIONAL LEGEND
ONDRÁŠEK SETS THE RECORD STRAIGHT

Zdeněk Ondrášek enjoyed the ideal introduction to international football at the age of 30, scoring a late winner as a substitute striker on his debut in a UEFA EURO 2020 qualifier against Group A table-toppers England in October 2019. The victory at Prague's Sinobo Stadium was revenge for England's 5-0 win at Wembley seven months earlier – the Czechs' heaviest international defeat since independence. They recovered from that opening-game setback and qualified for the now rescheduled UEFA EURO 2020 as group runners-up.

ONDRÁŠEK

1

Vladimir Šmicer won 80 caps for the Czech Republic, as well as one for Czechoslovakia.

DENMARK

ERIKSEN

They have been playing football since 1908 but Denmark's crowning moment came in 1992 when they walked away with the UEFA European Championship crown in one of the biggest-ever international football shocks.

Joined FIFA: 1908

Biggest win: 17-1 v. France, 1908

Highest FIFA ranking: 3rd

Home stadium: Parken Stadium, Copenhagen

Honours: 1 UEFA European Championship (1992)

STAR PLAYER
CHRISTIAN AID

A T-shirt produced as Denmark approached the 2018 FIFA World Cup summed up their tactics as passing the ball to **Christian Eriksen** and waiting for him to score. The playmaker's hat-trick had secured his side's place at the finals, in a 5-1 qualification play-off win away to the Republic of Ireland in November 2017 – 32 years after Denmark had beaten the same country 4-1, also in Dublin, to reach the 1986 FIFA World Cup. Midfielder Eriksen, who moved from Tottenham Hotspur to Italy's Internazionale in January 2020, top-scored for Denmark with 11 goals in the 2018 FIFA World Cup qualification campaign. He had reached 95 caps (joint-ninth for Denmark with defender Simon Kjaer) and 31 goals (seventh) by 2020.

16 SECONDS
Ebbe Sand scored the fastest-ever FIFA World Cup goal by a substitute when he netted a mere 16 seconds after coming onto the pitch in Denmark's clash with Nigeria at France 1998.

2 Midfielder Morten Wieghorst is the only player to be sent off twice while playing for Denmark – yet he also received a special award for fair play after deliberately missing a wrongly awarded penalty.

NATIONAL LEGENDS
BROTHERS IN ARMS

Denmark's two finest footballers came from the same family: **Michael** (104 games, 37 goals) and **Brian Laudrup** (82 games, 37 goals). The brothers spread their creative playmaking skills across Europe: Michael in Italy with Lazio and Juventus and in Spain with Barcelona and Real Madrid, Brian in Italy with Fiorentina and AC Milan, in Scotland with Rangers, and in England with Chelsea. Only Brian shared in Denmark's 1992 UEFA European Championship glory though – Michael had temporarily quit international football after falling out with then coach Richard Møller Nielsen.

MICHAEL LAUDRUP

BRIAN LAUDRUP

STAR PLAYER
IF THE SHIRT FITS

Danish striker Yussuf Poulsen had an eventful 2018 FIFA World Cup. In Denmark's opening game, he conceded a first-half penalty which was missed by Peru's Carlos Cueva, then scored the game's only goal and was officially voted man of the match. But he was booked in Denmark's first two games so missed their third against France. He wore his favoured middle name "YURARY" on the back of his Denmark shirt, despite wearing "POULSEN" for his German club RB Leipzig, because the club had already printed shirts with that name on them.

102

Morten Olsen captained Denmark at the 1986 FIFA World Cup and later became the first Dane to reach a century of caps, retiring in 1989 with four goals from 102 appearances.

OLSEN

MOST APPEARANCES:

1. Peter Schmeichel, 129
2. Dennis Rommedahl, 126
3. Jon Dahl Tomasson, 112
4. Thomas Helveg, 108
5. Michael Laudrup, 104

SCHMEICHEL

NATIONAL LEGEND
GOLDEN GLOVES

Peter Schmeichel, a European champion with Denmark in 1992, was rated by many as the world's best goalkeeper in the early 1990s. His son Kasper Schmeichel has since emulated his father by enjoying club success in England and becoming Denmark's first-choice keeper. Peter was a very animated fan in the stands at the 2018 FIFA World Cup as Kasper saved three spot kicks when Denmark lost their round-of-16 match against Croatia, 3-2 on penalties. He saved from Luka Modrić in extra time, and twice more in the shoot-out.

TOURNAMENT TRIVIA
THE UNEXPECTED IN 1992

Few Danish football fans will ever forget June 1992, their national team's finest hour, when they won the UEFA European Championship, despite not actually qualifying for the finals in Sweden. Ten days before the tournament opened, UEFA invited the Danes – who had finished second to Yugoslavia in their qualifying group – to take the Yugoslavs' place following their exclusion. Expectations were minimal, but then the inconceivable happened. Relying heavily on goalkeeper Peter Schmeichel, his defence, and the creative Brian Laudrup, Denmark caused one of the biggest shocks in football history by winning the tournament, culminating in a 2-0 victory over world champions Germany.

18

Christian Eriksen was the youngest player at the 2010 FIFA World Cup, aged 18 years and four months.

NATIONAL LEGEND
TOMASSON'S JOINT TOP

Jon Dahl Tomasson, Denmark's joint-top goalscorer with 52, became his national side's assistant manager in 2016, working with Norwegian-born head coach Åge Hareide. His final goal for Denmark came in a 3-1 defeat to Japan in the first round of the 2010 FIFA World Cup – tucking away the rebound after his penalty was saved by Eiji Kawashima. Tomasson won 112 caps, while Poul "Tist" Nielsen's 52 strikes came in just 38 appearances between 1910 and 1925. Pauli Jørgensen was also prolific, scoring 44 goals in just 47 games between 1925 and 1939.

TOMASSON

6-1
Denmark's 6-1 defeat of Uruguay in the first round of the 1986 FIFA World Cup in Neza ranks among the country's finest performances, although their adventure was ended by Spain in the last 16 as they lost 5-1.

TOP SCORERS:

1. Poul Nielsen, 52
= Jon Dahl Tomasson, 52
3. Pauli Jørgensen, 44
4. Ole Madsen, 42
5. Preben Elkjær, 38

GREECE

There is no argument about Greece's proudest footballing moment – their shock triumph at the 2004 UEFA European Championship, one of the game's greatest international upsets. It was only the Greeks' second appearance at a UEFA EURO finals.

Joined FIFA: 1929

Biggest win: 8-0 v. Syria, 1949

Highest FIFA ranking: 8th

Home stadium: Olympic Stadium, Athens

Honours: 1 UEFA European Championship (2004)

SAMARAS

3
Konstantinos "Kostas" Mitroglou played a crucial role as Greece qualified for the 2014 FIFA World Cup, scoring three goals in a 4-2 aggregate victory over Romania in a play-off.

17
Goalkeeper Stefanos Kapino became Greece's youngest international when he made his debut in November 2011 in a friendly against Romania at the age of 17 years and 241 days – 80 days younger than the previous record-holder, striker Thomas Mavros, had been when he faced the Netherlands in February 1972.

TOURNAMENT TRIVIA
GORGEOUS GEORGE

Georgios Samaras won and converted the last-minute penalty that sent Greece through to the knock-out stages of a FIFA World Cup for the first time, clinching a dramatic 2-1 victory over Group C opponents Côte d'Ivoire at the 2014 tournament in Brazil. The goal, following a foul by Giovanni Sio, was former Celtic striker Samaras's ninth goal for his country – his first coming on his debut against Belarus in February 2006. Samaras could actually have played international football for Australia because his father, Ioannis, was born in Melbourne and moved to Greece aged 13. Ioannis won 16 caps for Greece between 1986 and 1990, but he is a long way behind his son, who made 81 appearances.

38
Greece's oldest player was a goalkeeper, Kostas Chalkias – who was 38 years and 13 days old when he played his final international, against the Czech Republic in June 2012.

NATIONAL LEGEND
SIMPLY THEO BEST

Theodoros "Theo" **Zagorakis** – born near Kavala on 27 October 1971 – was captain of Greece when they won the UEFA European Championship in 2004, and the defensive midfielder picked up the prize for the tournament's best player. He is the second most-capped Greek footballer of all time, with 120 caps. But it was not until his 101st international appearance – ten years and five months after his debut – that he scored his first goal for his country, in a FIFA World Cup qualifier against Denmark in February 2005. He retired from international football after making a 15-minute cameo appearance against Spain in August 2007.

ZAGORAKIS

NATIONAL LEGEND
KING OTTO

German coach **Otto Rehhagel** became the first foreigner to be voted "Greek of the Year" in 2004 after leading the country to glory at that year's UEFA European Championship. He was also offered honorary Greek citizenship. His nine years in charge, after being appointed in 2001, made him Greece's longest-serving international manager. Rehhagel was 65 at EURO 2004, making him the oldest coach to win the UEFA European Championship – although that record was taken off him four years later when 69-year-old Luis Aragonés lifted the trophy with Spain.

REHHAGEL

TOP SCORERS:

1 Nikos Anostopoulos, 29
2 Angelos Charisteas, 25
3 Theofanis Gekas, 24
4 Dimitris Saravakos, 22
5 Mimis Papaioannou, 21

CHARISTEAS

2004
Greece's UEFA EURO 2004 triumph was the first time a country coached by a foreigner had triumphed at either the UEFA European Championship or the FIFA World Cup.

NATIONAL LEGEND
RIGHT ANGELOS

Only Nikos Anastopoulos has scored more goals for Greece than **Angelos Charisteas**, but no one can have struck a more important one than Charisteas, whose second-half header defeated hosts Portugal in the 2004 UEFA European Championship final. He had already scored the equaliser against Spain in the first round as well as the match-winner against holders France in the quarter-finals. Striker Charisteas made his international debut in February 2001, scoring twice in a 3-3 draw against Russia. He also went on to score Greece's sole goal in their unsuccessful trophy defence and opening-round exit at UEFA EURO 2008.

NATIONAL LEGEND
HIT AND MISS

In 2010, full-back Vasilios Torosidis, later Greece captain, scored the winner against Nigeria to secure his country's first-ever victory at a FIFA World Cup – having earlier in the game been kicked by Sani Kaita, for which the Nigerian midfielder was sent off. Torosidis was also in Greece's squad for the 2008 and 2012 UEFA European Championships and 2014 FIFA World Cup. There would be no third UEFA EURO appearance for Torosidis, however, as Greece finished bottom of their qualification group for UEFA EURO 2016, despite being the group's top seed. Their disastrous campaign included home and away defeats by the Faroe Islands.

1

Only one team – Greece – has beaten both the holders and the hosts on the way to winning either a UEFA European Championship or a FIFA World Cup. In fact, the Greeks beat hosts Portugal twice – in both the tournament's opening game and the final, with a quarter-final victory over defending champions France in between.

MOST APPEARANCES:

1 Giorgos Karagounis, 139
2 Theodoros Zagorakis, 120
3 Kostas Katsouranis, 116
4 Vasileios Torisidis, 101
5 Angelos Basinas, 100

KARAGOUNIS

NATIONAL LEGEND
GRIEF AND GLORY FOR GIORGOS

It was a bittersweet day for captain **Giorgos Karagounis** when he equalled the Greek record for international appearances, with his 120th cap against Russia in their final Group A game at UEFA EURO 2012. The midfielder scored the only goal of the game, giving Greece a place in the quarter-finals at Russia's expense – but a second yellow card of the tournament ruled him out of the match, which the Greeks lost to Germany. Karagounis was one of three survivors from Greece's UEFA EURO 2004 success, along with fellow midfielder Kostas Katsouranis and goalkeeper Kostas Chalkias.

HUNGARY

For a period in the early 1950s, Hungary possessed the most talented football team on the planet. They claimed Olympic gold at Helsinki in 1952 but finished as runners-up in the 1954 FIFA World Cup.

Joined FIFA: 1902
Biggest win: 13-1 v. France, 1927
Highest FIFA ranking: 18th
Home stadium:
Puskás Aréna, Budapest
Honours: -

KLEINHEISLER

NATIONAL LEGEND
LÁSZLÓ'S BREAKTHROUGH

An unlikely hero helped Hungary qualify for UEFA EURO 2016, their first international tournament since a first-round appearance at the 1986 FIFA World Cup. Midfielder **László Kleinheisler**, on his debut, scored the only goal in their qualifying play-off first leg away to Norway in November 2015, despite not having featured for his club Videoton that season. Hungary won the second leg 2-1, before German coach Bernd Storck's side reached the second round in France the following summer. They were helped to progress by a 3-3 draw against eventual champions Portugal, with captain Balázs Dzsudzsák scoring twice. Dzsudzsák equalled Hungary's international appearances record – with 108 – in a 2-0 defeat by Wales in November 2019.

5.4
Hungary's average of 5.4 goals per game at the 1954 FIFA World Cup remains an all-time high for the tournament.

37

Aged 37 years and 62 days, Zoltán Gera became the second oldest UEFA European Championship finals goalscorer at EURO 2016 – he is behind only Austria's Ivica Vastić, who was 38 years and 257 days old when he netted at EURO 2008.

SCORING RECORD
YEARS OF PLENTY

Hungary's dazzling line-up of the early 1950s was known as the Aranycsapat – or Golden Team. They set a record for international matches unbeaten, going 31 consecutive games without defeat between May 1950 and their July 1954 FIFA World Cup final loss to West Germany – a run that included clinching Olympic gold at Helsinki 1952. That 31-match tally has since been overtaken only by Brazil and Spain.

73

Hungary in the 1950s also set a record for most consecutive games scoring at least one goal: 73 matches.

NATIONAL LEGEND
GALLOPING MAJOR

In Hungarian football history, no one can compare with **Ferenc Puskás**, who netted 84 goals in 85 international matches for Hungary as well as 514 goals in 529 matches in the Hungarian and Spanish leagues. Blessed with a lethal left foot, he was known as the "Galloping Major" – by virtue of his playing for the army team Honved before joining Real Madrid and going on to play for Spain. During the 1950s, he was the top scorer and captain of the legendary Mighty Magyars (another nickname given to the Hungarian national team) and Honved.

TOP SCORERS:

1 Ferenc Puskás, 84
2 Sándor Kocsis, 75
3 Imre Schlosser, 59
4 Lajos Tichy, 51
5 György Sárosi, 42

PUSKÁS

TOURNAMENT TRIVIA
HUNGARY FOR IT

Hungary's 6–3 win over England at Wembley in 1953 remains one of the most significant international results ever as they became the first team from outside the British Isles to beat England in England – a record that had stood since 1901. The Hungarians had been undefeated for three years and were reigning Olympic champions, while England were the so-called "inventors" of football. The British press dubbed it "The Match of the Century". In the event, the match revolutionised the game in England, Hungary's unequivocal victory exposing England's rather naïve tactics.

1

Only one Hungarian has won the Ballon d'Or for player of the year: Flórián Albert in 1967.

NATIONAL LEGEND
NERVES AND STEEL

Gábor Király may now have won more caps, and earned more attention for his customary tracksuit bottoms – often compared to pyjama trousers – but Gyula Grosics is still recognised by many as Hungary's greatest goalkeeper. Unusual for a goalkeeper of his era, Grosics was comfortable with the ball at his feet and was willing to rush out of his area. The on-field confidence was not always displayed off it, however – and he was thought to be a nervous character, a hypochondriac and a loner. He allegedly asked to be substituted before the end of the match at Wembley in 1953.

66

Hungary hit a new personal low during qualifying for the 2018 FIFA World Cup: a 1–0 defeat to Andorra in June 2017, which ended Andorra's 66-match winless run.

KIRÁLY

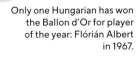

MOST APPEARANCES:

1 Balázs Dzsudzsák, 108
= Gábor Király, 108
3 József Bozsik, 101
4 Zoltán Gera, 97
5 Ronald Juhász, 95

NATIONAL LEGEND
GOLDEN HEAD

Sándor Kocsis, top scorer at the 1954 FIFA World Cup with 11 goals, was so good in the air that he was known as the "Golden Head". In 68 internationals, he scored an incredible 75 goals, including a then-record seven hat-tricks. His tally included two decisive extra-time goals in the 1954 FIFA World Cup semi-final against Uruguay, when Hungary had appeared to be on the brink of defeat.

49

NORTHERN IRELAND

Northern Ireland have played as a separate country since 1921 – before that, there had been an all-Ireland side. They last appeared at a major tournament in 2016, at the UEFA European Championship.

Joined FIFA: 1921
Biggest win: 7-0 v. Wales, 1930
Highest FIFA ranking: 20th
Home stadium: Windsor Park, Belfast
Honours: -

NATIONAL LEGEND
GEORGE IS BEST

One of the greatest players never to grace a FIFA World Cup, **George Best** (capped 37 times by Northern Ireland) nevertheless won domestic and European honours with Manchester United – including a European Champions Cup medal and the European Footballer of the Year award in 1968. He also played in the United States, Hong Kong and Australia before his "final" retirement in 1984.

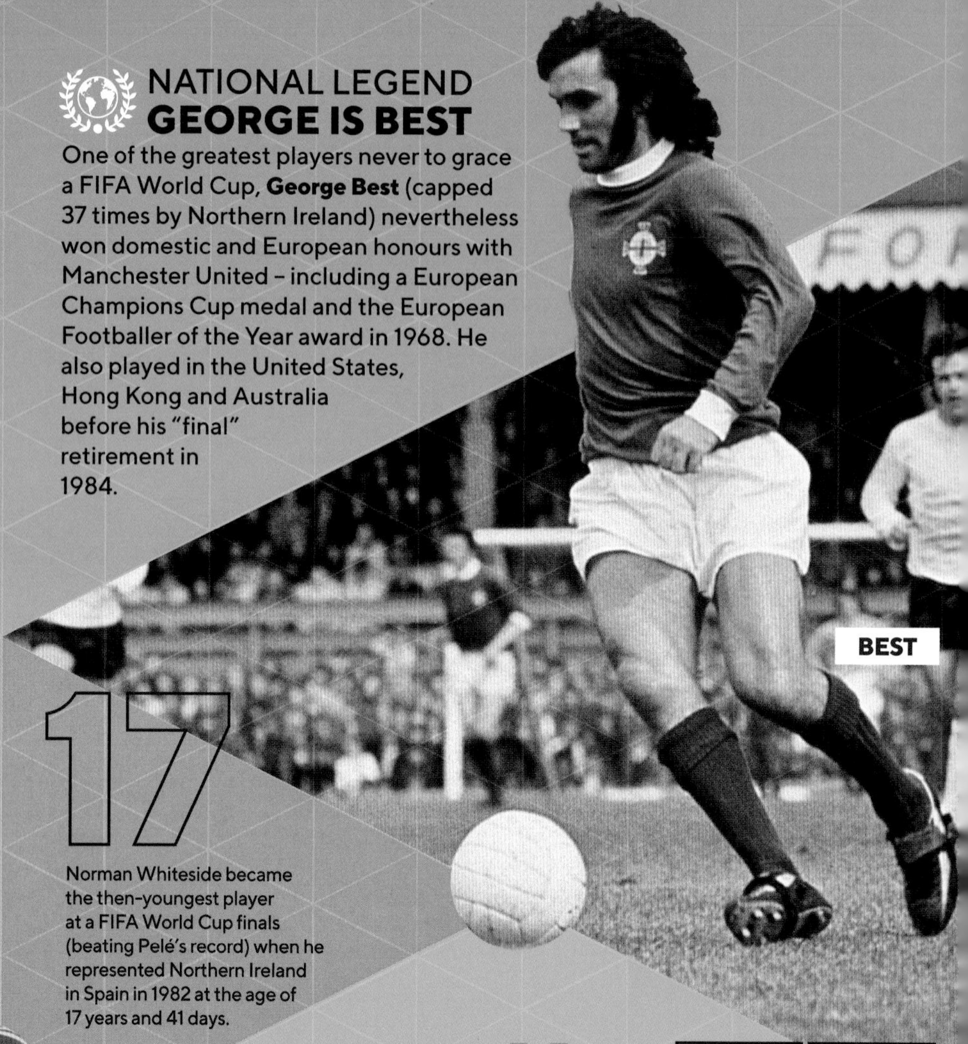

BEST

17

Norman Whiteside became the then-youngest player at a FIFA World Cup finals (beating Pelé's record) when he represented Northern Ireland in Spain in 1982 at the age of 17 years and 41 days.

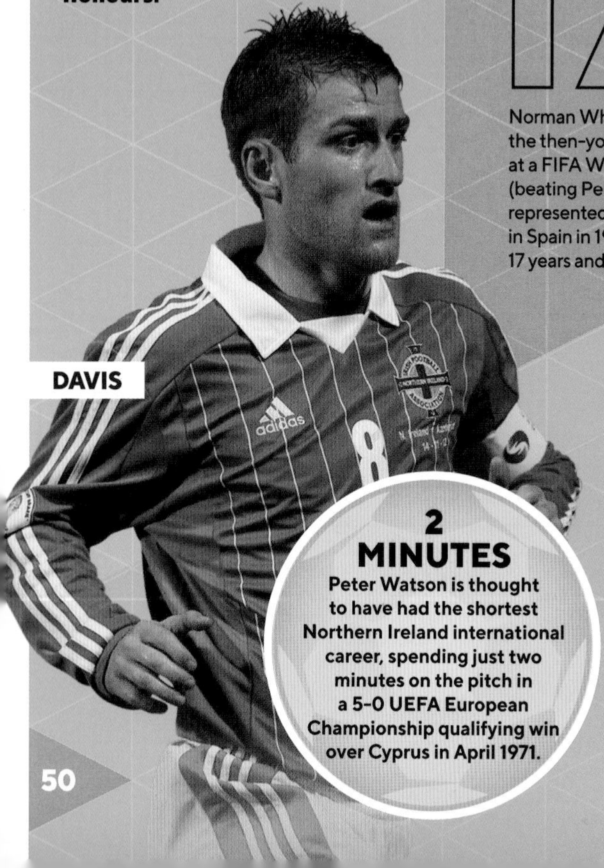

DAVIS

STAR PLAYER
THE BOY DAVIS

Midfielder **Steven Davis** became Northern Ireland's youngest post-war captain when he led the side out against Uruguay in May 2006, aged just 21 years, five months and 20 days. He remained captain for more than a decade, and perhaps his finest moment came in October 2015 when his two goals in a 3–1 defeat of Greece helped to secure Northern Ireland's place at the 2016 UEFA European Championship finals.

2 MINUTES

Peter Watson is thought to have had the shortest Northern Ireland international career, spending just two minutes on the pitch in a 5-0 UEFA European Championship qualifying win over Cyprus in April 1971.

77

Aaron Hughes ranks third among all Northern Ireland players, with 112 caps. The defender, however, was never known as a goalscorer. In fact, it took him until his 77th appearance, in August 2011, to register his first goal – against the Faroe Islands.

24

David Healy endured a four-year, 24-game scoring drought between October 2008 and November 2012 before hitting his 36th and final international goal against Israel in March 2013 and retiring from international football later that year, aged 34.

NATIONAL LEGEND
GIANT JENNINGS

Pat Jennings's record 119 appearances for Northern Ireland also stood as an international record at one stage. The former Tottenham Hotspur and Arsenal goalkeeper made his international debut, aged just 18, against Wales on 15 April 1964, and played his final game in the 1986 FIFA World Cup, against Brazil, on his 41st birthday. On 26 February 1983, Jennings became the first player in English football to make 1,000 senior appearances, and he marked the occasion with clean sheet in a 0-0 draw for Arsenal at West Bromwich Albion.

1958
Northern Ireland's captain at the 1958 FIFA World Cup was Tottenham Hotspur's cerebral Danny Blanchflower – the first 20th-century captain of an English club to win both the league and FA Cup in the same season, in 1960-61.

JENNINGS

NATIONAL LEGEND
HERO HEALY

Northern Ireland's leading goalscorer David Healy got off to the ideal start, scoring a brace on his international debut against Luxembourg in February 2000, but perhaps his two greatest days for his country came when he scored the only goal against Sven-Göran Eriksson's England in September 2005 – securing Northern Ireland's first victory over England since 1972 – and then, 12 months later, scoring a hat-trick to beat eventual champions Spain 3-2 in a 2008 UEFA European Championship qualifier.

MOST APPEARANCES:
1 Pat Jennings, 119
2 Steven Davis, 117
3 Aaron Hughes, 112
4 David Healy, 95
5 Mal Donaghy, 91

O'NEILL

NATIONAL LEGENDS
GIVING A GOOD ACCOUNT

Michael O'Neill coached Northern Ireland to their first major tournament, the 2016 UEFA European Championship, since Billy Bingham led them to the FIFA World Cups of 1982 and 1986. Northern Ireland also reached the play-offs for UEFA EURO 2020, but O'Neill resigned in April 2020 after the finals were postponed. He had been combining his national role with managing English Championship club Stoke City since November 2019. O'Neill, a winger as a a player, won 31 Northern Ireland caps before retiring in 2004. He was an accountant before being tempted into football management with Scotland's Cowdenbeath, and then Ireland's Shamrock Rovers, before taking the Northern Irish job in 2011. Only Bingham (118) managed Northern Ireland more times than O'Neill's 72 matches in charge.

TOURNAMENT TRIVIA
HOSTILE HOSTS

Northern Ireland topped their first-round group at the 1982 FIFA World Cup thanks to a 1-0 win over hosts Spain at a passionate Mestalla Stadium in Valencia. Watford striker Gerry Armstrong scored the goal, and the Northern Irish held on despite defender Mal Donaghy being sent off. A 4-1 second-round loss to France denied Northern Ireland a semi-finals place. Armstrong joined Spanish side RCD Mallorca the following year and, predictably, was regularly booed by rival fans.

TOP SCORERS:
1 David Healy, 36
2 Kyle Lafferty, 20
3 Colin Clarke, 13
   = Billy Gillespie, 13
5 Gerry Armstrong, 12
   = Joe Bambrick, 12
   = Steven Davis, 12
   = Iain Dowie, 12
   = Jimmy Quinn, 12

NORWAY

MOST APPEARANCES:

1 **John Arne Riise**, 110
2 **Thorbjørn Svenssen**, 104
3 **Henning Berg**, 100
4 **Erik Thorstvedt**, 97
5 **John Carew**, 91
= **Brede Hangeland**, 91

Although they played their first international, against Sweden, in 1908 and qualified for the 1938 FIFA World Cup, it would take a further 56 years, and the introduction of a direct brand of football, before Norway reappeared at a major international tournament.

Joined FIFA: 1908
Biggest win: 12-0 v. Finland, 1946
Highest FIFA ranking: 2nd
Home stadium: Ullevaal Stadion, Oslo
Honours: -

RIISE

NATIONAL LEGEND
LONG-DISTANCE RIISE

Fierce-shooting ex-Liverpool, AS Monaco and AS Roma left-back **John Arne Riise** marked the game in which he matched Thorbjørn Svenssen's Norwegian appearances record, against Greece in August 2012, by getting onto the scoresheet, albeit in a 3-2 defeat. He was also on the losing side when he claimed the record for himself, a 2-0 loss in Iceland the following month, before he scored his 16th international goal in his 106th match four days later as Norway beat Slovenia 2-1. Midfielder Bjorn Helge Riise, John Arne's younger brother, joined him at English club Fulham, and made 35 full international appearances.

15

Egil Olsen, one of Europe's most eccentric coaches, signed up for a surprise second spell as Norwegian national team coach in 2009, 15 years after he had led the unfancied Scandinavians to the 1994 FIFA World Cup finals.

NATIONAL LEGENDS
DOUBLE JEOPARDY

Sharing joint fifth place in Norway's scoring ranks are a pair who often led the line together in the late 1990s and early 2000s. Tore André Flo scored Norway's opener in a 2-1 defeat of Brazil at the 1998 FIFA World Cup, and Ole Gunnar Solskjær who, despite numerous injuries, scored his 23 goals in only 67 appearances, including one on his 1995 debut against Jamaica. In 2008, he became the youngest person to be given Norway's equivalent of a knighthood, aged 35.

OLSEN

0

Norway are the only country in the world to have played Brazil and never lost. Their record stands at won two, drawn two, lost zero.

SVENSSEN

NATIONAL LEGEND
ROCK STAR

Defender **Thorbjørn Svenssen** did not score a single goal in his 104 games for Norway between 1947 and 1962, but he did become the first Norwegian to reach a century of caps and, at the time, only the second footballer ever, behind only England's Billy Wright. Svenssen – nicknamed "Klippen", or "The Rock" – made his last appearance in May 1962, at the age of 38 years and 24 days. He died, aged 86, in January 2011.

15

Attacking midfielder **Martin Ødegaard** became Norway's youngest international when he made his debut against the United Arab Emirates in August 2014 at the tender age of 15 years and 253 days.

2

After beating Brazil in the first round at France 1998, Norway made it to an incredible no. 2 in FIFA's official world ranking.

HÅLAND

93

He may no longer hold Norway's record for the most international appearances but Thorbjørn Svenssen captained the country more than any other player, leading them out 93 times.

STAR PLAYER
STERLING ERLING

Norway's latest striking star **Erling Braut Håland** has proved himself a fast starter. Aged 16, he scored on his cup and league debuts for Molde FK in April and June 2017, respectively. Subsequent scoring feats have included four goals in the first 21 minutes away to SK Brann in July 2018, six goals in his first three UEFA Champions League appearances for Austria's Red Bull Salzburg in 2018-2019, and a hat-trick on his January 2020 debut for Germany's Borussia Dortmund in just 23 minutes, entering the fray as a substitute. Born in Leeds in July 2000, Håland had been eligible to play for England – his father Alf-Inge Håland, who won 34 Norway caps, was playing in England at the time – but he chose Norway and made his senior bow against Malta in September 2019. Håland won the Golden Boot at the FIFA U-20 World Cup 2019 in Poland, thanks to a tournament record nine goals in his side's 12-0 defeat of Honduras.

NATIONAL LEGEND
JUVE DONE IT ALL

Jørgen Juve netted his national record 33 international goals in 45 appearances between 1928 and 1937. He did not score as Norway claimed bronze at the Berlin 1936 Olympics, but he played when Norway beat Germany 2-0 in the quarter-finals, prompting Adolf Hitler and other Nazi leaders to storm out of the stadium in fury. After retiring in 1938, he worked as a legal scholar and sports journalist and wrote books on the Olympics and football.

JUVE

TOP SCORERS:

1 Jørgen Juve, 33
2 Einar Gundersen, 26
3 Harald Hennum, 25
4 John Carew, 24
5 Tore André Flo, 23
  = Ole Gunnar Solskjær, 23

TOURNAMENT TRIVIA
LONG-STAY TRAVELLERS

Norway's best finish at an international tournament was the bronze medal they clinched at the 1936 Summer Olympics in Berlin, losing to Italy in the semi-finals but beating Poland 3-2 in a medal play-off thanks to an Arne Brustad hat-trick. That year's side has gone down in Norwegian football history as the *Bronselaget*, or *Bronze Team*. However, they had entered the tournament with low expectations and were forced to alter their travel plans ahead of the semi-final against Italy on 10 August – Norwegian football authorities had originally booked their trip home for the previous day, not expecting their team to get so far.

POLAND

Poland first qualified for the FIFA World Cup in 1938 and finished in third place at both the 1974 and 1982 tournaments. They also notably co-hosted UEFA EURO 2012 with Ukraine, although they made a first-round exit.

Joined FIFA: 1921
Biggest win: 10-0 v. San Marino, 2009
Highest FIFA ranking: 5th
Home stadium: Stadion Narodowy, Warsaw
Honours: -

⚡ STAR PLAYER
☆ LOVING LEWANDOWSKI

Although **Robert Lewandowski** made his FIFA World Cup finals debut in Russia, he did not score as Poland finished bottom of Group H. Lewandowski, however, remains a much-feared striker – despite being rejected by Legia Warsaw aged 16 and, as a 20-year-old, failing to impress future Poland coach Franciszek Smuda, who chided the man who recommended him: "You owe me petrol money." Lewandowski eventually broke through with Lech Poznań, helped Borussia Dortmund to two *Bundesliga* titles in Germany and has won six more since joining Bayern Munich in 2014, on his way to becoming Poland's all-time top scorer.

LEWANDOWSKI

16

Prolific striker **Robert Lewandowski** set a European record for goals in a FIFA World Cup qualifying competition with 16 for the 2018 FIFA World Cup – a tally which included three hat-tricks.

🌐 NATIONAL LEGEND
PEERLESS PRESIDENTS

Grzegorz Lato is Poland's fourth most-capped player and third-highest scorer, the only Polish winner of the Golden Boot with his seven goals at the 1974 FIFA World Cup, and a member of the gold medal-winning team at the 1972 Summer Olympics. He was also a leading figure in Poland's co-hosting with Ukraine of the 2012 UEFA European Championship, having become president of the country's FA in 2008. He vowed: "I am determined to change the image of Polish football, to make it transparent and pure." He was succeeded as president in 2012 by **Zbigniew Boniek**, arguably Poland's finest-ever player.

BONIEK

🌐 NATIONAL LEGEND
MILIK DELIVERY

Arkadiusz Milik was the hero as Poland finally won a game at a UEFA European Championship in 2016 after three draws and three defeats in their two previous tournaments in 2008 and 2012. Milik struck in an opening win against Northern Ireland, kicking off what proved to be a run to the quarter-finals when only a penalty shoot-out defeat to Portugal ended Polish hopes. In fact, Poland did not trail for a single minute throughout the tournament until that 5-3 loss on spot kicks.

TOP SCORERS:

1 Robert Lewandowski, 61
2 Włodzimierz Lubański, 48
3 Grzegorz Lato, 45
4 Kazimierz Deyna, 41
5 Ernest Pohl, 39

4

Ernest Wilimowski wrote his name into FIFA World Cup history in 1938 when he scored four goals but still finished on the losing side. Poland went down 6-5 after extra time to Brazil in a first-round tie in Strasbourg, France.

TRIUMPH AND TRAGEDY

Jakub Błaszczykowski was one of his country's few players to come out of EURO 2012 with credit, despite going into the tournament in testing circumstances. He joined the rest of the squad only after attending the funeral of his father. As a ten-year-old, Błaszczykowski had witnessed his mother being stabbed to death by his father, who served 15 years in prison. Błaszczykowski was encouraged to pursue football by his uncle Jerzy Brzęczek, a former Poland captain and 1992 Olympic Games silver medallist. Błaszczykowski became the third Pole to reach 100 caps, doing so against Senegal in Poland's 2018 FIFA World Cup opener.

BŁASZCZYKOWSKI

NATIONAL LEGEND
STAYING ON LATER THAN LATO

Record-breaking Polish stalwart **Michał Żewłakow** bowed out of international football on familiar turf, even though his country was playing an away game. The versatile defender's 102nd and final appearance for his country was a goalless friendly in Greece in March 2011, at the Karaiskakis stadium in Piraeus where he used to play club football for Olympiacos. Żewłakow had overtaken Grzegorz Lato's appearances record for Poland in his previous match, an October 2010 friendly against Ecuador.

16

Aged just 16 years and 188 days, and on his debut, Włodzimierz Lubański scored Poland's third goal in a 9-0 victory over Norway in 1963 to become their youngest-ever scorer.

5

Poland had five different goalscorers when they beat Peru 5-1 at the 1982 FIFA World Cup: Włodzimierz Smolarek, Grzegorz Lato, Zbigniew Boniek, Andrzej Buncol and Włodzimierz Ciołek.

ŻEWŁAKOW

2000
Michał Żewłakow and brother Marcin became the first twins to line up together for Poland, against France in February 2000.

PIĄTEK

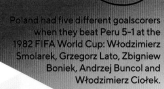

NATIONAL LEGEND
PIĄTEK ON POINT

Poland finally qualified for a UEFA European Championship in 2008 and have reached all subsequent UEFA EUROs – including as co-hosts with Ukraine in 2012. Robert Lewandowski (six goals) and strike partner **Krzysztof Piątek** led the line as they secured their place at the now-rescheduled 2020 finals by topping Group G, six points clear of Austria. Piątek scored five goals in his first ten internationals, including the winner in the Poles' penultimate qualifier away to Israel. Overseeing the campaign was former international Jerzy Brzęczek, who became coach in August 2018.

MOST APPEARANCES:

1	Robert Lewandowski,	112
2	Jakub Błaszczykowski,	108
3	Michał Żewłakow,	102
4	Grzegorz Lato,	100
5	Kazimierz Deyna,	97

PORTUGAL

At Russia 2018, Cristiano Ronaldo became the first Portuguese player – and fourth ever – to score at four different FIFA World Cups.

Despite producing some of Europe's finest-ever players, Portugal's international history was one of near misses – until they triumphed in the 2016 UEFA European Championship and the UEFA Nations League in 2019.

Joined FIFA: 1921

Biggest win:
8-0 v. Lichtenstein, 1994 & 1999, v. Kuwait, 2003

Highest FIFA ranking: 3rd

Home stadium:
Estadio de Luz, Lisbon

Honours: 1 UEFA European Championship (2016), 1 UEFA Nations League (2019)

STAR PLAYER
PRESIDENTIAL POWER

Cristiano Ronaldo dos Santos Aveiro was given his second name because his father was an admirer of United States President Ronald Reagan. The five-time FIFA World Player of the Year is the all-time leading goalscorer for Real Madrid and in the UEFA Champions League – a competition he has won five times. Already Portugal's top scorer, he became his country's most-capped player at the 2016 UEFA European Championship – and ended the competition lifting the trophy, despite going off injured 25 minutes into the final against France.

EUR 94M
Real Madrid paid a then-world record fee of EUR 94m in 2009 for Cristiano Ronaldo. He moved to Juventus in July 2018 for a fee of EUR 100m.

RONALDO

TOURNAMENT TRIVIA
HAPPY ÉDER AFTER

Substitute striker **Éder** was the unlikely hero when Portugal finally ended their long wait for an international trophy at UEFA EURO 2016. The forward – who spent the 2015-16 season on loan at French club Lille – scored the only goal of the final in Paris, in the 109th minute, to defeat host nation France. It was the latest opening goal scored in any UEFA European Championship final. Portugal, coached by Fernando Santos, drew their three first-round games to qualify as one of the best third-placed teams.

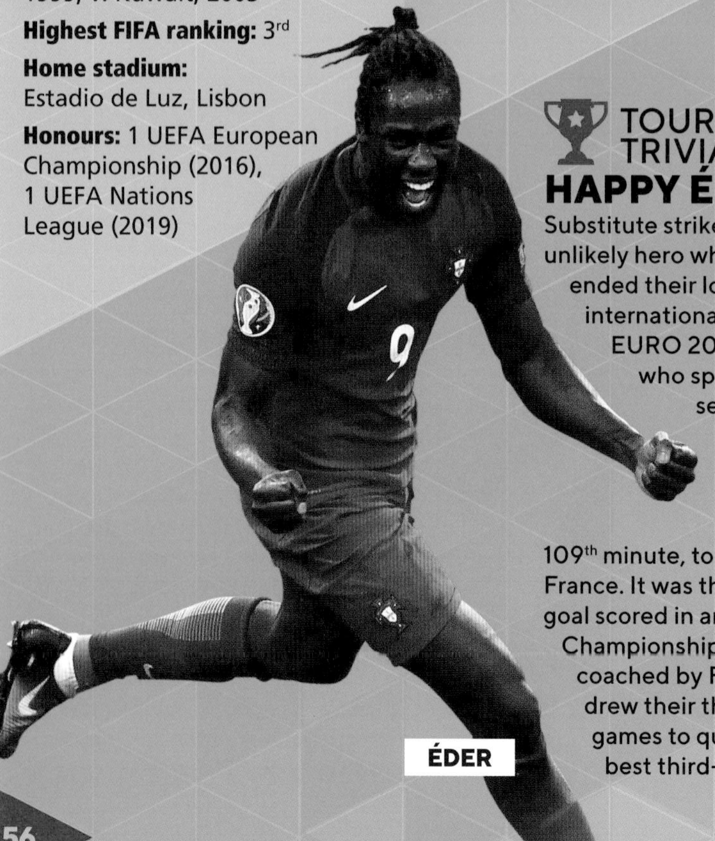

ÉDER

TOP SCORERS:

#	Player	Goals
1	Cristiano Ronaldo	99
2	Pauleta	47
3	Eusébio	41
4	Luís Figo	32
5	Nuno Gomes	29

MOST APPEARANCES:

1 Cristiano Ronaldo, 164
2 Luís Figo, 127
3 João Moutinho, 121
4 Nani, 112
5 Fernando Couto, 110

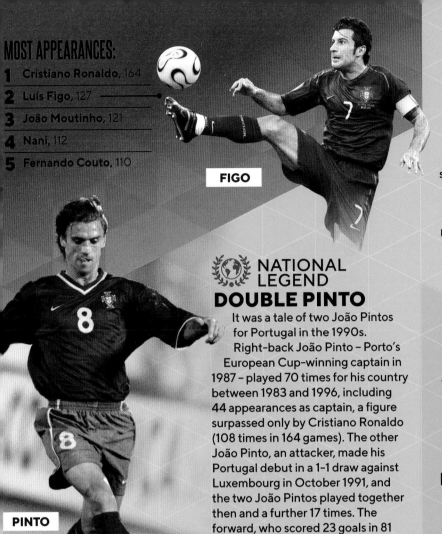

FIGO

PINTO

NICE ONE, SAN

Renato Sanches is Portugal's youngest player at an international tournament – he was 18 years and 301 days old for their 2016 UEFA European Championship opener against Iceland. He was one of the stars of the tournament, and was voted the best young player. His superb long-range strike against Poland in the quarter-finals made him the youngest scorer in any UEFA European Championship knock-out round, at the age of 18 years and 316 days. Ten days later, he became the youngest man to play in a UEFA European Championship final.

NATIONAL LEGEND
DOUBLE PINTO

It was a tale of two João Pintos for Portugal in the 1990s. Right-back João Pinto – Porto's European Cup-winning captain in 1987 – played 70 times for his country between 1983 and 1996, including 44 appearances as captain, a figure surpassed only by Cristiano Ronaldo (108 times in 164 games). The other João Pinto, an attacker, made his Portugal debut in a 1-1 draw against Luxembourg in October 1991, and the two João Pintos played together then and a further 17 times. The forward, who scored 23 goals in 81 appearances, is one of only three men to win the FIFA U-20 World Cup twice (along with Portuguese goalkeeper Fernando Brassard and Argentinian striker Sergio Agüero).

320

A phenomenal striker, Eusébio scored 320 goals in 313 Portuguese league matches and won the first European Golden Boot in 1968 (and a second in 1973).

1000

In a May 2018 FIFA World Cup warm-up against Tunisia, André Silva scored Portugal's 1,000th international goal in a 2-2 draw.

NATIONAL LEGEND
THE FAMOUS FIVE

Eusébio, Mário Coluna, José Augusto, António Simões and José Torres were the "Fabulous Five" in Benfica's 1960s dream team who also made up the spine of the Portuguese national side at the 1966 FIFA World Cup. Coluna, the "Sacred Monster", scored the vital third goal in the 1961 European Cup final and captained the national side in 1966. José Augusto, who scored two goals in the opening game against Hungary, went on to manage the national side and later the Portuguese women's team.

NATIONAL LEGEND
THE BLACK PANTHER

Born in Mozambique, **Eusébio da Silva Ferreira** was named Portugal's "Golden Player" to mark UEFA's 50th anniversary in 2004. Signed by Benfica in 1960 at the age of 18, he scored a hat-trick in his second game – against Santos in a friendly tournament in Paris – even outshining their young star, Pelé. He helped Benfica win a second European Cup in 1962, was named European Footballer of the Year in 1965 and led Portugal to third place in the 1966 FIFA World Cup, finishing as top scorer with nine goals.

EUSÉBIO

REPUBLIC OF IRELAND

Ever since Jack Charlton took the team to UEFA EURO '88, Ireland have been regulars at major international tournaments.

Joined FIFA: 1924
Biggest win: 8-0 v. Malta, 1983
Highest FIFA ranking: 6th
Home stadium: Aviva Stadium, Dublin
Honours: -

NATIONAL LEGEND
BRIEF RETURN OF THE MICK

Mick McCarthy holds all of the following records: the first man to captain the Republic of Ireland at a FIFA World Cup – Italy 1990 – the last man to manage them at the finals – Japan/Korea Republic 2002 – and, in 2018, the first man to have two spells as permanent manager. The Yorkshireman, whose father was Irish, was first coach between 1996 and 2004, and he began his second spell with successive 1-0 victories over Gibraltar. After setting up a EURO 2020 qualifying play-off against Slovakia, McCarthy stepped down in April 2020 following the postponement of the finals, and was succeeded by his assistant **Stephen Kenny**. The new man in charge took up coaching in his 20s, managing clubs in Ireland and Scotland before guiding the Republic of Ireland's U-21s to the 2021 UEFA EURO U-21s.

KENNY

MCCARTHY

64

Martin O'Neill, who played 64 times for Northern Ireland between 1971 and 1984, succeeded Italian veteran Giovanni Trapattoni as Republic of Ireland manager, who resigned after failing to lead the side to the 2014 FIFA World Cup finals.

STARPLAYER
BRADY BUNCH

Irish eyes were smiling again at Italy's expense in their final first-round group game at the 2016 UEFA European Championship, when **Robbie Brady** headed a late winning goal. It gave Martin O'Neill's team a place in the round of 16, where they took the lead against France through a Brady penalty, but eventually succumbed 2-1. Brady was the first Republic of Ireland player to score in consecutive UEFA European Championship games; Robbie Keane also achieved the feat at the 2002 FIFA World Cup.

BONNER

TOURNAMENT TRIVIA
WINNING JERSEY MISSING IN ACTION?

Irish fans' memories of their past FIFA World Cup adventures were reawakened in June 2017 when rapper M.I.A. appeared to be wearing one of goalkeeper **Packie Bonner**'s shirts in a photoshoot. Bonner starred at the 1988 European Championship and the 1990 and 1994 FIFA World Cups, and suggested that one of several red-and-yellow patterned jerseys he gave away for charity after USA '94 may have ended up with one of M.I.A.'s stylists. Bonner enhanced his national hero status by saving Daniel Timofte's penalty in the second-round shoot-out victory against Romania at Italy '90, before David O'Leary's winning spot kick clinched their place in the quarter-finals where they lost 1-0 to hosts Italy.

BRADY

CHARLTON

MOST APPEARANCES:

1. Robbie Keane, 146
2. Shay Given, 134
3. John O'Shea, 118
4. Kevin Kilbane, 110
5. Steve Staunton, 102

NATIONAL LEGEND
ROBBIE KEEN

Much-travelled striker **Robbie Keane** broke the Republic of Ireland's scoring record in October 2004 and added to it right up to 31 August 2016, when he marked his 146th and final appearance with his 68th goal in a 4-0 friendly victory against Oman. His most famous goals were last-minute equalisers against Germany and Spain at the 2002 FIFA World Cup. He marked the final game at the old Lansdowne Road with a hat-trick against San Marino in November 2006 and, four years later, won his 100th cap in the inaugural game at its replacement, the Aviva Stadium.

118 SECONDS

The Republic of Ireland hold the record for scoring the quickest penalty at the UEFA European Championship – after just 118 seconds of their 2016 clash with France.

NATIONAL LEGEND
CHAMPION CHARLTON

Jack Charlton became a hero after he guided the Republic of Ireland to their first major finals in 1988, his side defeating England 1-0 in their first game at the UEFA European Championship. Things got even better at their first FIFA World Cup finals two years later, with the unfancied Irish only losing to hosts Italy in the quarter-finals. Charlton quit in 1996 after failing to qualify for that year's UEFA European Championship in England. "In my heart of hearts, I knew I'd wrung as much as I could out of the squad I'd got," he later claimed.

KEANE

23

Robbie Keane's brace against Gibraltar in August 2016 took him to 23 goals in UEFA European Championship qualifiers: more than any other player.

TOP SCORERS:

1. Robbie Keane, 68
2. Niall Quinn, 21
3. Frank Stapleton, 20
4. John Aldridge, 19
   = Tony Cascarino, 19
   = Don Givens, 19

66

Only England's Billy Wright, with 70, played more consecutive internationals than **Kevin Kilbane**, whose 109th Republic of Ireland cap against Macedonia in March 2011 was also his 66th in a row, covering 11 years and five months.

KILBANE

4

Paddy Moore became the first player to score four goals in a FIFA World Cup qualifier when Ireland came from behind to draw 4-4 with Belgium on 25 February 1934.

NATIONAL LEGEND
KEANE CARRY ON

Few star players have walked out on their country quite as dramatically as Republic of Ireland captain **Roy Keane** in 2002 at their FIFA World Cup training camp in Saipan, Japan. The midfielder quit before a competitive ball had been kicked, complaining about a perceived lack of professionalism in the Irish preparations – and his loss of faith in manager Mick McCarthy. The Irish reached the second round without him, losing on penalties to Spain, but his behaviour divided a nation. When McCarthy stepped down, Keane and the FAI brokered a truce, and he returned to international duty in April 2004 under new boss Brian Kerr.

KEANE   **O'NEILL**

ROMANIA

Since 1938, Romania have qualified for the finals of the FIFA World Cup only four times in 16 attempts. The country's football highlight came in 1994 when, inspired by Gheorghe Hagi, they reached the quarter-finals.

Biggest win:
9-0 v. Finland, 1973

Highest FIFA ranking: 3rd

Home stadium: Arena Nationala, Bucharest

Honours: -

2

Romania conceded just two goals throughout the qualifying competition for the 2016 UEFA European Championship (the fewest of any team) – but then let in that same number in the tournament's opening match, a 2-1 defeat by hosts France.

NATIONAL LEGEND
MUCH ADO ABOUT MUTU

Romania lost only once when **Adrian Mutu** found the net – a feat made all the better since, with 35 goals, he is matched only by Gheorghe Hagi in the nation's all-time scoring ranks. His final international goal, an equaliser against Hungary in a March 2013 FIFA World Cup qualifier, was his first for 21 months.

MUTU

NATIONAL LEGEND
CENTURY MAN

Gheorghe Hagi, Romania's "Player of the Century", scored three goals and was named in the Team of the Tournament at the 1994 FIFA World Cup in the United States, at which Romania lost out on penalties to Sweden after a 2-2 draw in the quarter-finals. Hagi made his international debut in 1983, aged just 18, scored his first goal aged 19 (in a 3-2 defeat to Northern Ireland) and remains Romania's joint-top goalscorer with 35 goals in 125 games. Farul Constanța, in Hagi's hometown, named their stadium after him in 2000 – but fans stopped referring to it as such after he took the manager's job at rivals Timisoara.

HAGI

TOP SCORERS:

1	Gheorghe Hagi	35
=	Adrian Mutu	35
3	Iuliu Bodola	31
4	Viorel Moldovan	25
=	Ciprian Marica	25

TOURNAMENT TRIVIA
FAMOUS FOURSOME

Gheorghe Hagi, Florin Răducioiu, Ilie Dumitrescu and Gheorghe Popescu helped Romania light up the FIFA World Cup in the USA in 1994. Răducioiu (four), Dumitrescu (three) and Hagi (two) scored nine of their country's ten goals that summer, and the trio also converted their penalties in a quarter-final shoot-out against Sweden, only for misses by Dan Petrescu and Miodrag Belodedici to send the Romanians home. As well as being team-mates, Popescu and Hagi are also brothers-in-law – their wives, Luminiya Popescu and Marlilena Hagi, are sisters.

2

Romania only scored two goals in the 2016 UEFA European Championship: both from the penalty spot, scored by striker Bogdan Stancu.

MOST APPEARANCES:

1 **Dorinel Munteanu**, 134
2 **Gheorghe Hagi**, 124
3 **Gheorghe Popescu**, 115
4 **Răzvan Raț**, 113
5 **Ladislau Bölöni**, 102

BÖLÖNI

102

Midfielder **Ladislau Bölöni** became the first Romanian to win 100 caps in a 2–0 away defeat to the Republic of Ireland in March 1988. The last of his 23 goals came in a 3–3 draw with East Germany, and he bowed out with a 2–0 loss in the Netherlands.

NATIONAL LEGEND
ENDURING DORINEL

Nobody has played for Romania more than **Dorinel Munteanu**, although at one point his former team-mate Gheorghe Hagi's 125-cap record looked safe. Versatile defensive midfielder Munteanu was stuck on 119 appearances throughout an 18-month absence from the international scene before being surprisingly recalled at the age of 37 by manager Victor Piturca in February 2005. He ended his Romania career two years later, having scored 16 times in 134 games.

MUNTEANU

TROPHY TOURNAMENT TRIVIA
RUDOLF BY ROYAL APPOINTMENT

Romania played in the inaugural FIFA World Cup, in Uruguay in 1930, where they beat Peru 3–1 before being eliminated 4–0 by the hosts. Coach Constantin Rădulescu filled in as a linesman for some games, but not for those featuring his own side. It is claimed that the squad was picked by King Carol II. Their captain was Rudolf Wetzer, the only Romania player to score five goals in a game – in a pre-tournament 8–1 victory over Greece in May 1930.

6

Two yellow-card offences in six minutes in Romania's EURO 2000 quarter-final against Italy meant Gheorghe Hagi's final bow on the international stage was a red card and an early bath.

16

Right-back Cristian Manea became Romania's youngest international when he made his debut against Albania in May 2014, at the age of 16 years, nine months and 22 days, having played only five senior matches for his club Viitorul Constanța.

TOURNAMENT TRIVIA
BLONDE AMBITION

Despite topping Group G ahead of England, Colombia and Tunisia at the 1998 FIFA World Cup, that particular Romanian vintage is perhaps best remembered for their collective decision to dye their hair blond ahead of their final first-round game. The newly bleached Romanians struggled to a 1–1 draw against Tunisia, before being knocked out by Croatia in the round of 16, 1–0.

61

RUSSIA

Before the break-up of the Soviet Union (USSR) in 1992, the team was a world football powerhouse. While playing as Russia since August 1992, the good times have eluded them – although they were quarter-finalists at Russia 2018.

Joined FIFA: 1992

Biggest win:
9-0 v. Faroe Islands, 2019

Highest FIFA ranking: 3rd

Home stadium: Luzhniki Stadium, Moscow

Honours: -

SCORING RECORD
ARTEM'S TIME

A 9-0 victory over the Faroe Islands in Saransk in June 2019 was Russia's biggest win since the end of the Soviet Union era, with new captain **Artem Dzyuba** scoring four goals. He also scored four times when Liechtenstein were beaten 7-0 on 8 September 2014, this precisely a year after his first international goal, also against Liechtenstein. Dzyuba was eight-goal top scorer in Russia's 2016 UEFA European Championship qualifying campaign, but he did not score in the finals as they finished bottom of their group. He came good, however, at the 2018 FIFA World Cup, scoring three goals, including an equaliser in a shootout defeat of Spain in the second round.

NATIONAL LEGEND
GOLDEN BOY

Igor Netto captained the USSR national side to their greatest successes: gold at the 1956 Olympics in Melbourne and victory in the first-ever UEFA European Championship in France in 1960. Born in Moscow in 1930, Netto was awarded the Order of Lenin – the highest civilian honour in the Soviet Union – in 1957 and became an ice-hockey coach after retiring from football. He also scored 37 goals in 367 league games for Spartak Moscow, winning five Soviet championships.

NETTO

17
The youngest Soviet-era debutant was Eduard Streltsov, who hit a hat-trick on his debut against Sweden in June 1956, at the age of 17 years and 340 days, and then scored another treble in his second game, against India.

TOURNAMENT TRIVIA
HAPPY HOSTS

Expectations on the field for 2018 FIFA World Cup hosts Russia, at 70th the lowest team in the FIFA/Coca-Cola World Ranking, were not great, but in the opening game, they cruised past Saudi Arabia 5-0 and then downed Egypt 3-1 to guarantee a second-round place. Once there, Russia beat Spain on penalties before losing, again in a shoot-out, to Croatia in the last eight. Manager Stanislav Cherchesov, a former Russia goalkeeper, spoke of the pride felt nationwide by their unexpected progress.

4

Winger Denis Cheryshev scored four goals at the 2018 FIFA World Cup; he replaced Alan Dzagoev against Saudi Arabia and scored – making him the first-ever substitute to score in a FIFA World Cup opening game.

DZYUBA

MOST APPEARANCES:

1 Sergei Ignashevich, 127

2 Igor Akinfeev, 111

3 Viktor Onopko, 109

4 Vasili Berezutskiy, 101

5 Yuriy Zhirkov, 92

NATIONAL LEGEND
YURI WANTED AGAIN

Russia went out on the road after their better-than-expected performance as 2018 FIFA World Cup hosts. Home games were played away from Moscow – including a 5-1 UEFA Nations League trouncing of the Czech Republic in Rostov-on-Don and a goalless draw against Sweden in Kaliningrad. No squad member had won more than 50 caps until the March 2019 recall of 35-year-old wing-back Yuri Zhirkov, who had announced his international retirement after the FIFA World Cup. His recall came more than 14 years after his debut against Italy in 2005.

18

Igor Akinfeev became post-Soviet Russia's youngest international footballer when he made his debut in a friendly against Norway on 28 April 2004. The CSKA Moscow goalkeeper was just 18 years and 20 days old.

AKINFEEV

2

Although born in what is now Ukraine, Viktor Onopko played most of his club career in Russia and Spain and was twice named Russian Footballer of the Year – in 1993 and 1994.

NATIONAL LEGEND
KERZH LIFTS THE CURSE

Only one man was in Russia's squads for the 2002 FIFA World Cup finals and the next time they qualified, in 2014: Aleksandr Kerzhakov. He made his international debut as a 19-year-old a teenager in March 2002, and he played just eight minutes of the finals three months later. With five goals, he was Russia's leading scorer in qualifying for the 2014 finals, and Kerzhakov scored his 26th international goal to earn a 1-1 draw in Russia's opener against Korea Republic in Cuiaba. This goal equalled Russia's all-time scoring record, set in 2002 by **Vladimir Beschastnykh**.

TOP SCORERS:

1 Aleksandr Kerzhakov, 30

2 Vladimir Beschastnykh, 26

3 Artem Dzyuba, 24

4 Roman Pavlyuchenko, 21

5 Andrei Arshavin, 17
= Valeri Karpin, 17

BESCHASTNYKH

YASHIN

NATIONAL LEGEND
SUPER STOPPER

Lev Yashin made it into the FIFA World Cup All-Time Team. In a career spanning 20 years, Yashin played 326 league games for Dynamo Moscow – the only club side he ever played for – and won 78 caps for the Soviet Union, conceding, on average, less than a goal a game (only 70 in total). With Dynamo, he won five Soviet championships and three Soviet cups, the last of which came in his final full season in 1970. He saved around 150 penalties in his career, and kept four clean sheets in his 12 FIFA World Cup matches.

1

Only one goalkeeper has ever been named European Footballer of the Year: Lev Yashin in 1963 – the same year in which he won his fifth Soviet championship.

SCOTLAND

A country with a vibrant domestic league and a rich football tradition – it played host to the first-ever international football match, against England, in November 1872 – Scotland have rarely put in the performances on the international stage to match their lofty ambitions.

Joined FIFA: 1910
Biggest win:
11-0 v. Ireland, 1901
Highest FIFA ranking: 13th
Home stadium:
Hampden Park, Glasgow
Honours: -

DALGLISH

2
Kenny Dalglish joined Herbert Chapman and Brian Clough as one of the few managers to lead two different sides to the league title when he guided Blackburn Rovers to the summit of English football in 1994-95.

NATIONAL LEGEND
KING KENNY

Kenny Dalglish is Scotland's joint-top international goalscorer (with Denis Law) and remains the only player to have won more than a century of caps for the national side, with 102 in total – 11 more than the next highest, goalkeeper Jim Leighton. Dalglish made his name spearheading Celtic's domestic dominance in the 1970s, winning four league titles, four Scottish Cups and one League Cup. He then went on to become a legend at Liverpool, winning a hat-trick of European Cups (1978, 1981 and 1984) before leading the side as player-manager to a league and cup double in 1986.

TOP SCORERS:

1 Kenny Dalglish, 30
= Denis Law, 30
3 Hughie Gallacher, 23
4 Lawrie Reilly, 22
5 Ally McCoist, 19

LAW

4

Denis Law twice scored four goals in a match for Scotland, the first against Northern Ireland on 7 November 1962 – helping the Scots to win the British Home Championship – and then against Norway in a friendly on 7 November 1963.

WEIR

40

Rangers centre-back **David Weir**, Scotland's oldest-ever player, retired in October 2010 after winning 69 caps, his last coming at the ripe old age of 40 years and 150 days.

TOURNAMENT TRIVIA
UNOFFICIAL WORLD CHAMPIONS

One of the victories most cherished by Scotland fans is the 3-2 triumph over arch-rivals and reigning world champions England at Wembley in April 1967 – the first time Sir Alf Ramsey's team had lost since clinching the 1966 FIFA World Cup. Scotland's man of the match that day was ball-juggling left-half/midfielder Jim Baxter, while it was also the first game in charge for Scotland's first full-time manager, Bobby Brown. Less fondly recalled is Scotland's 9-3 trouncing by the same opposition at the same stadium in April 1961.

46

Steven Fletcher ended Scotland's 46-year wait for a hat-trick and his own six-year international goal drought when he scored three in his country's 6-1 victory over Gibraltar at Hampden Park in March 2015.

MOST APPEARANCES:

1 **Kenny Dalglish**, 102
2 **Jim Leighton**, 91
3 **Darren Fletcher**, 80
4 **Alex McLeish**, 77
5 **Paul McStay**, 76

STAR PLAYER
HANDY ANDREW

Scotland captain **Andrew Robertson** won the UEFA Champions League with Liverpool on 1 June 2019 and, a week later, scored the first goal of new Scotland manager Steve Clarke's reign in a 2-1 victory over Cyprus. A former defender himself, Clarke won six Scottish caps and was appointed after Alex McLeish's second spell in charge ended after a 3-0 reverse in Kazakhstan. Midfielder John McGinn dominated Scotland's scoring duties for the rest of 2019, scoring six goals in their last three games of the year, all victories, including his first international hat-trick in a 6-0 victory over San Marino.

ROBERTSON

NATIONAL LEGEND
DIVIDED LOYALTIES

Scottish-born winger Jim Brown played and scored for the USA side that lost to Argentina in the first FIFA World Cup in 1930. He had moved to New Jersey three years earlier and qualified through his US-citizen father. Two of his brothers also played professionally: younger brother John, a goalkeeper, was capped by Scotland, but Tom did not play at international level. Jim's son, George, appeared once for the USA, in 1957, while two of John's sons, Peter and Gordon, both played rugby for Scotland.

17

The youngest-ever Scotland captain is John Lambie, who led the team out at the age of 17 years and 92 days against Ireland in March 1886; the youngest since 1900 is Darren Fletcher, who was 20 years and 115 days old against Estonia in May 2004.

NATIONAL LEGEND
HOW GEMMILL DANCED TO THE MUSIC OF SCOTLAND'S WORLD CUP TIME

Archie Gemmill scored Scotland's greatest goal on the world stage in a surprise 3-2 victory over the Netherlands at the 1978 FIFA World Cup, jinking past three defenders before chipping the ball neatly over Dutch goalkeeper Jan Jongbloed. Amazingly, in 2008, this magical moment was turned into a dance in the English National Ballet's "The Beautiful Game", and was referenced in cult in 1990s film, *Trainspotting*, which is set in Edinburgh.

GEMMILL

STAR PLAYER
TRUST IN LEIGH

In his 13th appearance for his country, Celtic striker **Leigh Griffiths** hit the back of the net for the first time with an 87th-minute free-kick against old enemies England in a June 2017 FIFA World Cup qualifier – and promptly repeated the trick with another magnificent set-piece strike three minutes later. This put Scotland 2-1 ahead and they seemed set for a first home win against their neighbours since centre-back Richard Gough's sole goal in a 1985 Hampden Park clash. Scottish hearts were broken, however, when England captain Harry Kane volleyed an injury-time equaliser.

GRIFFITHS

SERBIA

The former Yugoslavia was one of the strongest football nations in Eastern Europe. Serbia broke from Montenegro in 2006 and last featured at a major tournament in 2018 at the FIFA World Cup.

Joined FIFA: 2006
Biggest win: 6-1 v. Azerbaijan, 2007, v. Bulgaria, 2008, v. Wales, 2012
Highest FIFA ranking: 19th
Home stadium: Rajko Mitić Stadium, Belgrade
Honours: -

NATIONAL LEGEND
STJEP UP

Yugoslavia/Serbia's all-time top goalscorer remains **Stjepan Bobek**, with 38 in 63 appearances. He also holds the record for the most goals in a Yugoslavia/Serbia top-flight game – in June 1948 he got nine for Partizan Belgrade in a 10-1 rout of 14 Oktobar. Although Partizan won the title that season, his 24 goals were four fewer than Franjo Wolfl of second-placed Dinamo Zagreb. Wolfl scored six goals in 12 international appearances and the pair combined to help Yugoslavia win the silver medal at the London 1948 Olympic Games. Bobek also was in Yugoslavia's squad that again won silver at the 1952 Games.

BOBEK

TOP SCORERS:

1 **Stjepan Bobek**, 38
2 **Milan Galić**, 37
= **Blagoje Marjanović**, 37
= **Savo Milošević**, 37
5 **Aleksandar Mitrović**, 34

17

Andrija Živković became Serbia's youngest senior international at the age of 17 years and 92 days when he played against Japan at the UEFA European U-19 Championship in 2013.

1930
The first man to captain and then coach his country at the FIFA World Cup was Milorad Arsenijević, who captained Yugoslavia to the semi-finals at the inaugural tournament in Uruguay in 1930 and then managed their squad in Brazil 20 years later.

STAR PLAYER
HITMAN MIT

Fiery striker **Aleksandar Mitrović** was named player of the tournament at the UEFA European U-19 Championship in 2013 when Serbia beat France 1-0 in the final, setting up Andrija Luković for the winning goal. Mitrović was Serbia's focal point at the 2018 FIFA World Cup, scoring six goals in qualifying and their goal in the 2-1 loss to Switzerland in Russia, his sixth of 2018 and 17th overall. Aleksandar Kolarov scored the only goal in Serbia's Group E opener against Costa Rica, but a 2-0 loss to Brazil saw them go home after the group stage.

MITROVIĆ

TOURNAMENT TRIVIA
A TAD SPECIAL

In September 2012 Serbia matched their record victory margin, crushing Wales 6-1 in a 2014 FIFA World Cup qualifier, with both Branislav Ivanović and Aleksandr Kolarov scoring. Other five-goal wins included 6-1 over Azerbaijan in 2007 and 5-0 against Romania two years later. The victory over Wales was also a notable occasion for forward Dušan Tadić, who scored his first goal in his eighth appearance for his country. After making his debut in 2008, he went on to win more than 60 caps, putting in some influential performances and chipping in with four goals on the way to the 2018 FIFA World Cup in Russia.

STAR PLAYER
BRAN POWER

Versatile defender **Branislav Ivanović**, who became Serbia's most-capped player with two appearances at the 2018 FIFA World Cup, has enjoyed scoring significant late goals against Portuguese opposition. His first goal for his country was an 88th-minute equaliser in a UEFA European Championship qualifier away to Portugal in September 2007. His stoppage-time header gave Chelsea victory over Benfica in the final of the UEFA Europa League in 2013, a year after suspension had ruled him out of the club's UEFA Champions League final triumph over Bayern Munich.

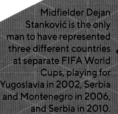

IVANOVIĆ

MOST APPEARANCES:

1 **Branislav Ivanović**, 105
2 **Dejan Stanković**, 103
3 **Savo Milošević**, 102
4 **Aleksander Kolarov**, 90
5 **Dragan Džajić**, 85

2

Two players have been named Serb Footballer of the Year in consecutive years since 2005: the first was Branislav Ivanović, in 2012 and 2013, and he was followed by his Chelsea team-mate Nemanja Matić in 2014 and 2015.

3

Midfielder Dejan Stanković is the only man to have represented three different countries at separate FIFA World Cups, playing for Yugoslavia in 2002, Serbia and Montenegro in 2006, and Serbia in 2010.

NATIONAL LEGEND
ACCLAIM FOR ANTIĆ

In April 2019, tributes were paid to **Radomir Antić** after his death aged 71 in Madrid. Antić was the only man to manage Spanish giants Barcelona, Real Madrid and Atlético Madrid – leading the latter to a Spanish league and cup double in 1995-96. Fellow Serbian Milinko Pantić, who scored Atlético's Copa del Rey final winner against Barcelona, described him as a "father". Antić also led Serbia at the 2010 FIFA World Cup in South Africa, the first finals to feature Serbia solely after Montenegro's independence. They exited after the first round but marked their campaign with a 1-0 Group D victory over Germany thanks to winger Milan Jovanović's first-half strike.

ANTIĆ

NATIONAL LEGEND
STAN'S THE MAN

Dejan Stanković scored twice on his international debut for Yugoslavia in 1998. He also twice scored memorable volleyed goals from virtually on the halfway line – once for Internazionale against Genoa in 2009-10, with a first-time shot from the opposing goalkeeper's clearance, and an almost identical finish against German club Schalke 04 in the UEFA Champions League the following season. Stanković tied Savo Milošević's Serbian appearances record with his final competitive international in October 2011, but went one better in October 2013 when he played the first ten minutes of a 2-0 friendly defeat of Japan in Novi Sad.

STANKOVIĆ

100

Savo Milošević was the first Serbian player to reach a century of international appearances – and he can claim to have played for his country in four different guises, representing Yugoslavia before and after it broke up, Serbia & Montenegro, and finally Serbia alone.

MILOŠEVIĆ

SLOVAKIA

STAR PLAYER
COOL DUDA

Slovakia made it to the second round at their first-ever UEFA European Championship finals in 2016 before succumbing 3-0 to reigning world champions Germany. **Ondrej Duda** became the first man to score for Slovakia at a EURO, grabbing an equaliser in their opening game against Wales just 52 seconds after coming on – the fastest goal in a European Championship by a substitute since Spain's Juan Carlos Valerón in 2004, when he needed just 36 seconds to score against Russia.

DUDA

Slovakia have finally begun to claim some bragging rights over their neighbours, the Czech Republic. The Slovakians qualified for their first FIFA World Cup in 2010, at which they upset defending champions Italy 3-2 and reached the second round.

Joined FIFA: 1994

Biggest win:
7-0, v. Liechtenstein, 2004, v. San Marino, 2007, v. San Marino, 2009

Highest FIFA ranking: 14th

Home stadium:
Tehelné pole, Bratislava

Honours: -

MOST APPEARANCES:

1 Marek Hamšík, 120

2 Miroslav Karhan, 107

3 Martin Škrtel, 104

4 Ján Ďurica, 91

= Peter Pekarík, 91

ŠKRTEL

THREE AND A HALF
Adam Nemec had to wait more than three and a half years between his Slovakia debut against Luxembourg in February 2011 and his first international goal, the only one of the game as his side beat Malta in September 2014.

6

Slovakia's qualification campaign for UEFA EURO 2016 included a national record six straight victories, including a surprise 2-1 win against defending champions Spain.

TOURNAMENT TRIVIA
MAREK OFF THE MARK

Slovakia's biggest win is 7-0, a result they have achieved three times – with wing-back Marek Čech the only man to play in all three games: against Liechtenstein in September 2004 and twice versus San Marino, in October 2007 and June 2009. He scored twice in the most recent match and, in fact, four of his five international goals since his 2004 debut came against San Marino – he also scored a brace in a 5-0 victory in November 2007.

STAR PLAYERS
ŠKRTEL POWER

Martin Škrtel and Marek Hamšík have shared many special moments together, including Slovakia's run to the last 16 of the 2010 FIFA World Cup and the UEFA European Championship in 2016. Škrtel bowed out of international football on 107 caps in a friendly against Paraguay in October 2019, when he played as captain for the first 30 minutes. The match was also a Slovakia farewell for defender Tomáš Hubočan (65 appearances) and striker Adam Nemec (43).

VITTEK

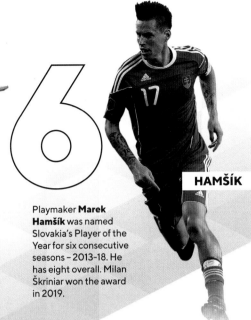

HAMŠÍK

6

Playmaker **Marek Hamšík** was named Slovakia's Player of the Year for six consecutive seasons – 2013-18. He has eight overall. Milan Škriniar won the award in 2019.

NATIONAL LEGEND
VLAD ALL OVER

Three relatives named Vladimir Weiss – different generations of the same family – have represented their country in international football, with two of them featuring at the 2010 FIFA World Cup. The first Vladimir made three appearances for Czechoslovakia, including the 1964 Olympics final in which he scored an own goal as Hungary triumphed 2-1. The second Vladimir won 19 caps for Czechoslavakia and 12 for Slovakia, and the third, then aged only 20, ended the 2010 FIFA World Cup with 12.

TOP SCORERS:

1 Marek Hamšík, 25

2 Róbert Vittek, 23

3 Szilárd Németh, 22

4 Marek Mintál, 14

= Miroslav Karhan, 14

NATIONAL LEGEND
RÓBERT THE HERO

At South Africa 2010, Slovakia's **Róbert Vittek** became only the fourth player from a FIFA World Cup debutant to score as many as four goals in one tournament. He hit one against New Zealand, two against defending champions Italy, and a late penalty in a second-round defeat to the Netherlands. The previous three players to have done so were Portugal's Eusébio in 1966, Denmark's Preben Elkjær in 1986, and Croatia's Davor Šuker in 1998.

STAR PLAYER
CUTTING EDGE HAMŠÍK

Playmaker **Marek Hamšík** often stood out from the crowd with his Mohawk hairstyle. However, he fulfilled a promise to shave it off if his club Napoli won the 2012 Coppa Italia. Two years earlier, he had captained Slovakia when they knocked holders Italy out in the 2010 FIFA World Cup first round. Hamšík became Slovakia's most-capped player with his 108th appearance in October 2018, marking the occasion with a goal in a 2-1 defeat to the Czech Republic. He then equalled and swiftly overtook Róbert Vittek as the nation's leading scorer with a brace as Azerbaijan were beaten 4-1 the following June.

8

Eight of Czechoslovakia's triumphant 1976 UEFA European Championship side were born in modern-day Slovakia, including captain Anton Ondruš and both their scorers in the 2-2 draw: Ján Švehlík and Karol Dobiaš.

107

Miroslav Karhan became the first Slovakia player to pass 100 caps and he retired in 2011 with 107 to his name.

KARHAN

SWEDEN

Twelve appearances at the FIFA World Cup finals (with a best result of second, as tournament hosts, in 1958) and three Olympic medals (including gold in London in 1948) bear testament to Sweden's rich history on the world football stage.

Joined FIFA: 1908
Biggest win: 12-0 v. Latvia, 1927, v. Korea Republic 1948
Highest FIFA ranking: 2nd
Home stadium: Friends Arena, Stockholm
Honours: -

4 Centre-back Olof Mellberg became the first Swedish man to play in four UEFA European Championship finals when he appeared at EURO 2012.

MOST APPEARANCES:

1. Anders Svensson, 148
2. Thomas Ravelli, 143
3. Andreas Isaksson, 133
4. Kim Källström, 131
5. Sebastian Larsson, 118

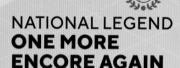

NATIONAL LEGEND
ONE MORE ENCORE AGAIN

One of the most famous and decorated Swedish footballers of modern times, **Henrik Larsson** (a star on the club scene with both Celtic and Barcelona), quit international football after the 2002 FIFA World Cup and again after the 2006 FIFA World Cup in Germany. He then made a further comeback in the 2010 FIFA World Cup qualifiers. With 37 goals in his 106 appearances, including five in his three FIFA World Cups, fans and officials clamoured for his return each time he tried to walk away. His son Jordan, also a striker, made his Sweden debut against Estonia in January 2018 and scored his first international goal to beat Moldova in a friendly two years later.

LARSSON

17 Alexander Isak became Sweden's youngest international scorer on 12 January 2017 when he netted the opener in a 6-0 friendly defeat of Slovakia in Abu Dhabi at the age of 17 years and 113 days.

SCORING RECORD
ANDERS KEEPERS

Midfielder **Anders Svensson** celebrated equalling Thomas Ravelli's Sweden appearances record by scoring in both his 142nd and 143rd games for his country: a long-range strike as Norway were beaten 4-2 and then the winning goal against the Republic of Ireland in a qualifier for the 2014 FIFA World Cup. He then became his country's most-capped player in a 1-0 victory over Kazakhstan, but he did not score. Svensson retired from international football in 2013, aged 37, after Sweden lost to Portugal in a 2014 FIFA World Cup qualifying play-off. He made 148 appearances, and scored 21 goals.

SVENSSON

NATIONAL LEGEND
IBRA-CADABRA

Few modern footballers can claim such consistent success – or boast such an unrepentant ego – as Swedish forward **Zlatan Ibrahimović**. His proclamations have included "There's only one Zlatan", "I am like Muhammad Ali" and – in response to criticism from Norway's John Carew – "What Carew does with a football, I can do with an orange". He christened the newly built Friends Arena in Solna with all four goals as hosts Sweden beat England 4-2 in a November 2012 friendly – his final strike topping the lot, a 30-yard overhead kick which won the FIFA Puskás Award for goal of the year.

TOP SCORERS:

1 Zlatan Ibrahimović, 62

2 Sven Rydell, 49

3 Gunnar Nordahl, 43

4 Henrik Larsson, 37

5 Gunnar Gren, 32

0

His clubs may have included Ajax, Juventus, both Milan giants, Barcelona, Paris Saint-Germain and Manchester United, but Zlatan Ibrahimović has never won the UEFA Champions League.

4

Substitute Jakob Johansson scored his first international goal four minutes after comiang on, in the second leg of the FIFA 2018 World Cup qualifying play-off against Italy, the only score of the tie.

IBRAHIMOVIĆ

2ND

Sweden's best result at a FIFA World Cup is runners-up. Englishman George Raynor, who led the Swedes to Olympic gold at London 1948, steered them to third place and the runners-up spot at the 1950 and 1958 FIFA World Cups, respectively.

STAR PLAYERS
NEW GOALDEN BOYS

Sweden's recent goalscoring heroes are not only centre-forward Marcus Berg, but also centre-backs Andreas Granqvist and Victor Lindelöf. Berg scored a record seven goals in hosts Sweden's run to the UEFA European U-21 Championship semi-finals in 2009 and top-scored with eight in 2018 FIFA World Cup qualifiers. Granqvist was his country's best marksman in their run to the World Cup quarter-finals and he then added a vital penalty in their UEFA Nations League Group B match against Turkey. Sweden secured promotion with a 2-0 defeat of Russia, with Lindelöf and Berg scoring the goals.

NATIONAL LEGEND
GRE-NO-LI OLYMPIC AND ITALIAN GLORY

Having conquered the world by leading Sweden to gold at the 1948 Olympics in London, Gunnar Gren, Gunnar Nordahl and **Nils Liedholm** were snapped up by AC Milan. Their three-pronged "Gre-No-Li" forward line led the Italian giants to their 1951 *Scudetto*. Nordahl, who topped the *Serie A* scoring charts five times between 1950 and 1955, remains Milan's all-time top scorer with 221 goals in 268 games. Gren and Liedholm went on to appear for the Swedish national team in the 1958 FIFA World Cup, where they finished runners-up.

STAR PLAYER
SEB STEPS UP

Midfielder **Sebastian Larsson**, renowned for his long-range strikes and set pieces, spent much of his career in England after joining Arsenal as a 16-year-old. He helped Sweden reach the 2018 FIFA World Cup quarter-finals, where they were defeated ... by England. Now fifth on Sweden's all-time appearance list with 118, Larsson won his 100th cap in Sweden's last pre-Russia 2018 friendly against Peru. He also scored twice from the penalty spot in a 4-0 victory over Malta in October 2019 to help Sweden qualify for UEFA EURO 2020. These were his long-awaited first international goals since a 2-0 victory over France at the 2012 UEFA European Championship.

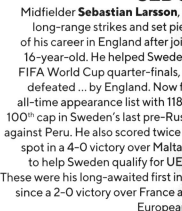

LIEDHOLM

LARSSON

SWITZERLAND

Switzerland may not be an international football powerhouse, but it is the home of both FIFA and UEFA. Switzerland co-hosted UEFA EURO 2008 with Austria, and reached the semi-finals of the inaugural UEFA Nations League in 2019.

TOURNAMENT TRIVIA
CLEAN SHEET WIPE-OUT

Switzerland remain the only team to exit the FIFA World Cup without conceding a goal in regulation time, which they did in 2006. However, in the shoot-out defeat to Ukraine in the second round, following a goalless 120 minutes, they failed to score a single penalty and lost 3-0. Despite being beaten three times in the shoot-out, goalkeeper **Pascal Zuberbühler's** performances in Germany earned him a Swiss record for consecutive clean sheets at an international tournament.

ZUBERBÜHLER

Joined FIFA: 1905
Biggest win:
9-0 v. Lithuania, 1924
Highest FIFA ranking: 3rd
Home Stadium:
Stade de Suisse Wankdorf, Bern
Honours: -

NATIONAL LEGEND
FREI-S AND LOWS

In April 2011, citing abuse from his own fans during recent matches, **Alexander Frei** announced his retirement from international football following a string of underwhelming results with the national side. He stepped down as Switzerland's all-time leading goalscorer with 42 in 84 games. Frei was joined in international retirement by strike partner Marco Streller, who had scored 12 goals in 37 games.

FREI

2004
After being compared to a llama by an angry Swiss sports press for spitting at Steven Gerrard at UEFA EURO 2004, Alexander Frei, Switzerland's all-time top scorer, adopted a llama at Basel Zoo as part of his apology to the nation.

3

Yann Sommer is only the third goalkeeper to score a FIFA World Cup own goal, after Spain's Andoni Zubizarreta in 1998 and Noel Valladeres of Honduras in 2014. Sommer saw a penalty from Costa Rica rebound off his head and into the net in 2018.

TOP SCORERS:
1 Alexander Frei, 42
2 Max Abegglen, 34
= Kubilay Türkyilmaz, 34
4 André Abegglen, 29
= Jacques Fatton, 29

MOST APPEARANCES:

1 **Heinz Hermann**, 118

2 **Alain Geiger**, 112

3 **Stephan Lichtsteiner**, 108

4 **Stéphane Chapuisat**, 103

5 **Johann Vogel**, 94

Karl Rappan, who pioneered pressurising defending and positional fluidity, managed Switzerland in four separate spells between 1937 and 1963.

STAR PLAYER
LEADING LIGHT LICHTSTEINER

Captain Stephan Lichtsteiner went into the 2018 FIFA World Cup as only the fourth Swiss player to reach a century of caps. The attacking right-back – who won 14 titles with Italian giants Juventus before joining Arsenal in June 2018 – went on to skipper Switzerland as they clinched top spot in the UEFA Nations League group they shared with Belgium and Iceland in late 2018. The *Schweizer Nati* scored 14 goals across their four games, emphatically more than fellow semi-finalists the Netherlands (eight), England (six) and Portugal (five).

STAR PLAYER
SHAQIRI LOYALTY TEST

Playmaker **Xherdan Shaqiri** scored one of the most spectacular goals of the UEFA European Championship in 2016, an overhead kick from outside the penalty area to give Switzerland a 1-1 draw in their second-round match with Poland – the Poles, however, prevailed on penalties. Two years earlier, he had scored the 50th hat-trick in FIFA World Cup history during his side's 3-0 triumph over Honduras in Manaus. Kosovo-born Shaqiri indicated he would be prepared to switch international allegiance to his native land – which became a full UEFA and FIFA member in 2016 – though FIFA ruled against it.

NATIONAL LEGEND
NEARLY MAN HERMANN

Switzerland's most-capped player Heinz Hermann unfortunately found his playing career coinciding with his country's lengthy spell between major tournaments. Midfielder Hermann scored 15 goals in 118 appearances for his country between 1978 and 1991, and was named Swiss Footballer of the Year four times. His career fell in the void between Switzerland's first-round exit from the 1966 FIFA World Cup and their progress to the second round of the 1994 FIFA World Cup.

SHAQIRI

NATIONAL LEGEND
WHO'S HÜGI

Only two men have scored more than three goals in one game for Switzerland, and **Josef Hügi** leads the way with a five-goal haul. His 23 goals in 34 games for his country included five on 12 October 1960 as France were beaten 6-2 in Basel. Hügi found the net six times at the 1954 FIFA World Cup, including a hat-trick in a 7-5 quarter-final defeat to Austria, as he finished second top scorer at the tournament. His six FIFA World Cup finals goals remains a national record. At the 1924 Paris Olympic Games, Paul Sturzenegger netted four in a 9-0 win over Lithuania.

HÜGI

2-1
The Swiss were the first team at the 2018 FIFA World Cup to come from behind to win, beating Serbia 2-1.

Legendary Swiss international player and manager **Jakob "Köbi" Kuhn** was only 22 years old when he was sent home from the 1966 FIFA World Cup for missing a curfew.

KUHN

TURKEY

MOST APPEARANCES:

1 Rüştü Reçber, 120
2 Hakan Şükür, 112
3 Bülent Korkmaz, 102
4 Emre Belözoğlu, 101
5 Arda Turan, 100

Turkey qualified for the FIFA World Cup only twice in the 20th century. Since 2000, however, Turkish fans have had plenty to cheer about, including a third-place finish at the 2002 FIFA World Cup in Japan and Korea Republic.

Joined FIFA: 1923

Biggest win:
7-0 v. Syria, 1949, v. Korea Republic, 1954, v. San Marino, 1996

Highest FIFA ranking: 5th

Home stadium:
Atatürk Olympic Stadium, Istanbul

Honours: -

REÇBER

NATIONAL LEGEND
RÜŞTÜ TO THE RESCUE

With his distinctive ponytail and charcoal-black warpaint, Turkey's most-capped international, **Rüştü Reçber** always stood out, but perhaps never more so than as a star of Turkey's third-place performance at the 2002 FIFA World Cup, as he was named in the FIFA World Cup All Star Team. He was on the bench by UEFA EURO 2008 but played in the quarter-final after first-choice goalkeeper Volkan Demirel was sent off in the final group game and suspended – and Reçber was the hero again, saving from Croatia's Mladen Petrić in a penalty shoot-out to send Turkey into their first UEFA European Championship semi-final, a narrow defeat to Germany.

NATIONAL LEGEND
TAKE FAT

It was the end of an epic era when **Fatih Terim**'s third spell as national manager finished abruptly in July 2017, but Terim remains the dominant force in Turkish football history. After coaching Galatasaray to the UEFA Cup in 2000 – the nation's first European trophy – he led Turkey on their surprise run to the UEFA European Championship semi-finals in 2008. Turkey led in the semi-final only to concede a last-minute winner to Germany. Terim returned to Galatasaray in 2009 but became national manager for the third time in 2013.

TERIM

136
Fatih Terim managed Turkey for 136 matches, winning 70, drawing 34 and losing 32.

STAR PLAYER
WORK HARD, PLAY ARDA

Wing wizard Arda Turan – Turkey's captain at UEFA EURO 2016 – survived cardiac arrhythmia, swine flu and a car crash to emerge as one of Turkish football's leading lights. His international achievements include key goals at EURO 2008, the first a stoppage-time winner against Switzerland, then Turkey's late opener when overturning a two-goal deficit against the Czech Republic in a first-round qualification decider. Since leaving Galatasaray, he has enjoyed great success in Spanish club football, winning European and domestic trophies with Atlético Madrid and Barcelona.

STAR PLAYER
FROM ONE EMRE TO ANOTHER

After missing out on the 2018 FIFA World Cup, Turkey, blending youth and age under new coach Şenol Güneş, qualified for UEFA EURO 2000 in second place of Group H behind world champions France. Striker **Enes Ünal**, who became the Turkish top flight's youngest scorer on his Bursaspor debut aged 16 in August 2013, scored his first two international goals in their final qualifier, a 2–0 victory over Andorra in November 2019. Captain for the campaign was 39-year-old Emre Belözoğlu, a key member of the Turkey's best-ever tournament finish – third – at the 2002 FIFA World Cup. This Emre is not to be confused with Emre Mor, who in 2016 became – at 18 – Turkey's youngest-ever player at a UEFA European Championship.

ÜNAL

15

Zeki Riza Sporel scored Turkey's first goal in international football, against Romania on 26 October 1923. He actually hit a brace that day in a 2–2 draw – the first of 16 games for Turkey in which he hit 15 goals.

94

The last-ever FIFA World Cup "golden goal" was scored by Turkey substitute İlhan Mansız, instantly ending and winning their 2002 quarter-final against Senegal four minutes into extra time. By the 2006 FIFA World Cup, the old system of two 15-minute periods and penalties – if necessary – had returned.

SCORING RECORD
SUPER ŞÜKÜR

Turkey beat Korea Republic 3–2 to claim third place at the 2002 FIFA World Cup, their finest-ever performance in the competition, helped in no small part by an 11-second strike from Hakan Şükür. Şükür's total of 51 goals (in 112 games) is more than double his nearest competitor in the national team ranking. His first goal came in only his second appearance, as Turkey beat Denmark 2–1 on 8 April 1992. He went on to score four goals in a single game twice – in the 6–4 win over Wales on 20 August 1997 and in the 5–0 crushing of Moldova on 11 October 2006.

17

Playmaker Nuri Şahin became both Turkey's youngest international and youngest goalscorer on the same day. Şahin was 17 years and 32 days old when he made his debut against Germany in Istanbul on 8 October 2005, and his goal, one minute from time, gave Turkey a 2–1 win.

NATIONAL LEGEND
TWIN TURKS

Hamit Altıntop (right) was born ten minutes before identical twin brother **Halil** (left) – and he led the way throughout their professional footballing careers too. Both began playing for German amateur side Wattenscheid 09, before defender-cum-midfielder Hamit signed for Schalke 04 in the summer of 2003 and attacking midfielder Halil followed suit in 2006. They played together for one season, before Hamit was bought by Bayern Munich. Both helped Turkey reach the semi-finals of UEFA EURO 2008 – losing to their adopted homeland Germany – although Hamit was voted among UEFA's 23 best players of the tournament.

ŞÜKÜR

TOP SCORERS:

1 **Hakan Şükür**, 51
2 **Burak Yilmaz**, 24
3 **Tuncay Şanlı**, 22
4 **Lefter Küçükandonyadis**, 21
5 **Nihat Kahveci**, 19
= **Metin Oktay**, 19
= **Cemil Turan**, 19

11

Hakan Şükür scored the fastest-ever FIFA World Cup finals goal – he needed only 11 seconds to score Turkey's opener in their third-place play-off against Korea Republic at the 2002 FIFA World Cup.

HALIL ALTINTOP

HAMIT ALTINTOP

UKRAINE

ZINCHENKO

Since gaining independence in 1991, Ukraine has become a football force in its own right. They reached the quarter-finals at Germany 2006 and were co-hosts of UEFA EURO 2012.

Joined FIFA: 1992
Biggest win:
9-0 v. San Marino, 2013
Highest FIFA ranking: 11th
Home stadium: (rotation)
Honours: -

TOURNAMENT TRIVIA
GET ZIN IN

Midfielder or left-back **Oleksandr Zinchenko** promised hope for the future even as Ukraine made a first-round exit from UEFA EURO 2016. Two weeks before the tournament, he became the country's youngest ever goalscorer in a 4-3 friendly win over Romania before becoming, in Ukraine's tournament opener against Germany, his nation's youngest player at a major finals at the age of 19 years and 179 days. Since moving from Russia to England, where he won multiple trophies with Manchester City, he has continued to thrive for Ukraine, helping them top their UEFA Nations League B group in 2018. Zinchenko got their promotion campaign off to a perfect start with a stoppage-time winner to seal an opening 2-1 victory away to the Czech Republic.

No one has found the net quicker after kick-off for Ukraine than Andriy Yarmolenko. The winger scored just 14 seconds into the 3-2 friendly defeat against Uruguay in September 2011.

STAR PLAYER
PY IN THE SKY

Andriy Pyatov became Ukraine's most-capped goalkeeper when he made his 93rd appearance in a 2-2 draw away to Serbia in November 2019, which clinched his country's place at UEFA EURO 2020. It took Pyatov past former squad-mate Oleksandr Shovkovskiy – not the first time that he had claimed a national record from his predecessor. Pyatov went 752 minutes without conceding a goal between March and November 2013, surpassing Shovkovskiy's best of 728 minutes. Pyatov's resistance ended when Mamadou Sakho scored France's opener in a 3-0 play-off win that denied Ukraine a place at the 2014 FIFA World Cup.

PYATOV

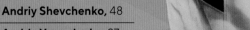

TOP SCORERS:

1 Andriy Shevchenko, 48
2 Andriy Yarmolenko, 37
3 Yevhen Konoplyanka, 21
4 Serhiy Rebrov, 15
5 Oleh Husyev, 13

NATIONAL LEGEND
REB ALERT

Serhiy Rebrov scored Ukraine's first-ever FIFA World Cup goal, giving them a 1-0 win over Northern Ireland in an August 1996 qualifier for the 1998 tournament. He was part of the squad for Ukraine's first FIFA World Cup finals in 2006, scoring against Saudi Arabia to help his side toward the quarter-finals, where they lost 3-0 to eventual champions Italy. After spells in England and Turkey, Rebrov returned to Kyiv and, in 2014, went into management, steering Dynamo to two Ukrainian league titles.

MOST APPEARANCES:

1. **Anatoliy Tymoshchuk**, 144
2. **Andriy Shevchenko**, 111
3. **Ruslan Rotan**, 100
4. **Oleh Husyev**, 98
5. **Andriy Pyatov**, 93

TYMOSHCHUK

NATIONAL LEGEND
LEADING FROM THE FRONT

Oleh Blokhin, Ukraine's coach on their first appearance at a major tournament finals, made his name as a striker with his hometown club Dynamo Kyiv. Born in 1952, when Ukraine was part of the Soviet Union, Blokhin scored a record 211 goals in another record 432 appearances in the USSR national league. He also holds the goals and caps records for the USSR, with 42 in 112 games. Always a high flyer, Blokhin led Ukraine to the finals of the 2006 FIFA World Cup in Germany, where they lost to eventual winners Italy 3-0 in the quarter-finals after knocking Switzerland out in the second round.

NATIONAL LEGEND
ROCKET MAN

Andriy Shevchenko was the first Ukrainian to reach a century of international appearances – but defensive midfielder **Anatoliy Tymoshchuk** overtook him and retired in 2016 as the country's most-capped player with 144 appearances. He also had the rare honour of seeing his name in space when Ukrainian cosmonaut Yuri Malenchenko was launched into orbit in 2007 while wearing a Zenit St Petersburg shirt with Tymoshchuk on the back.

11 SECONDS

Oleh Blokhin was renowned for his speed – when Olympic gold medallist Valeriy Borzov trained the Kyiv squad in the 1970s, Blokhin recorded a 100 metres time of 11 seconds, just 0.46 seconds slower than Borzov's own 1972 medal-winning run.

18

Serhiy Rebrov was 18 years and 24 days old when he made his debut against the USA in June 1992, becoming Ukraine's youngest international

3

Three Ukrainians have won the Ballon d'Or, although only Andriy Shevchenko (2006) has done so since Ukraine gained independence from the Soviet Union.

8

There were eight different scorers in Ukraine's 9-0 thrashing of San Marino in a FIFA World Cup qualifier in 2013 – still the country's biggest-ever win.

NATIONAL LEGEND
SUPER SHEVA

Andriy Shevchenko was a promising boxer as a youngster before deciding to focus on football full time. He lifted trophies at every club he played for and retired as Ukraine's second-most capped player and top goalscorer with 48 goals in 111 games, which included two at the 2006 FIFA World Cup, where he captained his country in their first-ever major finals appearance, and a double to secure a 2-1 comeback win over Sweden in Ukraine's first match co-hosting UEFA EURO 2012. Shevchenko was Ukraine's assistant coach at the European Championship four years later, and replaced Mikhail Fomenko as head coach after the tournament.

SHEVCHENKO

WALES

In a land where rugby union has long been the main national obsession, recent progress – including a semi-final appearance at UEFA EURO 2016 – has inspired unprecedented excitement and optimism.

Joined FIFA: 1906
Biggest win:
11-0 v. Ireland, 1888
Highest FIFA ranking: 8th
Home stadium:
Cardiff City Stadium, Cardiff
Honours: -

100 MILLION

Gareth Bale cost Real Madrid a world record EUR 100 million (GBP 86 million) when he moved from Tottenham Hotspur in August 2013.

BALE

NATIONAL LEGEND
ALL HAIL BALE

It was rather predictable that Wales' first goalscorer at the 2016 UEFA European Championship – their first finals since the 1958 FIFA World Cup – would be **Gareth Bale**. The Real Madrid man – a four-time UEFA Champions League winner – opened the scoring with a free kick in a 2-1 first-round win over Slovakia, and repeated the trick in their next game against England. Before Bale, only France's Michel Platini in 1984 and Germany's Thomas Hässler in 1992 had scored twice from direct free kicks at one UEFA EURO finals. Once Wales' youngest international, he became their leading goalscorer in style with a hat-trick in a 6-0 rout of China PR in March 2018.

20

Midfielder Aaron Ramsey became Wales's youngest captain, aged 20 years and 90 days, when he wore the armband against England in March 2011. The previous record was set in April 1964 by Mike England, who was 22 years and 135 days old when he skippered the side against Northern Ireland.

NATIONAL LEGEND
BILLY IDOL

Winger Harry Wilson became Wales' youngest full international when he replaced Hal Robson-Kanu in a 2014 FIFA World Cup qualifier in October 2013. At 16 years and 207 days, he was 108 days younger than previous record-holder Gareth Bale. Wales' oldest international is Billy Meredith, whose 48th and final international came at the age of 45 years and 229 days in March 1920. Meredith's international career span 25 years, another Welsh record.

CHARLES

TOURNAMENT TRIVIA
FAMILY MATTERS

Wales's only FIFA World Cup finals appearance came in 1958 when they fell 1-0 to eventual champions Brazil and Pelé's first international goal. It was a family affair in more ways than one. Left-winger Cliff Jones was joined in the squad by cousin Ken, a back-up goalkeeper who never played for his country. Their father, Ivor, and uncle, Bryn, both played for Wales too. Mainstays in 1958 were Mel and **John Charles**. John, dubbed "The Gentle Giant", excelled at both centre-back and centre-forward. He scored Wales's first goal in Sweden, a 1-1 draw against Hungary. Mel is one of only four Welshmen to score four times in a full international.

TOP SCORERS:

1 **Gareth Bale**, 33

2 **Ian Rush**, 28

3 **Ivor Allchurch**, 23

= **Trevor Ford**, 23

4 **Dean Saunders**, 22

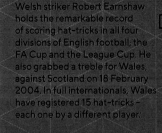

15

Welsh striker Robert Earnshaw holds the remarkable record of scoring hat-tricks in all four divisions of English football, the FA Cup and the League Cup. He also grabbed a treble for Wales, against Scotland on 18 February 2004. In full internationals, Wales have registered 15 hat-tricks – each one by a different player.

SPEED

NATIONAL LEGEND
HEADLINING GIGGS

Ryan Giggs, the most-decorated Welsh player of all-time, took over as the country's national coach in 2018 – despite having no previous full-time managerial experience. Giggs scored 12 goals in 64 internationals between 1991 and 2007. At domestic level, he was a one-club man, winning 13 English league titles, four FA Cups, three League Cups, two UEFA Champions Leagues and one FIFA Club World Cup with Manchester United. He also appeared in more than 1,000 first-team matches before retiring, aged 40, in 2014. After Wales failed to reach the 2018 FIFA World Cup, Giggs replaced Chris Coleman and guided the side to UEFA EURO 2020, their second EURO and third major finals.

GIGGS

NATIONAL LEGEND
SHOCK LOSS OF A MODEL PROFESSIONAL

The football world was united in shock and grief following the sudden death of Wales manager **Gary Speed** in November 2011. Former Leeds United, Everton, Newcastle United and Bolton Wanderers midfielder Speed, once the country's most-capped outfield player, was found at his home in Cheshire, England. The 42-year-old had been manager for 11 months, overseeing a series of encouraging performances that saw a rise in the world ranking from 116th to 48th and a prize for FIFA's Best Movers of 2011. An official memorial game was played in Cardiff in February 2012 between Wales and Costa Rica, the country against whom he had made his international debut in May 1990.

1906

Pioneer movie-makers Sagar Mitchell and James Kenyon filmed Wales v. Ireland in March 1906, making it the first international football match to be captured on film.

18

Ryan Giggs was criticised by some fans for failing to play in friendlies – he missed 18 in a row in one spell.

NATIONAL LEGEND
OH, BROTHER

Chris Gunter was 29 when he made his 93rd Wales appearance against Albania in November 2018, passing former binman-turned-Everton-goalkeeper Neville Southall as his country's most-capped player. Versatile full-back Gunter's parents had a dilemma after a 3-1 victory over Belgium in their 2016 UEFA European Championship quarter-final, thanks to goals by captain Ashley Williams, Hal Robson-Kanu and Sam Vokes – his brother Marc's wedding in Mexico coincided with the semi-final against Portugal. They opted to watch Chris in Lille, where Wales lost 2-0, bringing their memorable run to an end. Gunter was on the bench as a brace from Aaron Ramsey clinched their place at UEFA EURO 2020 in a 2-0 victory over Hungary in November 2019.

GUNTER

MOST APPEARANCES:

1 **Chris Gunter**, 96

2 **Neville Southall**, 92

3 **Wayne Hennessey**, 89

4 **Ashley Williams**, 86

5 **Gary Speed**, 85

EUROPE : OTHER TEAMS

For some of the smaller countries in Europe, the thrill of representing their nation is more important than harbouring dreams of world domination.

Country: Iceland
Joined FIFA: 1947
Most appearances:
Rúnar Kristinsson, 104
Top scorer:
Eiður Guðjohnsen/Kolbeinn
Sigþórsson, 26

Country: San Marino
Joined FIFA: 1988
Most appearances:
Andy Selva, 74
Top scorer: Andy Selva, 8

Country: Finland
Joined FIFA: 1908
Most appearances:
Jari Litmanen, 137
Top scorer:
Jari Litmanen, 32

Country: Luxembourg
Joined FIFA: 1910
Most appearances: Mario
Mutsch, 102
Top scorer: Léon Mart, 16

Country: Gibraltar
Joined FIFA: 2016
Most appearances:
Liam Walker, 44
Top scorer:
Lee Casciaro, 3

Country: Austria
Joined FIFA: 1905
Most appearances:
Andreas Herzog, 103
Top scorer: Toni Polster, 44

Country: Georgia
Joined FIFA: 1992
Most appearances:
Levan Kobiashvili, 100
Top scorer:
Shota Arveladze, 26

Country: North Macedonia
Joined FIFA: 1994
Most appearances:
Goran Pandev, 108
Top scorer:
Goran Pandev, 34

Country: Azerbaijan
Joined FIFA: 1992
Most appearances:
Rashad Sadygov, 111
Top scorer:
Gurban Gurbanov, 14

Country: Bosnia and
Herzegovina
Joined FIFA: 1996
Most appearances:
Edin Džeko, 107
Top scorer: Edin Džeko, 58

Country: Slovenia
Joined FIFA: 1992
Most appearances:
Boštjan Cesar, 101
Top scorer: Zlatko Zahovič, 35

Country: Armenia
Joined FIFA: 1992
Most appearances:
Sargis Hovsepyan, 132
Top scorer:
Henrikh Mkitaryan, 29

Country: Albania
Joined FIFA: 1932
Most appearances:
Lorik Cana, 93
Top scorer:
Erjon Bogdani, 18

Country: Belarus
Joined FIFA: 1992
Most appearances:
Alyaksandr Kulchy, 102
Top scorer:
Maksim Romaschenko, 20

Country: Andorra
Joined FIFA: 1996
Most appearances:
Ildefons Lima, 128
Top scorer:
Ildefons Lima, 11

Country: Montenegro
Joined FIFA: 2007
Most appearances:
Fatos Bećiraj, 69
Top scorer:
Stevan Jovetić, 24

Country: Kosovo
Joined FIFA: 2015
Most appearances:
Amir Rrahmani, 29
Top scorer:
Vedat Muriqi, 8

SIGURDSSON

TOURNAMENT TRIVIA
UNDERDOGS HAVE THEIR DAY

Iceland became the smallest nation to qualify for a FIFA World Cup with a 2-0 victory over Kosovo in October 2017 thanks to goals from star midfielder **Gylfi Sigurðsson** and Jóhann Berg Guðmundsson. Striker Alfreð Finnbogason netted their first FIFA World Cup finals goal, in a 1-1 draw with two-time winners Argentina. Unlike in their first UEFA European Championship appearance two years earlier, Iceland missed out on the knock-out stages after going down 2-0 to Nigeria and 2-1 to Croatia. Manager and part-time dentist Heimir Hallgrimsson resigned after the finals.

TOURNAMENT TRIVIA
FINALLY, FINLAND

Ten-goal **Teemu Pukki** starred as Finland qualified for a major international tournament for the first time, at the 33rd attempt, clinching a place at UEFA EURO 2020 as Group B runners-up behind Italy. Pukki's strikes included a brace in the crucial penultimate qualifier, a 3-0 win over Liechtenstein in November 2019. Only Luxembourg had taken part in more qualifying contests – 35 – without reaching a finals. Pukki scored ten times in his first 59 matches, but has since netted 15 in his last 21 and ten in eight. He now trails Mikael Forsell, 29, and Jari Litmanen 32, in Finland's top goalscorers chart – Litmanen also leads the appearances list with 134.

PUKKI

137

In 2016, Georgia became the lowest-ranked side ever to defeat Spain. The Georgians were 137th in the FIFA ranking – 131 places below their opponents.

JÄNISCH

SCORING RECORD
SELVA SERVICE

San Marino, with a population of under 30,000, remain near the bottom of FIFA's world ranking but they finally had something to celebrate in November 2014 thanks to a goalless draw with Estonia – their first-ever point in a UEFA European Championship qualifier – which ended a run of 61 successive defeats. They have avoided defeat only five times and have never recorded a competitive victory. In fact, San Marino's only win was a 1-0 friendly triumph over Liechtenstein in April 2004. Andy Selva, who retired in 2016 after making his debut in 1998, is San Marino's top scorer with eight goals.

SCORING RECORD
REBORN BOURG

A long and painful wait finally ended for traditional whipping boys Luxembourg when they beat Northern Ireland 3-2 in September 2013. It was the *Red Lions'* first home win in a FIFA World Cup qualifier for 41 years, since overcoming Turkey 2-0 in October 1972. It was also five years to the day since their last FIFA World Cup qualifying victory, a 2-1 triumph in Switzerland in 2008. Luxembourg's goals came from Aurélien Joachim, Stefano Bensi and **Mathias Jänisch**. The winning goal, with three minutes remaining, was the first of Jänisch's international career.

330,000
With a population of 182,000, only FIFA Confederations Cup 2013 qualifiers Tahiti have been a smaller nation at an international finals than Iceland (population 330,000), who played at both the 2018 FIFA World Cup and UEFA EURO 2016.

NATIONAL LEGEND
SUPER PAN

North Macedonia celebrated 100 years of football in the country with a friendly against future world champions Spain in August 2009 – and striker **Goran Pandev** marked the occasion by becoming his country's all-time leading scorer. His first-half brace gave the hosts a 2-0 lead and although Spain came back to win 3-2, Pandev replaced 16-goal Georgi Hristov at the top of North Macedonia's scoring charts. Pandev has played the majority of his club career in Italy after signing for Internazionale from local team FK Belasica as an 18-year-old in 2001.

PANDEV

15

The break-up of the Soviet Union in 1990 led to 15 new footballing nations, although Russia initially played on at the 1992 UEFA European Championship as CIS, or the Commonwealth of Independent States – albeit without the involvement of Estonia, Latvia and Lithuania.

LIMA

★ STAR PLAYER
HAPPY DAYS FOR ILDEFONS

Andorra's long-serving captain **Ildefons Lima** had double cause for celebration on 9 June 2017. Not only did he equal Óscar Sonejee's record of 106 international appearances, but Andorra also beat Hungary 1-0 in a 2018 FIFA World Cup qualifier – only their second-ever competitive victory and first in 66 matches. The winning goal came from Lima's central defensive partner Marc Rebés, his first for Andorra in his ninth game. The Andorrans ended a run of 56 consecutive defeats in UEFA European Championship qualifiers in October 2019 with a 1-0 victory over Moldova, thanks to a goal by another centre-back, Marc Vales.

★ STAR PLAYER
ED BOY

Edin Džeko became Bosnia and Herzegovina's all-time leading scorer with a second-half hat-trick in an 8-1 2014 FIFA World Cup qualifier victory over Liechtenstein in September 2012. The goals not only took him past previous record-holder Elvir Bolić, but also ahead of Džeko's international team-mate Zvjezdan Misimović, whose brace earlier in the game had briefly put him in the lead. The pair jostled for position at the top of the charts for a while before Džeko took over for good. Džeko then became his country's most-capped international when he played against Austria in the UEFA Nations League in September 2018, scoring the only goal of the game for good measure.

DŽEKO

> **5**
> Iceland picked an unchanged starting 11 for all five of their games at **UEFA EURO 2016**, making them the first team to do so in the competition's history.

54

The British Overseas Territory of Gibraltar became UEFA's 54th member state just in time to take part in qualifiers for UEFA EURO 2016, but they were deliberately kept apart from neighbours Spain in the draw.

SINDELAR

🏆 TOURNAMENT TRIVIA
KOS FOR CELEBRATION

Kosovo made their debut in international competition in the 2018 FIFA World Cup qualifiers. Two years later, they marked their first UEFA European Championship qualifiers by finishing third behind England and the Czech Republic in Group A, clinching a play-off against North Macedonia. Top scorer for coach Bernard Challandes' side – who rose 62 places in the FIFA/Coca-Cola World Ranking in just 17 months, peaking at 115th in October 2019 – was striker **Vedat Muriqi**. His four goals doubled his national record tally. Muriqi scored in a crucial 2-0 victory over Montenegro, as did defender Amir Rrahmani, who holds the fledgling nation's record for the most appearances.

MURIQI

🌍 NATIONAL LEGEND
MORE SIND AGAINST

Austria's star player **Matthias Sindelar** refused to play for a new, merged national team when Germany annexed Austria in 1938. Sindelar, born in modern-day Czech Republic in February 1903, was the inspirational leader of Austria's *Wunderteam* of the 1930s. He scored 27 goals in 43 games for Austria, who went 14 internationals unbeaten between April 1931 and December 1932, won the 1932 Central European International Cup and silver at the 1936 Olympics.

17

Iceland striker Eiður Guðjohnsen made history on his international debut away to Estonia in April 1996 when he was 17. He was a substitute for his father, Arnór Guðjohnsen, aged 34.

STAR PLAYER
BY JOVE

Stevan Jovetić struck seven goals in seven games for Montenegro between September 2016 and June 2017, taking him past strike partner and captain **Mirko Vučinić** as the country's leading scorer with 23. His 2018 FIFA World Cup qualifying hat-trick helped to down Armenia 4-1 in June 2017. Vučinić's 17 goals included a winner against Switzerland in a EURO 2012 qualifier, which he celebrated by removing his shorts and wearing them on his head – antics that earned him a yellow card.

VUCINIC

STAR PLAYER
XHAKA CLAN

Granit and Taulant Xhaka, both born in Swiss city Basel to Kosovo Albanian parents, became the first brothers to face each other on opposing sides at a UEFA European Championship on 11 June 2016 – midfielder Granit, 23, for Switzerland, 25-year-old defender Taulant for Albania. Granit and Switzerland won 1-0, and their mother was seen in the stands that day wearing a half-and-half football shirt, supporting both her sons.

STAR PLAYER
A SEQUEL TO HAMLET

Striker Hamlet Mkhitaryan played twice for post-Soviet state Armenia in 1994 before tragically dying two years later from a brain tumour at the age of just 33. His son, **Henrikh Mkhitaryan**, just seven when his father died, has gone on to become the country's all-time leading scorer – and one who often dedicates his achievements to his late father. The younger Mkhitaryan became Armenia's joint-top scorer, alongside Artur Petrosyan, with a goal against Denmark in June 2013. While Petrosyan's goals came in 69 games, Mkhitaryan's 11 were scored in 39 – and he pulled away on his own, with a 12th international strike, in a 2-2 draw with Italy in October 2013.

MKHITARYAN

NATIONAL LEGEND
KULCHY COUP

Midfielder Alyaksandr Kulchy became the first player to win 100 caps for Belarus, skippering the side against Lithuania in a June 2012 friendly. He also ended ex-Arsenal and Barcelona playmaker Alexander Hleb's run of four successive Belarus footballer of the year awards by claiming the prize in 2009. Hleb, whose younger brother Vyacheslav has also played for Belarus, had previously won the accolade in 2002 and 2003 as well, only for Belarus's all-time Top scorer Maksim Romaschenko to take it in 2004.

100
Slovenia's Boštjan Cesar made his 100th appearance against Scotland in October 2017, but it was marred by a late red card and he retired after one more game.

TOURNAMENT TRIVIA
KAZAK JOY, SCOTTISH MISERY

Some 27,000 Kazakhstan fans celebrating a national new year had even more reason for joy in March 2019 with perhaps the country's finest footballing result, a surprise 3-0 trouncing of Scotland in their opening UEFA EURO 2020 qualifier in Astana – despite being ranked 117th in the world. Yuriy Pertsukh, Yan Vorogovskiy and Baktiyar Zaynutdinov were the goalscoring heroes in the first game in charge for new Kazakhstan coach, former Czech Republic midfielder and manager Michael Bílek. Kazakhstan had failed to register a win in their ten qualifiers for the 2018 FIFA World Cup.

XHAKA

SOUTH AMERICA

South America is renowned for the unmatched passion of its fans and exciting skills of its players. Its teams have won the FIFA World Cup on nine occasions and the *Copa América*, launched in 1916, is the longest surviving national team competition.

Confederation founded: 1916

Number of associations: 10

Headquarters: Luque, Paraguay

Most continental championship wins: Uruguay, 15

12

With the exception of the *Centenario* tournament in 2016, 12 teams have competed in each *Copa América* since 1993: the ten CONMEBOL countries, along with two invited nations.

The first FIFA World Cup was held in South America: Uruguay hosted and won the tournament in 1930.

21

Brazil have competed at all 21 FIFA World Cups – more than any other nation – and have won five, also a record.

RIVALDO

RONALDO

The first football club established in South America was the Lima Cricket and Football Club, in Peru in 1859.

10

With only ten member associations, CONMEBOL has the fewest of any FIFA confederation.

ARGENTINA

Copa América champions on 14 occasions, FIFA Confederations Cup winners in 1992, Olympic gold medallists in 2004 and 2008 and, most treasured of all, FIFA World Cup winners in 1978 and 1986: few countries have won as many international titles as Argentina.

Joined FIFA: 1912

Biggest win:
12-0 v. Ecuador, 1942

Highest FIFA ranking: 1st

Home stadium:
Estadio Antonio Vespucio Liberti (El Monumental), Buenos Aires

Honours: 2 FIFA World Cups (1978, 1986), 14 *Copa Américas* (1921, 1925, 1927, 1929, 1937, 1941, 1945, 1946, 1947, 1955, 1957, 1957, 1959, 1991, 1993)

MESSI

STAR PLAYER
LEO BRAVO

Lionel Messi was sent off just two minutes into his national debut, against Hungary in August 2005 after coming on as a substitute, but went on to become Argentina's all-time record goalscorer, youngest FIFA World Cup scorer (against Serbia and Montenegro in 2006, aged 19), youngest captain (at 23 years old during the 2010 FIFA World Cup) and the winner of the Golden Ball for best player at the 2014 FIFA World Cup, where his four Man of the Match awards equalled the record for one tournament.

19

Lionel Messi became only the second substitute to hit a *Copa América* hat-trick when he came off the bench to score three times in Argentina's 5-0 victory over Panama in the opening round of the 2016 *Copa América Centenario*. There were just 19 minutes between his first and third goals.

STAR PLAYER
MASCHERANO'S GOLDEN GLOW

Before the introduction of the FIFA World Cup in 1930, eight Uruguayans had won football gold at both the 1924 and 1928 Summer Olympics. Only one man, Hungary's Dezso Novak in 1964 and 1968, had achieved a similar double before Argentina's defensive midfielder **Javier Mascherano** at Athens 2004 and Beijing 2008. Carlos Tevez got the only goal against Paraguay in 2004, while Ángel Di Mária struck the winner against Nigeria four years later in a game played in such heat that officials allowed water breaks. Mascherano – nicknamed "The Little Chief" – became Argentina's most-capped player at the 2018 FIFA World Cup, before retiring from international football following their 4-3 second round exit to eventual champions France.

3

Argentina are one of only three teams, alongside France and Brazil, to have won the FIFA World Cup, FIFA Confederations Cup and Olympic Games gold medals.

MASCHERANO

ROMERO

1

Only one member of Cesar Menotti's 1978 FIFA World Cup-winning Argentina squad was from a foreign club: Mario Kempes, who scored twice in the final and won the Golden Boot.

STAR PLAYER
HERO ROMERO

No man has kept goal for Argentina more than **Sergio Romero**. He won an Olympic Games gold medal in 2008 but had to wait until September 2009 for his senior international debut against Paraguay. Romero, who reached 96 caps in 2018 but was missed in that summer's FIFA World Cup with a knee injury, had been ever-present for Argentina at both the 2010 and 2014 FIFA World Cups, helping them reach the 2014 final with two saves in a semi-final penalty shoot-out victory over the Netherlands. The 1-0 final defeat to Germany denied him the FIFA World Cup winner's medal earned by compatriot keepers Ubaldo Fillol (58 caps) in 1978 and Nery Pumpido (36) eight years later

TOURNAMENT TRIVIA
MESSI ENDINGS

Argentina reached – and lost – a final for the third consecutive year when Chile won a penalty shoot-out at the 2016 *Copa América Centenario*. This final – just as in 2015, when the then hosts Chile took the shoot-out 4-1 – ended goalless after 120 minutes before Chile triumphed 4-2. Argentina had also fallen to Germany in the 2014 FIFA World Cup final. In fact, Argentina last won the *Copa América* in 1993 and the FIFA World Cup in 1986. Messi ended the 2016 final in despair, failing in the shoot-out and, at age 29, suddenly retiring – though he was back a few months later. His 2019 *Copa América* also finished unhappily when he received the second red card of his career in the third-place play-off, although Argentina did win the game against Chile 2-1.

14

Argentina have finished *Copa América* runners-up more times than any other country, 14, three more than Brazil, most recently in 2015 and 2016.

NATIONAL LEGEND
BEGINNER'S LUCK

Aged just 27 years and 267 days old, Juan José Tramutola became the FIFA World Cup's youngest-ever coach when Argentina opened their 1930 campaign by beating France 1-0. Argentina went on to reach the final, only to lose 4-2 to Uruguay. Top scorer at the 1930 FIFA World Cup was Argentina's Guillermo Stábile, with eight goals in four games – the only internationals he played. He later won six *Copa América* titles as his country's longest-serving coach between 1939 and 1960.

NATIONAL LEGEND
DIVINE DIEGO

To many, **Diego Maradona** is the greatest footballer ever. The Argentinian legend became famous as a ball-juggling child during half-time intervals at Argentinos Juniors matches, but he was distraught to be left out of Argentina's 1978 FIFA World Cup squad and was then sent off for retaliation at the 1982 tournament. As the triumphant Argentina captain in Mexico in 1986, Maradona scored the notorious "Hand of God" goal and then a spectacular individual strike within five minutes of each other in a quarter-final win over England. He again captained Argentina to the FIFA World Cup final in 1990, in Italy – the country where he inspired Napoli to *Serie A* and UEFA Cup success.

2
Midfielder Marcelo Trobbiani played just two minutes of FIFA World Cup football – the last two minutes of the 1986 final, after replacing winning goalscorer Jorge Burruchaga.

MARADONA

STAR PLAYER
THE KIDS ARE ALRIGHT

Sergio Agüero struck in the final, and ended the tournament as six-goal top scorer, when Argentina won the FIFA World U-20 Championship for a record sixth time in 2007, in Canada, beating the Czech Republic 2-1. Agüero married Giannina Maradona – the youngest daughter of Argentina legend Diego – and in 2009 she gave birth to Diego's first grandchild, Benjamin. Sergio Agüero is widely known by his nickname of "Kun", after a cartoon character he was said to resemble as a child.

AGÜERO

12

Argentina were responsible for the biggest win in *Copa América* history, when five goals by José Manuel Moreno helped them thrash Ecuador 12-0 in 1942.

NATIONAL LEGEND
THE ANGEL GABRIEL

Gabriel Batistuta, nicknamed "Batigol", is the only man to have scored hat-tricks in two separate FIFA World Cups. Argentina's former all-time leading goalscorer grabbed the first treble against Greece in 1994 and the second against Jamaica four years later. Hungary's Sándor Kocsis, France's Just Fontaine and Germany's Gerd Müller each scored two hat-tricks in the same FIFA World Cup. Batistuta, born in Avellaneda on 1 February 1969, also set an Italian league record by scoring in 11 consecutive *Serie A* matches for his club Fiorentina at the start of the 1994–95 season.

BATISTUTA

TOURNAMENT TRIVIA
HOME *COPA* COMFORTS

No country has hosted or co-hosted the *Copa América* more often than Argentina's nine times, starting in 1916 – and they are due to make it ten when the next tournament comes around. Originally scheduled for 2020, but postponed to 2021, the tournament will be co hosted with Colombia. The "northern" – Colombia – section will feature Brazil, Ecuador, Peru and Venezuela. Argentina will welcome Bolivia, Chile, Paraguay and Uruguay, while the two guest nations will be Australia and Qatar, hosts of the next FIFA World Cup. Knockout rounds in Argentina's section will see quarter-finals in Buenos Aires (at "El Monumental") and La Plata and a semi-final in Córdoba, before Colombia stages the final in Barranquilla.

TOURNAMENT TRIVIA
YELLOW GOODBYE

Some 20 years before France were forced to wear local Argentine team Club Atlético Kimberley's kit at the 1978 FIFA World Cup, Argentina themselves faced similar embarrassment before their first-round match against West Germany. The Argentinians had neglected to bring along a second kit and a colour clash with their opponents meant borrowing the yellow shirts of Swedish side IFK Malmö. Despite taking a third-minute lead, Argentina lost 3-1 and departed the tournament bottom of Group A.

20

Argentina's national stadium, "El Monumental" in Buenos Aires, hosted its first game in 1938, but the original design was not completed until 20 years later – largely thanks to the GBP 97,000 River Plate received for a transfer fee from Juventus for Omar Sívori.

SÍVORI

NATIONAL LEGEND
FITTER, JAVIER

Only **Javier Mascherano** has won more caps for Argentina than Javier Zanetti, who made 143 international appearances – despite being surprisingly left out of squads for both the 2006 and 2010 FIFA World Cups. Zanetti, who played at full-back or in midfield, also played more *Serie A* matches than any other non-Italian – and all for Inter Milan, with whom he won the treble of Italian league, Italian Cup and UEFA Champions League in 2009 10. Despite those achievements, he and Inter team-mate Esteban Cambiasso failed to make Diego Maradona's squad for the 2010 FIFA World Cup.

MOST APPEARANCES:

1	Javier Mascherano,	147
2	Javier Zanetti,	143
3	Lionel Messi,	138
4	Roberto Ayala,	114
5	Diego Simeone,	104

ZANETTI

NATIONAL LEGEND
SECOND TIME LUCKY

Luisito Monti is the only man to play in a FIFA World Cup final for two different countries. The centre-half, born in Buenos Aires on 15 May 1901 but with Italian family origins, was highly influential in Argentina's run to the 1930 final. They lost the game 4-2 to Uruguay – after Monti allegedly received mysterious pre-match death threats. Following a transfer to Juventus the following year, he was allowed to play for Italy and was on the winning side when the *Azzurri* beat Czechoslovakia in the 1934 final. Another member of the 1934 team was Raimundo Orsi, who had also played for Argentina before switching countries in 1929.

TOURNAMENT TRIVIA
NUMBERS GAME

Argentina's FIFA World Cup squads of 1978 and 1982 were given numbers based on alphabetical order rather than positions, which meant the no. 1 shirt was worn by midfielders Norberto Alonso in 1978 and Osvaldo Ardiles in 1982. The only member of the 1982 squad whose shirt number broke the alphabetical order was no. 10, Diego Maradona. Italian club Napoli retired the number 10 in tribute to Maradona, who starred for the team at his peak.

NATIONAL LEGEND
FRINGE PLAYERS

Daniel Passarella was a demanding captain when he led his country to glory at the 1978 FIFA World Cup. He was the same as coach. After taking over the national side in 1994, he refused to pick anyone unless they had their hair cut short – and ordered striker Claudio Caniggia to get rid of his "girl's hair".

PASSARELLA

Martin Palermo missed all three penalties he took during Argentina's 1999 *Copa América* clash with Colombia. The first hit the crossbar, the second flew over and the third was saved. Colombia won the match 3-0.

3

BRAZIL

No country has captured the soul of the game to the same extent as Brazil. The only nation to appear in every FIFA World Cup finals, Brazil have won the competition a record five times.

Joined FIFA: 1923

Biggest win:
10-1 v. Bolivia, 1949

Highest FIFA ranking: 1st

Home stadium:
Maracanã, Rio de Janeiro

Honours: 5 FIFA World Cups (1958, 1962, 1970, 1994, 2002), 9 *Copa Américas* (1919, 1922, 1949, 1989, 1997, 1999, 2004, 2007, 2019), 4 FIFA Confederations Cups (1997, 2005, 2009, 2013)

26

1970 FIFA World Cup star Tostão retired at the age of 26 in 1973, after an eye injury.

STAR PLAYER
TAKING AIM WITH NEYMAR

Neymar became the youngest man to reach a century of caps for Brazil in a 1–1 friendly draw against Senegal in Singapore in October 2019, aged 27 years and 247 days – three years younger than the previous record-holder Roberto Carlos. The world's most expensive footballer after his GBP 198 million transfer from Barcelona to Paris Saint-Germain in 2017, Neymar reached the landmark despite injuries ending his involvement in the 2014 FIFA World Cup, having netted four goals, and the 2019 *Copa América*, a tournament Brazil went on to win. He did convert the last spot kick as Brazil beat Germany on penalties to win Brazil's first football Olympic gold in Rio's Maracanã stadium in 2016.

NEYMAR

43

Brazilian legend Rivaldo retired at the age of 43 in 2014 – more than a decade after the highlight of his career, helping Brazil win the 2002 FIFA World Cup.

NATIONAL LEGEND
BRAZIL HAVE HAD THEIR BIG PHIL

The return of "Big Phil" **Luiz Felipe Scolari** as Brazil coach in November 2012 was meant to culminate, in 2014, with a repeat of his success spearheading the country to triumph at the 2002 FIFA World Cup. Although his second reign did bring glory at the 2013 FIFA Confederations Cup, the following year's FIFA World Cup on home turf will be remembered for the many unwanted records his team set and the embarrassment with which their efforts ended – most notably, the 7–1 defeat by Germany in their Belo Horizonte semi-final. Scolari was relieved of his role just days after a 3–0 defeat to the Netherlands in the third place play-off.

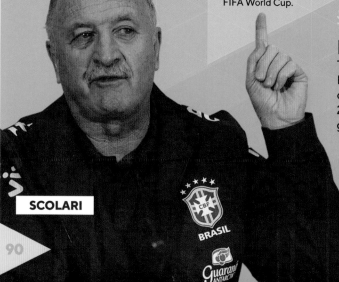

SCOLARI

THE KING

Pelé is considered by many as the greatest player of all time, a sporting icon par excellence and not only for his exploits on the pitch. When, for instance, he scored his 1,000th goal, Pelé dedicated it to the poor children of Brazil. He began playing for Santos at the age of 15 and won his first FIFA World Cup two years later, scoring twice in the final. Despite numerous offers from European clubs, the economic conditions and Brazilian football regulations at the time allowed Santos to keep hold of their prized asset for almost two decades, until 1974.

TOP SCORERS:

1. **Pelé**, 77
2. **Ronaldo**, 62
3. **Neymar**, 61
4. **Romário**, 55
5. **Zico**, 48

3
All-time leading scorer of the Brazilian national team, Pelé is the only footballer to be a member of three FIFA World Cup-winning squads.

PELÉ

7
Pelé leads the way with seven hat-tricks for Brazil, followed by Zico and Romário on four – but only one-time Flamengo and Barcelona centre-forward Evaristo de Macedo has scored five goals in one game for Brazil, against Colombia in March 1957.

© TM FIFA

TOURNAMENT TRIVIA
CLOSE ENCOUNTERS

Brazil have been involved in many memorable games. Their 3–2 defeat to Italy in 1982 is regarded as one of the classic games in FIFA World Cup finals history. Paolo Rossi scored all three of Italy's goals, with Brazil coach Telê Santana much criticised for his all-out attack approach when only a 2–2 draw was needed. Brazil's 1982 squad, with players such as Sócrates, Zico and Falcão, is considered one of the greatest teams never to win the tournament. In 1994, a 3–2 win over the Netherlands in the quarter-finals – their first competitive meeting in 20 years – was just as thrilling, with all the goals coming in the second half.

1954
The world-renowned yellow and blue kit now worn by Brazil was not adopted until 1954, as a replacement for their former all-white strip.

TOURNAMENT TRIVIA
LAND OF FOOTBALL

No country is more deeply identified with football success than Brazil, who have won the FIFA World Cup a record five times – in 1958, 1962, 1970, 1994 and 2002. They are also the only team never to have missed a FIFA World Cup finals and are favourites virtually every time the competition is staged. After winning the trophy for a third time in Mexico in 1970, Brazil kept the Jules Rimet Trophy permanently. Sadly, it was stolen from the association's headquarters in 1983 and was never recovered.

NATIONAL LEGEND
JOY OF THE PEOPLE

Garrincha, one of Brazil's greatest legends, was really Manuel Francisco dos Santos at birth but his nickname meant "Little Bird" – inspired by his slender, bent legs. Despite the legacy of childhood illness, he was a star right-winger at Botafogo from 1953 to 1965. He and Pelé were explosively decisive newcomers for Brazil at the 1958 FIFA World Cup finals. In 1962 Garrincha was voted player of the tournament. He died in January 1983 at just 49. His epitaph was the title often bestowed on him in life: "The Joy of the People".

GARRINCHA

NATIONAL LEGEND
LETTING LÚCIO

Elegant centre-back **Lúcio** set a FIFA World Cup record during the 2006 tournament by playing for 386 minutes without conceding a foul – only ending in Brazil's 1-0 quarter-final defeat to France. While mostly noted for his leadership and control at the back, he also had an eye for goal – heading the late winner that gave Brazil a 3-2 triumph over the USA in the 2009 FIFA Confederations Cup final. The following year he was part of Italian club Inter Milan's treble success, clinching the Italian league and cup as well as the UEFA Champions League.

LÚCIO

1000

Brazil played their 1,000th match on 14 November 2012, with Neymar's second-half equaliser securing a 1-1 draw against Colombia in New Jersey, USA.

TOURNAMENT TRIVIA
EARLY ARRIVAL... AND DEPARTURE

Brazil became the first country outside host nation Russia to secure a place at the 2018 FIFA World Cup, when they beat Paraguay 3-0 on 28 March 2017 after just 14 of South American confederation CONMEBOL's scheduled 18 qualification rounds. They had been sixth of ten South American nations in the group when Tite took over as manager in summer 2016, but he led them to eight consecutive victories and comfortable qualification. Yet despite high hopes for the 2018 tournament – and surpassing Germany as the FIFA World Cup's all-time highest scorers, with 229 goals – they bowed out 2-1 to Belgium in the quarter-finals.

STAR PLAYER
ALISSON WONDERLAND

Liverpool and Brazil goalkeeper Alisson went 14 hours and 59 minutes without conceding a goal for club or country before being finally beaten by a Paolo Guerrero penalty in the 2019 *Copa América* final – but Peru's goal in a 3-1 Brazil victory was the only one he let in all tournament. It was glorious 2019 for Alisson – winner of The Best FIFA Men's Goalkeeper award – as he also won the *Copa América*, UEFA Champions League and FIFA Club World Cup. He was joined as a triple medal-winner by team-mate Roberto Firmino.

TOURNAMENT TRIVIA
PLAYING *COPA* CATCH-UP

Brazil won just three of the first 33 *Copa América* tournaments yet have now won five of the last nine editions, after triumphing on home soil in 2019. It was also their first South American crown in 12 years. Brazil beat Peru 3-1 in the final in Rio's Maracanã stadium, despite the absence of injured superstar Neymar and Gabriel Jesus being sent off. The centre-forward set up Everton's opening goal and then scored Brazil's second before being dismissed for collecting two yellow cards. Brazil, even with ten men, extended their lead through a penalty from substitute Richarlison, allowing veteran captain Dani Alves to lift the trophy.

3

Right-back **Djalma Santos** is one of only two players to be voted into the official all-star team of a FIFA World Cup on three different occasions.

SANTOS

ALVES

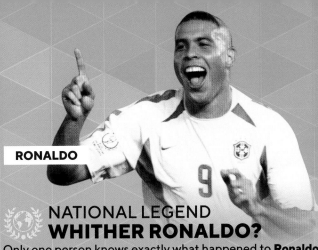

RONALDO

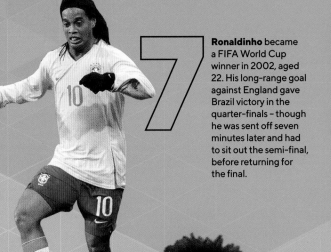

RONALDINHO

7 Ronaldinho became a FIFA World Cup winner in 2002, aged 22. His long-range goal against England gave Brazil victory in the quarter-finals – though he was sent off seven minutes later and had to sit out the semi-final, before returning for the final.

NATIONAL LEGEND
WHITHER RONALDO?

Only one person knows exactly what happened to **Ronaldo** in the hours before the 1998 FIFA World Cup final – the man himself. He sparked one of the biggest mysteries in FIFA World Cup history when his name was left off the teamsheet before the game, only for it to reappear just in time for kick-off. It was initially reported that Ronaldo had an ankle injury, and then a upset stomach. Finally, team doctor Lídio Toledo revealed the striker had been rushed to hospital after suffering a convulsion in his sleep, but that he had been cleared to play after neurological and cardiac tests. He did score both goals in the final four years later as Brazil beat Germany 2-0, giving him the Golden Boot with eight overall. Only Germany's Miroslav Klose has scored more FIFA World Cup goals than his 15.

ROMÁRIO

MARCELO

STAR PLAYER
INAUSPICIOUS START

Left-back/left-winger **Marcelo** achieved the dubious "honour" of being the first player to score the opening goal of a FIFA World Cup finals in his own net. He inadvertently gave Croatia the lead in the 2014 tournament's curtain-raiser in São Paulo, but Brazil did come back to win 3-1, thanks to a pair of goals from Neymar and one from Oscar. Marcelo, who a couple of weeks earlier had scored for his club, Real Madrid, as they won the UEFA Champions League final, also became the first Brazil player ever to score past his own goalkeeper in the FIFA World Cup finals.

MOST APPEARANCES:

1 **Cafu**, 142
2 **Roberto Carlos**, 125
3 **Dani Alves**, 118
4 **Lúcio**, 105
5 **Neymar**, 101
= **Cláudio Taffarel**, 101

NATIONAL LEGEND
ROM NUMBERS

Brazilian goal poacher supreme **Romário** is one of the few footballers to claim more than 1,000 career goals. He is also the last man to win both the FIFA World Cup and the Golden Ball award as the best player at the same tournament, something he achieved in 1994 when his five goals – including the semi-final winner against Sweden – helped Brazil to their fourth title. The former Barcelona and Fluminense forward moved into politics after retiring from playing to become elected as an MP, as did his 1994 FIFA World Cup strike partner Bebeto.

TOURNAMENT TRIVIA
SUPER POWERS' POWER CUT

There was a new addition to the annual international calendar in 2011: the *Superclásico de las Américas*, a two-legged event between Brazil and Argentina. Brazil were the first winners, thanks to a goalless draw followed by a 2-0 win. They dramatically retained the crown in 2012. Brazil won the first leg at home 2-1, but the return game in Chaco was postponed after a power cut. The rearranged game ended 2-1 to Argentina, but Brazil won 4-3 on penalties.

CHILE

Chile were one of four founding members of CONMEBOL, South America's football confederation, in 1916. Their greatest glories were hosting and finishing third at the 1962 FIFA World Cup and winning their first two *Copa América* titles in 2015 and 2016.

Joined FIFA: 1912

Biggest win:
7-0 v. Venezuela, 1979, v. Armenia, 1997, v. Mexico, 2016

Highest FIFA ranking: 3rd

Home stadium:
Estadio Nacional Julio Martínez Prádanos, Santiago

Honours: 2 *Copa Américas* (2015, 2016)

SALAS

NATIONAL LEGEND
SALAS DAYS

Chile's third leading scorer **Marcelo Salas** formed a much-feared striking partnership with Iván Zamorano during the late 1990s and early 21st century. Salas scored four goals as Chile reached the round of 16 at the 1998 FIFA World Cup in France despite not winning a game. The striker spent two years in international retirement, from 2005 to 2007, but returned for the first four games of qualification for the 2010 FIFA World Cup. He scored twice in Chile's 2-2 draw with Uruguay on 18 November 2007, but his international career ended for good three days later, following a 3-0 defeat to Paraguay.

2

Argentinians Marcelo Bielsa and Jorge Sampaoli coached Chile to consecutive FIFA World Cup round-of-16 exits in 2010 and 2014, their first ever back-to-back finals.

SCORING RECORD
LUCKY LEO

For many years, Leonel Sánchez held the Chilean record for international appearances, scoring 23 goals in 84 games. But he was lucky to remain on the pitch for one of them. Sánchez escaped an early bath despite punching Italy's Humberto Maschio in the face during their so-called "Battle of Santiago" clash at the 1962 FIFA World Cup, when English referee Ken Aston could have sent off more than just the two players he did dismiss. Sánchez, a left-winger who was born in Santiago on 25 April 1936, finished the 1962 FIFA World Cup as one of six four-goal leading scorers – along with Garrincha, Vavá, Valentin Ivanov, Drazan Jerković and Flórián Albert.

STAR PLAYER
SÁNCHEZ SETS MORE CHILE RECORDS

The winning spot kick against Argentina to secure Chile's first *Copa América* in 2015 was struck by the well-travelled **Alexis Sánchez**, then of Arsenal in England, following spells in Italy with Udinese and in Spain with Barcelona. Sánchez holds the record as Chile's youngest international, having made his debut against New Zealand in April 2006 at the age of 17 years and four months. At the 2017 FIFA Confederations Cup, Sánchez passed Marcelo Salas to become Chile's all-time record goalscorer. Then, in 2018, and while with Manchester United, he took over at the top of the appearances list too.

SÁNCHEZ

NATIONAL LEGEND
VIDAL ESCAPES TO VICTORY

Hosts Chile's 2015 *Copa América* campaign nearly careered off the road, literally. Star midfielder **Arturo Vidal** crashed his red Ferrari after over-enjoying a night out, having scored twice in a 3-3 draw with Mexico. Coach Jorge Sampaoli resisted public pressure to drop him for the deciding match of the group after Vidal promised to donate his tournament fee to charity and a 5-0 thrashing of Bolivia – he grabbed another double – sealed Chile's quarter-final place. Vidal was named Man of the Match in the final and was selected for the 2015 *Copa América* team of the tournament.

VIDAL

48

Chile went precisely 48 years between victories at a FIFA World Cup, from a 1-0 third-place play-off success against Yugoslavia on 16 June 1962 to a first-round victory by the same scoreline over Honduras on 16 June 2010.

BEAUSEJOUR

1930
Chile forward Carlos Vidal – nicknamed "Little Fox" – was the first man to miss a penalty at a FIFA World Cup, seeing his spot kick saved by France goalkeeper Alex Thépot in 1930.

99
Chile waited 99 years for their first *Copa América* triumph, winning the tournament in 2015. They won the tournament the following year, too.

MOST APPEARANCES:

1 **Alexis Sánchez**, 132

2 **Gary Medel**, 126

3 **Claudio Bravo**, 123

4 **Mauricio Isla**, 115

= **Gonzalo Jara**, 115

= **Arturo Vidal**, 115

STAR PLAYER
DEJU VU, BRAVO

You wait 90 years to win the *Copa América* for the first time – and then a second triumph comes around 12 months later. Just as in 2015, Chile beat Argentina in the final of the 2016 *Copa América* – this time in the USA, in the *Copa América Centenario* to mark the 100th anniversary of the tournament. Both finals ended goalless and went to a shoot-out, with Chile winning 4-1 on penalties in 2015 and 4-2 the following year. Goalkeeper and captain **Claudio Bravo** was named the tournament's best goalkeeper on both occasions – as he was again when Chile competed in their first FIFA Confederations Cup in Russia in 2017, yet this time they finished runners-up following a 1-0 defeat to Germany in the final. Bravo had been a shoot-out hero again in the semi-final, after another 0-0 draw, saving three Portugal spot kicks.

BRAVO

SCORING RECORD
BRAVO, BEAUSEJOUR

Chile's first goal at the 2010 FIFA World Cup in South Africa came from **Jean Beausejour** in a 1-0 win over Honduras. He then scored Chile's third in an opening-game 3-1 triumph over Australia in Brazil four years later, becoming the first Chilean player ever to score at more than one FIFA World Cup. In goal and captain at both tournaments was Claudio Bravo, Chile's most-capped goalkeeper of all time.

4
Eduardo Vargas scored four times as Chile matched their record win – and their biggest in a competitive match – by beating Mexico 7-0 in their June 2016 quarter-final at that summer's *Copa América Centenario*.

VARGAS

URUGUAY

Uruguay were the first country to win a FIFA World Cup, in 1930, and with a population of under four million, they remain the smallest to do so. They claimed the game's greatest prize for a second time in 1950.

Joined FIFA: 1916

Biggest win:
9-0 v. Peru, 1927

Highest FIFA ranking: 2nd

Home stadium: Estadio Centenario, Montevideo

Honours: 2 FIFA World Cups (1930, 1950), 15 *Copa Américas* (1916, 1917, 1920, 1923, 1924, 1926, 1935, 1942, 1956, 1959, 1967, 1983, 1987, 1995, 2011)

3

It took just three minutes for Edinson Cavani to score his first international goal, after coming on as a substitute for his Uruguay debut against Colombia in February 2008.

CAVANI

3.4M

Uruguay's population of 3.4 million and area of 176,000 sq km makes it the smallest nation to have lifted the FIFA World Cup trophy. The next smallest in terms of population is Argentina with 43 million.

STAR PLAYER
CAV FAITH

Edinson Cavani not only helped Uruguay finish fourth at the 2010 FIFA World Cup and win a record 15th *Copa América*, the devout Christian also won praise when playing for Italian club Napoli from the Archbishop of Naples Crescenzio Sepe, who declared: "God serves himself by having Cavani score goals." Yet his 2015 *Copa América* ended unhappily with a sending off at the end of a quarter-final defeat to hosts and eventual champions Chile. Cavani had retaliated after a clash with Gonzalo Jara.

NATIONAL LEGEND
CLASS APART

Óscar Tabárez, a former schoolteacher known as "The Maestro", led Uruguay to the second round of the 1990 FIFA World Cup and returned for a second spell in 2006, taking them back to the tournament in 2010 – and a fourth-place finish. When he took charge of his 168th Uruguay game in 2016, he passed West Germany's Sepp Herberger for the most matches coached for one team. Tabárez became the first international manager to oversee 200 matches when winger Brian Rodríguez gave Uruguay a 1-0 friendly win over Peru in the Montevideo's Estadio Centenario in October 2019.

TABÁREZ

16

There were 16 years between Óscar Tabárez's first and second stints in charge of Uruguay. In that time, they failed to win a single FIFA World Cup finals game.

TOURNAMENT TRIVIA
DIFFERENT BALL GAME

Uruguay were the inaugural hosts – and the first winners – of the FIFA World Cup in 1930, having won football gold at the Olympics of 1924 in Paris and 1928 in Amsterdam. Uruguay beat arch-rivals Argentina 4-2 in the 1930 final, a game in which two different footballs were used – Argentina's choice in the first half, in which they led 2-1, before Uruguay's was used for their second-half comeback. Uruguay declined the chance to defend their title in 1934, refusing to travel to host country Italy in pique at only four European nations visiting in 1930.

STAR PLAYER
GET IN, GODÍN

Centre-back Diego Godín was the third man to reach win 100 caps for Uruguay, and he became their most-capped player in the final of the 2019 China Cup, as Uruguay beat Thailand 4-0. Godín has a knack for scoring crucial goals, especially three in May and June 2014. The first secured a first Spanish league title in 18 years for his club Atlético Madrid; he then gave them the lead in the UEFA Champions League final (although they lost 4-1 to Real Madrid); and he headed the late goal that beat Italy and secured Uruguay's place in the FIFA World Cup round of 16.

GODIN

1901
Uruguay's 3-2 home defeat to neighbours Argentina, in Montevideo on 16 May 1901, was the first official international match outside the UK.

MOST APPEARANCES:

1 **Diego Godín**, 135

2 **Maxi Pereria**, 125

3 **Edinson Cavani**, 116

= **Fernando Muslera**, 116

5 **Luis Suárez**, 113

3

Forward Héctor Scarone, currently Uruguay's fourth-top scorer with 31 goals in 52 internationals, won three titles with Uruguay: the FIFA World Cup in 1930, and football gold at the Olympic Games of 1924 in Paris and 1928 in Amsterdam.

TOURNAMENT TRIVIA
HAPPY ANNIVERSARY

A so-called *Mundialito* or "Little World Cup", was staged in December 1980 and January 1981 to mark the 50th anniversary of the FIFA World Cup – and, as in 1930, Uruguay emerged triumphant. The tournament was meant to involve all six countries who had previously won the tournament, though 1966 champions England turned down the invitation and were replaced by 1978 runners-up the Netherlands. Uruguay beat Brazil 2-1 in the final, a repeat of the scoreline from the final match of the 1950 FIFA World Cup. The *Mundialito*-winning Uruguay side was captained by goalkeeper Rodolfo Rodríguez and coached by Roque Máspoli, who had played in goal in that 1950 final.

STAR PLAYER
BITE CLUB

Notoriety has cast many shadows over the career of **Luis Suárez**. He earned infamy with a deliberate goal-line handball in the last minute of extra time when Uruguay and Ghana were level in their 2010 FIFA World Cup quarter-final – then celebrated wildly when Asamoah Gyan missed – and Uruguay won the resulting shoot-out. Worse followed, however, at the 2014 FIFA World Cup, when he bit into the shoulder of Italian defender Giorgio Chiellini, earning himself a nine-match international ban and a four-month suspension from all football. His scoring instincts are much more admirable – his international goals total includes four during Uruguay's triumphant 2011 *Copa América* campaign.

SUÁREZ

TOP SCORERS:

1 **Luis Suárez**, 59

2 **Edinson Cavani**, 50

3 **Diego Forlán**, 36

4 **Héctor Scarone**, 31

5 **Ángel Romano**, 28

SOUTH AMERICA: OTHER TEAMS

With only ten nations in South America, CONMEBOL is competitive. Though there are minnows who don't have the history or prowess of Brazil or Argentina, the rest of South America has still produced wonderful stories football over the years.

Country: Colombia
Joined FIFA: 1938
Most appearances: Carlos Valderrama, 111
Top scorer: Radamel Falcao, 34
Honours: 1 *Copa América* (2001)

Country: Peru
Joined FIFA: 1925
Most appearances: Roberto Palacios, 128
Top scorer: Paulo Guerrero 39
Honours: 2 *Copa Américas* (1939, 1975)

Country: Bolivia
Joined FIFA: 1926
Most appearances: Ronald Raldes, 102
Top scorer: Joaquín Botero, 20
Honours: 1 *Copa América* (1963)

Country: Paraguay
Joined FIFA: 1925
Most appearances: Paulo da Silva, 150
Top scorer: Roque Santa Cruz, 32
Honours: 2 *Copa Américas* (1953, 1979)

Country: Ecuador
Joined FIFA: 1930
Most appearances: Iván Hurtado, 168
Top scorer: Agustín Delgado, Enner Valencia, 31
Honours: -

Country: Venezuela
Joined FIFA: 1952
Most appearances: Juan Arango, 129
Top scorer: Salomón Rondon, 30
Honours: -

STAR PLAYER
MINA MAKES HIS MARK

Colombian centre-back Yerry Mina surprised even himself at the 2018 FIFA World Cup in Russia when he proved not only a tower of strength in defence but was his team's three-goal leading scorer. That equalled the record tally for a defender at the finals. Colombia lost their opening game to Japan, but Mina scored the first goal of their next game, a 3-0 defeat of Poland. He then struck again with the lone goal which beat Senegal and sent Colombia into the round of 16. Mina headed the last-minute equaliser in a 1-1 draw with England before Colombia lost on penalties.

26
The number of minutes it took all-time leading goalscorer Salomón Rondón to complete a hat-trick as Venezuela won the 2019 Kirin Cup with a 4-1 defeat of Japan in Suita.

STAR PLAYER
HERO GUERRERO

Veteran playmaker **Paolo Guerrero** had to wait a very long time before he could lead Peru at the 2018 FIFA World Cup, their first appearance in the finals for 36 years. He scored in a 2-0 win over Australia, but Peru went out at the group stage. That goal was his record-extending 35th for Peru and it came 14 years after his debut. He achieved even more at the 2019 *Copa América*, when his three goals made him joint top scorer. Guerrero led Peru to the final, and scored, but his side ultimately lost 3-1 to Brazil.

GUERRERO

4

Bolivia's only win at *Copa América* came as hosts in 1963. They led Brazil 2-0 and 4-2 in their final match, only for Máximo Alcócer to clinch a 5-4 victory with just four minutes left.

GARECA

ICONIC MOMENT
ECUADOR'S EARTHQUAKE TRIBUTE

Ecuador reached the knockout stages of the 2016 *Copa América Centenario* – the first time they had advanced from the opening round since 1987. They drew with Brazil (0-0) and Peru (2-2) and defeated Haiti 4-0. Head coach Gustavo Quinteros dedicated their progress to the more than 600 people killed by an earthquake in the country's Manabí region on 16 April 2016. Ecuador's opening goal against Haiti was scored by then West Ham United striker Enner Valencia, who had netted three times at the 2014 FIFA World Cup – the first Ecuadorian to score more than once in a FIFA World Cup finals match.

TEAM TRIVIA
CROSSING CONTINENTS

South American coaches have worked all around the world yet, in 2019, three Europeans were in charge of South American nations: Portugal's José Peseiro in Venezuela and Carlos Queiroz in Colombia, and Dutchman Jordi Cruyff – son of the legendary Johan – in Ecuador. However, Peru's Argentinian coach **Ricardo Gareca** was bullish after leading Peru to the 2018 FIFA World Cup and the 2019 *Copa América* final, this following knockout wins over Uruguay and holders Chile. He declared: "We know who we are. We should work on our own style, our own culture."

44

Peru were coached at the 1982 FIFA World Cup by Tim, who had been waiting an unprecedented 44 years to return to the FIFA World Cup finals – after playing once as striker for his native Brazil in the 1938 tournament.

35,742
The smallest national stadium in South America is the Estadio Olímpico Atahualpa, Quito, Ecuador, which holds 35,742.

TEAM TRIVIA
HIGH LIFE

Bolivia and Ecuador play their home internationals at higher altitudes than any other teams on earth. Bolivia's showpiece Estadio Hernando Siles stadium, in the capital La Paz, is 3,637 metres (11,932 feet) above sea level, while Ecuador's main Estadio Olímpico Atahualpa, in Quito, sits 2,800 metres (9,185 feet) above sea level. Opposing teams have complained that the rarefied nature of the air makes it difficult to breathe, let alone play, but a FIFA ban on playing competitive internationals at least 2,500 metres (8,200 feet) above sea level, first introduced in May 2007, was suspended entirely in May 2008.

VALDERRAMA

NATIONAL LEGEND
TALKING HEAD

Colombia's record international remains frizzy-haired midfielder **Carlos Valderrama** who played 111 times for *Los Cafeteros*, scoring 11 goals, between 1985 and 1998. Valderrama stood out for both his hairstyle and his playmaking talent when he captained Colombia in a golden era for the national team. He was voted South American Footballer of the Year in 1987 and 1993 while appearing in the finals of the FIFA World Cup on three successive occasions in 1990, 1994 and 1998. Valderrama was a hugely popular figure at the 2018 finals in Russia when he undertook television pundit duties, still parading his famous hairstyle.

HURTADO

NATIONAL LEGEND
ABOVE-PAR PARAGUAY

Paraguay's two most-capped players, centre-back Paulo da Silva (148 appearances, first against Bolivia on 27 July 2000) and goalkeeper Justo Villar (120 caps, debut v. Guatemala, 3 March 1999) were mainstays in their country's most successful FIFA World Cup performance: topping their group in 2010 and reaching the quarter-finals, only losing to eventual champions Spain. Both were still in the side in October 2016, helping Paraguay win a FIFA World Cup qualifier in Argentina for the first time – thanks to a Derlis González strike.

SCORING RECORD
NOT SO FAB

Colombia full-back Frank Fabra endured a bittersweet *Copa América* first at the 2016 *Centenario* tournament when he scored for both teams in one match – no other player had done this in the competition's 100-year history. He found the net at both ends as his side lost 3-2 to Costa Rica in the first round, although Colombia did recover to qualify for the next stage and ultimately reached the semi-finals.

168

With 168 caps, **Iván Hurtado** of Ecuador is the most capped South American footballer of all time.

NATIONAL LEGEND
WINNING RON

Bolivia's most-capped player, centre-back **Ronald Raldes**, scored just his second-ever international goal against Ecuador at the 2015 Copa América, helping secure Bolivia's first victory in the tournament since 1997. Their failure to qualify for the 2018 FIFA World Cup means that 1930, 1950 and 1994 remain their only finals – but the 2018 campaign did include back-to-back wins for the first time since 1998, including a surprise 2-0 victory over Argentina thanks in part to a goal from Marcelo Martins – who had gone ten internationals without scoring beforehand.

RONDON

RALDES

10 MILLION
Yerry Mina became the first Colombian to join Barcelona in 2018, costing them GBP 10m from Brazil's Palmeiras.

TEAM TRIVIA
GOING CARACAS FOR FOOTBALL

Venezuela is the only CONMEBOL nation not to qualify for a FIFA World Cup, yet it achieved a record high 25th position in the FIFA/Coca-Cola World Ranking in November 2019, despite baseball and boxing long being the dominant sports in the country. After lavish investment in new stadiums, Venezuela staged its first *Copa América* in 2007 as captain and record cap-holder Juan Arango helped them through to the knockout stages for the first time. Much-travelled striker **Salomón Rondon** became Venezuela's first man to reach 30 goals for his country with a hat-trick in a 4-1 victory away to Japan in November 2019.

3

All three of Paraguayan Paulo da Silva's international goals came against Chile – two on 21 November 2007 in Santiago and the third, almost nine years later, on 1 September 2016.

SCORING RECORD
FALCAO FIGHTS BACK

Colombia captain and leading goalscorer **Radamel Falcao** made a remarkable recovery to play at the 2018 FIFA World Cup finals in Russia. Four years earlier, it had been feared a knee injury might bring his goal-hungry career to a premature end. In 2009, FC Porto bought Falcao for GBP 2m, and it proved a bargain as he led them to a 2011 treble of league, cup and UEFA Europa League. Following a move to Spain's Atlético Madrid, he repeated the Europa League triumph 12 months later. He then moved to AS Monaco, where he was top scorer in their 2016–17 Ligue 1 title win.

FALCAO

73

Keeping clean sheets for Colombia all the way through the 2001 *Copa América* was Óscar Córdoba, who went on to make 73 appearances between 1993 and 2006.

TOURNAMENT TRIVIA
RUID AWAKENING

Peru ended a 31-year wait to beat Brazil with a 1-0 win in the first round of the 2016 *Copa América Centenario*. It put Ricardo Gareca's side in the quarter-finals and eliminated Dunga's Brazilians. The goal was contentious, however, as Raúl Ruidíaz seemed to knock the ball into the goal with his hand from Andy Polo's cross. Ruidíaz insisted he had used his thigh and denied comparisons to Diego Maradona's "Hand of God" goal at the 1986 FIFA World Cup, claiming his strike was "thanks to God". Peru's previous win over Brazil – 2016 was only the fourth ever – had been in April 1985, when Julio César Uribe got the only goal in a friendly in Brasilia. Their other *Copa América* defeats of Brazil were in 1953 and 1975.

TOURNAMENT TRIVIA
COOL DUDAMEL

Venezuela suffered some bad defeats when missing out on the 1998 FIFA World Cup. They ended with no wins and 13 defeats in 16 games, scoring 13 and conceding 41 goals. The losses included 4-1 to Peru, 6-1 to Bolivia and 6-0 to Chile, for whom Iván Zamorano scored five. But their goalkeeper Rafael Dudamel had a moment to savour against Argentina in October 1996, when he scored with a direct free kick late in the game. Venezuela still lost 5-2. Dudamel became Venezuela coach in April 2016 and, two months later, led them to the quarter-finals of the *Copa América Centenario*.

NATIONAL LEGEND
HIGHS AND LOWS FOR LOLO

Teodoro "Lolo" Fernández scored six goals in two games for Peru at the 1936 Summer Olympics, including five in a 7–3 defeat of Finland and another in a 4–2 victory over Austria, though the that match was ruled void. Peru withdrew from the tournament in protest, while Austria went on to claim silver. But Fernández and his team-mates had a happier ending at the *Copa América* three years later, with Peru crowned champions and Fernández finishing as top scorer with seven goals.

FERNÁNDEZ

AFRICA

The African confederation organised its inaugural Cup of Nations in 1957, only a year after it was founded. Now with more than 50 member associations, it can claim to be largest of the international confederations, with a rich football history to match.

Founded: 1956

Number of associations: 55 (+1 non-FIFA member)

Headquarters: Cairo, Egypt

Most continental championship wins: Egypt, 7 (1957, 1959, 1986, 1998, 2006, 2008, 2010)

5

UNAF (Southern Africa)

WAFU-UFOA
(West Africa)

CECAFA
(East Africa)

UNIFFAC
(Central Africa)

COSAFA
(Southern Africa)

Africa is split into five regional federations based on location, with one non-FIFA member, Réunion.

6

Six African nations competed in the 2010 FIFA World Cup, more than any other edition of the tournament. They were hosts South Africa, Algeria, Cameroon, , Côte d'Ivoire, Ghana and Nigeria.

ETO'O

18

Samuel Eto'o scored 18 goals in the CAF Africa Cup of Nations, more than any other player.

In 1934, Egypt became the first African team to reach the FIFA World Cup finals. Africa had to wait until 1978 for their first win though, a 3-1 win for Tunisia over Mexico.

2

Nigeria became the first African side to reach consecutive FIFA World Cup knockout stages – in 1994 and 1998.

NORTH AFRICA

The most successful regional zone within Africa, the north of the continent has produced the most successful CAF Africa Nations Cup side of all time, Egypt, along with the first African team to win a FIFA World Cup match, Tunisia.

Country: Algeria
Joined FIFA: 1964
Most appearances:
Lakhdar Belloumi, 100
Top scorer:
Abdelhafid Tasfaout, 36
Honours: 2 Africa Cup of Nations (1990, 2019)

Country: Egypt
Joined FIFA: 1923
Most appearances:
Ahmed Hassan, 184
Top scorer:
Hossam Hassan, 69
Honours: 7 Africa Cup of Nations (1957, 1959, 1986, 1998, 2006, 2008, 2010)

Country: Libya
Joined FIFA: 1964
Most appearances:
Ahmed Saad, 108
Top scorer: Fawzi Al-Issawi, 40
Honours: -

Country: Morocco
Joined FIFA: 1960
Most appearances:
Noureddine Naybet, 115
Top scorer:
Ahmed Faras, 29
Honours: 1 Africa Cup of Nations (1976)

Country: Sudan
Joined FIFA: 1948
Most appearances:
Muhannad El Tahir, 79
Top scorer:
Nasr El-Din Abbas, 27
Honours: 1 Africa Cup of Nations (1970)

Country: Tunisia
Joined FIFA: 1960
Most appearances:
Sadok Sassi, 116
Top scorer:
Issam Jemâa, 36
Honours: 1 Africa Cup of Nations (2004)

TOURNAMENT TRIVIA
MOKHTAR RUNS AMOK

Egypt had to play only two matches to qualify for the 1934 FIFA World Cup, becoming the first African representatives at the tournament. Both qualifiers were against a Palestine side under the British mandate – and the Egyptians won both games handsomely, 7-1 in Cairo and 4-1 in Palestine. Captain and striker Mahmoud Mokhtar scored a hat-trick in the first leg, a brace in the second. Turkey were also meant to contest qualifiers against the two sides, but withdrew, leaving the path to the finals free for Egypt.

4

Four nations founded CAF, but South Africa were expelled before they could join on account of the apartheid regime, the other three competing in the first Africa Cup of Nations: Egypt, Ethiopia and Sudan.

BOUNEDJAH

TOURNAMENT TRIVIA
ALGERIA HYSTERIA

Playmaker Riyad Mahrez had been billed as the star of the show – and he was indeed one of four Algerian players named in the team of the tournament – but striker Baghdad Bounedjah was the hero as his deflected long-range strike won the 2019 CAF Africa Cup of Nations final against Senegal in Egypt. Manager and former Algeria international midfielder Djamel Belmadi had only taken charge the previous August. This was Algeria's second second African championship, having previously won it in 1990. It was the first tournament to be staged in the middle of the year and 24 teams competed, up from 16. Three countries made their tournament debuts: Burundi, Mauritania – both finished bottom of their groups – and Madagascar, who lost 3-0 to Tunisia in the quarter-finals. Algeria dominated the individual prizes, with Ismaël Bennacer named best player while Raïs M'Bolhi was best goalkeeper.

STAR PLAYER
SALAH THE FOOTBALLING PHAROAH

Egypt winger **Mohamed Salah** has established himself as one of the world's outstanding players in recent years. Salah scored a hat-trick against Zimbabwe in the 2014 World Cup qualifiers before his goals for both Egypt and Swiss club Basel earned an GBP 11m transfer to Chelsea. Salah ended up at Liverpool in 2017 and was voted footballer of the year in 2018 by both the Football Writers' Association and Professional Footballers' Association; he suffered a shoulder injury early in Liverpool's defeat against Real Madrid in the UEFA Champions League final in 2018 but was on the scoresheet a year later when the Reds claimed the title against Tottenham Hotspur.

SALAH

TOURNAMENT TRIVIA
HAIL HALLICHE

Algeria became the first African nation to score four goals in one game at a FIFA World Cup finals when they defeated Korea Republic 4-2 in Porto Alegre in their Group H contest at Brazil 2014. The Algerians went on to finish second in the group, behind winners Belgium, and thus qualified for the knock-out stages for the first time. In the round of 16, they faced one of the tournament favourites, Germany, and they only departed after losing a thrilling match 2-1 after extra time. Centre-back Rafik Halliche had made seven FIFA World Cup appearances by the end of 2014 – a new Algerian record.

1-0
Morocco were the first North African country to reach the round of 16 of a FIFA World Cup in 1986, although they were knocked out, 1-0, by eventual finalists West Germany.

15
Sudan's 3-1 away win in Chad in September 2019 was their first in 15 FIFA World Cup qualifiers – following three draws and 11 defeats. Striker Ramad Agab hit their first-ever FIFA World Cup hat-trick.

NATIONAL LEGEND
HOMEGROWN HERO

Of the six African countries at the 2010 FIFA World Cup, Algeria's was the only squad with an African coach – Rabah Saâdane, in his fifth separate stint in charge since 1981. He previously led his country to the 1986 FIFA World Cup in Mexico, where they were eliminated in the first round. In 2010, only two countries failed to score a single goal: Algeria and Honduras. However, the Algerians did concede just twice in their three games: 1-0 defeats to Slovakia and the USA, and a surprise goalless draw with England – Algeria's first-ever FIFA World Cup clean sheet.

SAADANE

TOURNAMENT TRIVIA
MOROCCAN ROLL

At Mexico 1986, Morocco became the first African team to top a FIFA World Cup group, finishing above England, Poland and Portugal. Their 3-1 victory over Portugal in their final group game was crucial, following goalless draws against the other two teams – including an England side who lost captain Bryan Robson to a dislocated shoulder and vice-captain Ray Wilkins to a red card. **Abderrazak Khairi** scored two of the goals against Portugal, while Lothar Matthäus's winning strike for Germany in the round of 16 came with just two minutes remaining.

KHAIRI

BOUTAIB

TOURNAMENT TRIVIA
DOUBLE CUP UPSET

In 2018, Morocco suffered double heartbreak in Russia. The Moroccan FA had lodged a bid with FIFA for the hosting rights to the 2026 finals, only for the FIFA Congress to choose the combined bid from Canada, Mexico and the United States. Morocco did not have better luck on the pitch either, going out at the end of the group stage after losing to IR Iran and Portugal and drawing 2-2 with Spain thanks to goals from **Khalid Boutaib** and Youssef En-Nesyri.

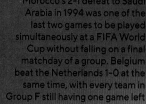

Morocco's 2-1 defeat to Saudi Arabia in 1994 was one of the last two games to be played simultaneously at a FIFA World Cup without falling on a final matchday of a group. Belgium beat the Netherlands 1-0 at the same time, with every team in Group F still having one game left to play. Since France 1998, every match has had different kick-off times – apart from the last two fixtures in every group, which now kick off at the same time.

TOURNAMENT TRIVIA
LUCKY ESCAPE

Libya would probably still hold the record for the highest score by an African nation if not for the fact that their Arab Nations Cup match against Oman in April 1966 was abandoned after 80 minutes. They were leading 21-0 at the time. The biggest recorded victory for an African team was Sudan's 15-0 win over Muscat and Oman in 1965.

TOURNAMENT TRIVIA
NO HOME WIN FOR EGYPT

Although they are easily the most successful team in CAF Africa Cup of Nations history, seven-time champions Egypt did not add to their tally as hosts in 2019. One year after making their third FIFA World Cup appearance in 2018 they lost 1-0 to South Africa in the round of 16.

MAHREZ

STAR PLAYER
MAHREZ THE MARVEL

When first approached by Leicester City in January 2014, Algerian winger **Riyad Mahrez** had never even heard of the team, but he still signed for just GBP 380,000. His slight build had raised doubts about his ability to thrive in England. The first Algerian to win a Premier League winner's medal recalled growing up as a sports-mad "street footballer", saying: "I was always with a ball – that's why I was so skinny, I would miss dinner."

2016
In early 2016, Riyad Mahrez became the first African to be voted England's Footballer of the Year by his fellow professionals. He helped Leicester City win their first top-division championship, the 2015-16 Premier League title.

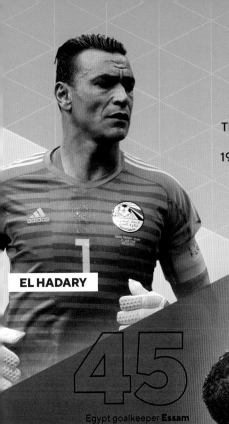

EL HADARY

OFFICIAL INFLUENCE

The first African to referee a FIFA World Cup final was Morocco's Said Belqola, who controlled the 1998 climax in which hosts France beat Brazil 3-0. Perhaps his most notable moment was sending off France's Marcel Desailly in the 68th minute – brandishing only the third red card to be shown in a FIFA World Cup final. Belqola was 41 at the time. He sadly died from cancer just under four years later.

36

Morocco's qualification for the 1970 FIFA World Cup ended a 36-year African exile from the finals. No African countries played at the 1966 FIFA World Cup in England, with 16 possible candidate countries all boycotting the event because FIFA wanted the top African team to face a side from Asia or Oceania in a qualification play-off.

45

Egypt goalkeeper **Essam El-Hadary**, at 45 years and 161 days, became the oldest player in World Cup history when he played in a 2-1 defeat by Saudi Arabia in 2018.

TOURNAMENT
TRIVIA

ABOUD AWAKENING

After the political upheaval in Libya in 2011, little was expected of the country's footballers at the 2012 Africa Cup of Nations. Yet they brought some joy to supporters with a surprise 2-1 victory over Senegal in their final first-round match – the first time Libya had ever won an Africa Cup of Nations match outside their own country. Their kit bore the new flag of the country's National Transitional Council. Among the star performers were Ihaab al Boussefi – scorer of both goals against Senegal – and goalkeeper and captain **Samir Aboud**, at 39 the oldest player in the tournament.

ABOUD

NATIONAL LEGEND
SO FARAS, SO GOOD

Ahmed Faras not only heads Morocco's all-time scoring charts with 42 goals between 1965 and 1979, he was also the captain who lifted the country's only Africa Cup of Nations trophy in 1976. He was also named the tournament's best player after scoring three goals in six games. He had previously come on twice as a sub when Morocco made their FIFA World Cup finals debut in 1970, the first African representatives since 1934.

1934

Abdelrahman Fawzi became the first African footballer to score at a FIFA World Cup when he pulled a goal back for Egypt against Hungary in the first round of the 1934 tournament.

NATIONAL LEGEND
STRIKING RIVALS

A homegrown hero regained top spot in Tunisia's scoring ranks after Gabes-born Issam Jemâa overtook Francileudo Santos to total 36 goals in 80 appearances between 2005 and 2014. Jemâa moved from Esperance to play his club football in France for RC Lens, SM Caen, AJ Auxerre and Stade Brestois and in the Gulf for Kuwait SC, Al-Salliya (Qatar) and Dubai CSC. By contrast, Brazil-born Santos did not visit Tunisia until his late teens and accepted citizenship at the age of 24 in 2004.

JEMÂA

SUB-SAHARAN AFRICA

From the *Super Eagles* to the Black Stars, and from *Bafana Bafana* to *Les Éléphants*, Sub-Saharan football has delivered some of the biggest African stars of all time, and also hosted the first African FIFA World Cup in South Africa in 2010.

Country: South Africa
Rejoined FIFA: 1992
Most appearances: Aaron Mokoena, 107
Top scorer: Benni McCarthy, 31
Honours: 1 Africa Cup of Nations (1996)

Country: Ghana
Joined FIFA: 1958
Most appearances: Asamoah Gyan, 109
Top scorer: Asamoah Gyan, 51
Honours: 4 CAF Africa Cup of Nations (1963, 1965, 1978, 1982)

Country: Cameroon
Joined FIFA: 1962
Most appearances: Rigobert Song, 137
Top scorer: Samuel Eto'o, 56
Honours:
5 Africa Cup of Nations (1984, 1988, 2000, 2002, 2017)

Country: Nigeria
Joined FIFA: 1960
Most appearances: Vincent Enyeama/Joseph Yobo, 101
Top scorer: Rashidi Yakini, 37
Honours: 3 CAF Africa Cup of Nations (1980, 1994, 2013)
1 Olympic Games (1996)

Country: Gabon
Joined FIFA: 1966
Most appearances: Didier Ovono, 114
Top scorer: Pierre-Emerick Aubameyang, 25
Honours: -

Country: Mali
Joined FIFA: 1964
Most appearances: Seydou Keita, 102
Top scorer: Seydou Keita, 25
Honours: -

Country: Senegal
Joined FIFA: 1964
Most appearances: Henri Camara, 99
Top scorer: Henri Camara, 29
Honours: -

Country: Liberia
Joined FIFA: 1964
Most appearances: Joe Nagbe, 77
Top scorer: George Weah, 18
Honours: -

Country: Zimbabwe
Joined FIFA: 1965
Most appearances: Peter Ndlovu, 100
Top scorer: Peter Ndlovu, 38
Honours: -

Country: Côte d'Ivoire
Joined FIFA: 1964
Most appearances: Didier Zokora, 123
Top scorer: Didier Drogba, 65
Honours: 2 CAF Africa Cup of Nations (1992, 2015)

Country: Zambia
Joined FIFA: 1964
Most appearances: Kennedy Mweene, 121
Top scorer: Godfrey Chitalu, 79
Honours: 1 CAF Africa Cup of Nations (2012)

Country: Togo
Joined FIFA: 1964
Most appearances: Emmanuel Adebayor, 87
Top scorer: Emmanuel Adebayor, 32
Honours: -

Country: Botswana
Joined FIFA: 1978
Most appearances: Joel Mogorosi, 92
Top scorer: Jerome Ramatlhakwane, 24
Honours: -

1985
The first African country to win an official FIFA tournament was Nigeria, when their Golden Eaglets beat West Germany in the final of the 1985 FIFA World U-16 Championship.

STAR PLAYER
WELL DONE, ODION

Nigeria striker **Odion Ighalo** was not only the top scorer in qualifying for the 2019 CAF Africa Cup of Nations with seven goals, but he also claimed the Golden Boot at the tournament itself. His five goals included strikes in a 2-1 semi-final defeat to eventual champions Algeria and in a 1-0 third-place play-off victory over China PR. Ighalo signed for his boyhood club Manchester United in January 2019 – although he had to wait three games to make his debut due to coronavirus fears after he joined from Chinese club Shanghai Shenhua. Only five men have scored more for Nigeria than Ighalo's 16, although he has some way to go to catch up with 37-goal Rashidi Yekini.

STAR PLAYER
BROTHERS IN ARMS

The Boateng brothers made FIFA World Cup history by playing against each other at the 2010 finals in South Africa. Both were also selected for the "replay" in 2014. In 2010, Jérôme played left-back for Germany while elder half-brother Kevin-Prince, who had switched nationalities a month earlier, was in the Ghana midfield. Germany won 1-0 in South Africa, while the return in Brazil ended up 2-2. Kevin-Prince was the only brother to play a full 90 minutes, in South Africa. He was substituted during the game in Brazil while Jérôme was replaced in both games. Of the total 180 minutes, they were on the pitch together for "only" 117 minutes.

4

Ghana went through four different managers during their qualifiers for the 2006 FIFA World Cup, with Serbian coach Ratomir Dujković finally clinching the country a place at the finals for the very first time.

NATIONAL LEGEND
MAD FOR MADIBA

Apart from the Dutch and Spanish sides competing in the 2010 FIFA World Cup final, one of the star attractions in Johannesburg's Soccer City stadium on 11 July 2010 was South Africa's legendary former president **Nelson Mandela**. The frail 91-year-old – known affectionately by his tribal name of "Madiba" – was driven onto the pitch before the game in a golf cart and given a rapturous reception by the crowd. It marked his one and only public appearance at the tournament. He had been a high-profile presence at the FIFA vote in 2004 which awarded South Africa hosting rights for 2010.

NATIONAL LEGEND
GOING FOR A SONG

Two players have been sent off at two separate FIFA World Cups: Cameroon's Rigobert Song, against Brazil in 1994 and Chile four years later, and France's Zinédine Zidane – red-carded against Saudi Arabia in 1998 and against Italy in the 2006 final. Song's red card against Brazil made him the youngest player to be dismissed at a FIFA World Cup – he was just 17 years and 358 days old. Song, born in Nkanglikock, is Cameroon's most-capped player with 137 appearances – and he claimed winner's medals in the final of both the 2000 and 2002 CAF Africa Cup of Nations.

116

Zambians believe the world record for goals in a calendar year should belong to their own Godfrey Chitalu and not to Lionel Messi. In 2012, Messi scored 91 goals for Argentina and Barcelona, but the Zambian FA insists that Chitalu had scored 116 goals, apparently unnoticed abroad, in 1972.

NATIONAL LEGEND
JOLLY ROGER

Cameroon striker **Roger Milla**, famous for dancing around corner flags after his goals, became the FIFA World Cup's oldest scorer against Russia in 1994 – aged 42 years and 39 days. Milla, born in Yaoundé on 20 May 1952, had retired from professional football for a year before Cameroon President Paul Biya persuaded him to join the 1990 FIFA World Cup squad. He finally ended his international career after the 1994 FIFA World Cup in the United States, finishing with 77 caps and 43 goals to his name.

15

Fifteen-year-old Samuel Kuffour became the youngest footballer to win an Olympic medal when Ghana took bronze at the 1992 Olympics in Barcelona – 27 days before his 16th birthday.

NATIONAL LEGEND
THE FOURMOST

The only two African footballers to play at four FIFA World Cups – and the only three to be named in the squads for four – are all from Cameroon. Striker Samuel Eto'o became the latest in 2014, after also playing in 1998, 2002 and 2010. He emulated defender Rigobert Song, who was in the Cameroon squad in 1994, 1998, 2002 and 2010. Goalkeeper Jacques Songo'o was named in the country's squads for the four FIFA World Cups between 1990 and 2002, but he only actually played in the 1994 and 1998 versions.

1992
Zimbabwe's leading scorer Peter Ndlovu was the first African footballer to appear in the English Premier League when he appeared for Coventry City in August 1992.

STAR PLAYER
GABON ON SONG

Gabon's leading international goalscorer **Pierre-Emerick Aubameyang** ended Yaya Touré's four-year reign as CAF African Footballer of the Year in 2016. Touré had joined Cameroon's Samuel Eto'o as a four-time winner, but Aubameyang's 41 goals for Borussia Dortmund and his country relegated Touré to second. Born in Laval, France, Aubameyang launched his career in Italy with AC Milan, and was the first Bundesliga player to win the award. He later joined Arsenal in 2018 for a club record GBP 56m. Aubameyang, who played once for France under-21s, made his Gabon debut in 2009.

AUBAMEYANG

3

In 2014, Ghana's Asamoah Gyan became the first African to score at three separate FIFA World Cups, and his 11 matches took him level with Cameroon's François Omam-Biyik.

NATIONAL LEGEND
SUPER FRED

In 2007, Frédéric Kanouté became the first non-African-born player to be named African Footballer of the Year. The striker was born in Lyon, France, and played for France U-21s. But the son of a French mother and Malian father opted to play for Mali in 2004, scoring 23 goals in 37 appearances before retiring from international football after the 2010 CAF Africa Cup of Nations. As well as going down in history as one of Mali's greatest ever players, he is also a hero to fans of Spanish side Sevilla FC, for whom he scored 143 goals, winning two UEFA Cups along the way. Only three men have scored more goals for the club.

NATIONAL LEGEND
PRESIDENT GEORGE

George Weah made history in December 2017 when he became the first former African footballer to become president of his country. In Liberia's first democratic handover in decades, Weah succeeded Ellen Johnson Sirleaf, Africa's first elected female president. Weah, raised in a slum in the capital Monrovia, is the only former FIFA World Player of the Year whose country has never qualified for the World Cup finals. He starred in attack for Monaco, Paris Saint-Germain and AC Milan, played for Chelsea and Manchester City, and dipped into his own earnings to help pay for his national team's travel costs and kit.

WEAH

14

Cameroonian Roger Milla's goals in the 1990 FIFA World Cup helped him win the African Footballer of the Year award for an unprecedented second time – 14 years after he had first received the trophy.

7

Benni McCarthy of South Africa and Egypt's Hossam Hassan both scored seven goals at the 1998 CAF Africa Cup of Nations. No player has scored more than five in a single tournament since then.

NATIONAL LEGEND
FIRST ADE

Togo's all-time leading goalscorer – and 2008 African Footballer of the Year – **Emmanuel Adebayor** was captain during the country's only FIFA World Cup finals appearance, in Germany in 2006. They failed to win a game, but Adebayor's European club career was more successful, with stints in France with FC Metz and AS Monaco, in Spain with Real Madrid, in England with Arsenal, Manchester City, Tottenham Hotspur and Crystal Palace, and in Turkey with İstanbul Başakşehir and Kayserispor.

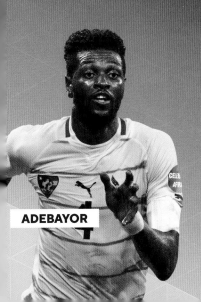

ADEBAYOR

NATIONAL LEGEND
SHOOTING STAR

Peter Ndlovu ended his international career with 38 goals in 100 games for Zimbabwe between 1991 and 2007 – before being appointed the country's assistant manager in 2011. The man nicknamed "the Bulawayo Bullet" had spearheaded in 2004 the first Zimbabwe side to reach a CAF Africa Cup of Nations finals, following that up with repeat qualification two years later. His international team-mates included brother Adam, who tragically died in a car accident near Victoria Falls in Zimbabwe in December 2012. Peter was also in the car and although he suffered very serious head injuries and broken bones he managed to survive.

NDLOVU

DISCIPLINARY-RELATED
HISTORY LESSON

Senegal made FIFA World Cup history in 2018 as the first country to be eliminated on yellow cards. *The Lions of Teranga* and Japan finished their group on four points apiece, but the tiebreaker came down to a new fair play regulation. They drew their match 2-2 and finished with the same points, the same goal difference and the same number goals scored, but Senegal "lost" 6-5 on bookings so Japan went into the second round, and Senegal went home.

DROGBA

NATIONAL LEGEND
HOT DROG

Didier Drogba may have been raised in France, but he was born in Côte d'Ivoire and remains one of the African country's favourite sons for his actions both on and off the pitch. He scored a record 65 goals in 104 appearances for *Les Éléphants* and was credited with influence off the pitch, too, calling for a ceasefire in the civil war-torn nation. He also pushed for a CAF Africa Cup of Nations qualifier against Madagascar in June 2007 to be moved from the capital Abidjan to rebel army stronghold Bouaké in an effort to encourage reconciliation.

DISCIPLINARY-RELATED
KNOCKED OUT ON PENALTIES

Botswana goalkeeper and captain Modiri Marumo was sent off in the middle of a penalty shoot-out against Malawi in May 2003 after punching opposing goalkeeper Philip Nyasulu in the face. Botswana defender Michael Mogaladi had to go in goal for the rest of the shoot-out, which Malawi won 4-1. "I over-reacted in an exchange of words between myself and my counterpart," admitted Marumo. "I hope my apology would be recognized and I pledge my commitment in serving the nation."

ASIA & OCEANIA

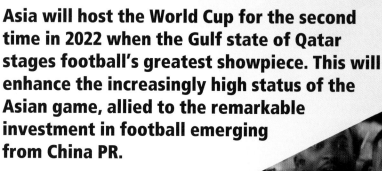

Asia will host the World Cup for the second time in 2022 when the Gulf state of Qatar stages football's greatest showpiece. This will enhance the increasingly high status of the Asian game, allied to the remarkable investment in football emerging from China PR.

AFC

Confederation founded: 1954

Number of associations:
46 (+1 non-FIFA member)

Headquarters: Bukit Jalil, Kuala Lumpur, Malaysia

Most continental championship wins: Japan, 4

OFC

Confederation founded: 1966

Number of associations:
11 (+3 non-FIFA members)

Headquarters: Auckland, New Zealand

Most continental championship wins: New Zealand, 5

88

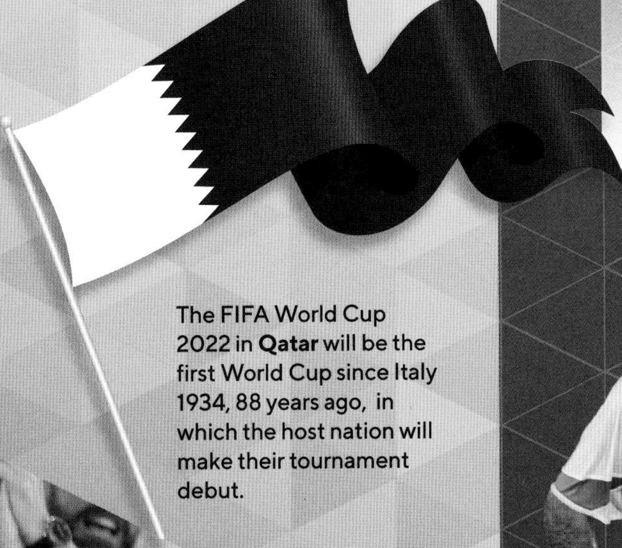

The FIFA World Cup 2022 in **Qatar** will be the first World Cup since Italy 1934, 88 years ago, in which the host nation will make their tournament debut.

Indian fans displayed their ever-growing enthusiasm for football with their huge support for the country's staging of the FIFA U-17 World Cup in 2017.

DAEI

10

To mark the 60th anniversary of its foundation in 2014, the AFC created a Hall of Fame for Asian players, inducting ten players to begin with, including **Ali Daei** (IR Iran), **Harry Kewell** (Australia) and Yasuhiko Okudera (Japan).

KEWELL

1964

Israel won the Asian Cup in 1964, but they were expelled from the AFC ten years later before becoming a full member of UEFA in 1984.

12

The Asian Football Confederation was founded by 12 members in 1954 but has since grown to 47, although the Northern Mariana Islands are not a FIFA member.

AUSTRALIA

Driven by new generations of players, many starring for top European clubs, Australia have become regular FIFA World Cup qualifiers. In 2015, they hosted and lifted the AFC Asian Cup for the first time.

Joined FIFA: 1922

Biggest win:
31-0 v. American Samoa, 2001

Highest FIFA ranking: 14th

Home stadium:
Stadium Australia, Sydney

Major honours:
4 OFC Nations Cups (1980, 1996, 2000, 2004), 1 AFC Asian Cup (2015)

STAR PLAYER
A MILE AHEAD

Australia captain **Mile Jedinak** has scored his country's last three FIFA World Cup goals – all from the penalty spot. He found the net in their 3-2 defeat to the Netherlands in 2014, then four years later scored in a 2-1 defeat to France and a 1-1 draw with Denmark as Australia bowed out in the first round. Midfielder Jedinak had also scored a hat-trick to secure Australia's place in Russia – including two penalties – as the *Socceroos* saw off Honduras 3-1 on aggregate in their November 2017 play-off following a goalless first leg.

JEDINAK

NATIONAL LEGEND
HERO HARRY

Harry Williams holds a proud place in Australian football history as the first Aboriginal player to represent the country in internationals. He made his debut in 1970 and was part of the first Australian squad to compete at a FIFA World Cup finals, in West Germany in 1974. Despite holding Chile to draw, the Australians finished bottom of their group, losing to both East Germany and eventual champions West Germany.

WILLIAMS

5
Tim Cahill's total of five FIFA World Cup goals is only three fewer than all other Australians put together.

TOURNAMENT TRIVIA
ARNOLD ON THE SPOT

Australia were overthrown as AFC Asian Cup holders at the 2019 tournament, knocked out 1-0 in the quarter-finals by the hosts, the United Arab Emirates. The Socceroos coach was Graham Arnold, who had scored 19 goals in 54 appearances for Australia as a striker before assisting Guus Hiddink's between 2000 and 2006 and briefly taking charge himself in 2007. Australia's 2019 round-of-16 victory over Uzbekistan, 4-2 on penalties, meant that Arnold had been involved in all seven of the country's international penalty shoot-outs – including four as a player, as assistant manager for the 2006 FIFA World Cup qualifying play-off triumph over Uruguay, and as head coach for their AFC Asian Cup quarter-final loss to Japan in 2007.

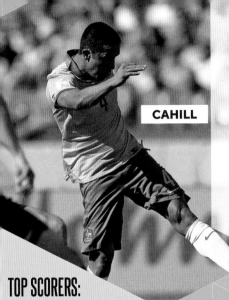
CAHILL

NATIONAL LEGEND
CAHILL MAKES HISTORY

Tim Cahill scored Australia's first two FIFA World Cup goals, netting in the 84th and 89th minutes of a comeback 3-1 win over Japan in 2006, but he saved the most spectacular for last, a first-time volley in a 3-2 defeat to the Netherlands in 2014. Cahill also received his second yellow card of the competition later in that game and so missed Australia's final match. He scored twice in 2006, once in 2010 – when he was also red-carded – and twice in 2014. He retired from international football in November 2018, having won 108 caps and scored 50 goals – more than half of them (26) with his head.

TOP SCORERS:

1 **Tim Cahill**, 50
2 **Damian Mori**, 29
3 **Archie Thompson**, 28
4 **John Aloisi**, 27
5 **Attila Abonyi**, 25
= **John Kosmina**, 25

MOST APPEARANCES:

1 **Mark Schwarzer**, 109
2 **Tim Cahill**, 108
3 **Lucas Neill**, 96
4 **Brett Emerton**, 95
5 **Alex Tobin**, 87

29

Damian Mori's then-Australian record tally of 29 goals, in just 45 internationals, included no fewer than five hat-tricks: trebles against Fiji and Tahiti, four-goal hauls against the Cook Islands and Tonga, and five in Australia's 13-0 rout of the Solomon Islands in a 1998 FIFA World Cup qualifier.

SCORING RECORD
AUSSIES ON THE SPOT

Australia are the only team to reach the FIFA World Cup finals via a penalty shoot-out – in their qualifying play-off against Uruguay in November 2005. The Aussies lost the first leg 1-0 in Montevideo, but Mark Bresciano levelled the aggregate score in Sydney, and it remained 1-1 after extra time. Goalkeeper **Mark Schwarzer** made two crucial saves as Australia won the shoot-out 4-2, with John Aloisi scoring the winning spot kick. In 2011, Schwarzer also passed Alex Tobin as Australia's most-capped footballer when he made his 88th appearance in the AFC Asian Cup final defeat to Japan. Tobin had been in defence when Schwarzer made his international debut against Canada in 1993.

3.69

Damian Mori never played at a FIFA World Cup but he did claim a world record for scoring the fastest recorded goal ever – after just 3.69 seconds for his club side Adelaide City against Sydney United in 1996.

91

Tough-tackling Australia veteran Lucas Neill had to wait until his 91st international appearance before scoring his first goal for his country: the final strike in a 4-0 victory over Jordan in June 2013 that boosted their chances of reaching the 2014 FIFA World Cup.

1000

In March 2015, Mile Jedinak scored Australia's 1,000th international goal, a stunning free kick in a 2-2 friendly draw against world champions Germany.

SCHWARZER

3

Josip Simunić, in 2006, was not the first player at a FIFA World Cup to receive three yellow cards in one game. The same had happened in an earlier game involving Australia, when their English-born midfielder Ray Richards was belatedly sent off against Chile at the 1974 FIFA World Cup.

THOMPSON

SCORING RECORD
ARCHIE COSMIC

On 9 April 2001, Australia set an international record by beating Tonga 22-0 in a 2002 FIFA World Cup qualifier, but they went even better two days later by trouncing American Samoa 31-0. This included an unprecedented 13 goals from striker **Archie Thompson**, while team-mate David Zdrilic found the net "only" eight times. Both outscored the previous international record-holder, Iran's seven-goal Karim Bagheri. Thompson's debut goal against Tonga and his 13 in his next appearance meant he scored as many goals in his first two appearances (14) as he managed in his subsequent 51 games for his country.

JAPAN

Japan co-hosted the FIFA World Cup in 2002 when the team reached the second round for the first time. AFC Asian Cup wins in 1992, 2000, 2004 and 2011 were all celebrated keenly as proof of surging standards.

Joined FIFA: 1950

Biggest win:
15-0 v. Phillippines, 1967

Highest FIFA ranking: 9th

Home stadium:
rotation

Major honours:
4 AFC Asian Cups (1992, 2000, 2004, 2011)

50
Shinji Okazaki's 50 goals for his country include hat-tricks in consecutive matches, against Hong Kong and Togo in October 2009.

NATIONAL LEGEND
HONDA INSPIRES

Skilful midfielder **Keisuke Honda** is Japan's top scorer at the FIFA World Cup – with four goals – and the only Japanese player to have found the net at three final competitions. It all started at South Africa in 2010 when he scored in Japan's victories over Cameroon and Denmark, and continued with a goal in the defeat against Costa Rica in Brazil four years later. Honda won two man-of-the-match awards at the 2010 FIFA World Cup and was named player of the tournament when Japan won the 2011 AFC Asian Cup. After Japan had exited the 2018 tournament – after he had scored against Senegal – Honda retired from international football.

HONDA

STAR PLAYER
OKAZAKI'S A-OK

In March 2016, **Shinji Okazaki** became only the fifth man to reach 100 appearances for Japan when he took to the field against Syria. Two months later, the striker ended the season with an English Premier League winner's medal, having scored five goals in Leicester City's 5,000-1 triumph (and one in the FA Cup). He was also on the scoresheet during Japan's 3-1 victory over Denmark in Bloemfontein at the 2010 FIFA World Cup, along with Keisuke Honda and Yasuhito Endo – the first time an Asian side had scored three goals in a FIFA World Cup match since 1966, when Korea DPR gave Portugal a run for their money in a famous 5-3 quarter-final win for the Europeans.

OKAZAKI

TOP SCORERS:

1 Kunishige Kamamoto, 75

2 Kazuyoshi Miura, 55

3 Shinji Okazaki, 50

4 Hiromi Hara, 37
= Keisuke Honda, 37

50
Despite hanging up his international boots in 2000 after an impressive 55 goals in 89 matches, Kazuyoshi Miura was far from finished with the game. On 12 March 2017, aged 50 years and 14 days, Miura scored for Yokohama FC against Thespakusatsu Gunma in J.League Division 2.

TOURNAMENT TRIVIA
POLITICAL FOOTBALL

Japan were surprise bronze medallists at the 1968 Olympic Football Tournament in Mexico City, with Star striker Kunishige Kamamoto finishing as top scorer with seven goals. He remains Japan's all-time top marksman with 75 goals in 76 games (Japan consider Olympic Games matches to be full internationals). Since retirement, he has combined coaching with being elected to Japan's parliament and serving as vice-president of the country's football association.

At Russia 2018, Keisuke Honda came on after 72 minutes of Japan's Group H game against Senegal and, six minutes later, scored his team's second equaliser in a 2-2 draw in Ekaterinburg.

ENDO

SCORING RECORD
FIFTEEN SECONDS OF FAME

Japan fell at the final hurdle in their attempt to win a fifth AFC Asian Cup title in 2019, losing 3-1 in the final to surprise champions Qatar. This was the first time that Japan had reached the final but failed to win. Japan had warmed up for the tournament in style, beating Kyrgyzstan 4-0 in November 2018 in a game notable for their two goals in a mere 15 seconds to go three up. Substitute striker Yuya Osako hit a 72nd-minute strike, and fellow sub and midfielder Shoya Nakajima found the net almost immediately after the restart with his first touch after coming on.

21

No team has ever scored more goals in one AFC Asian Cup tournament than Japan's 21 in six matches in Lebanon in 2000. Nine different players scored, with Akinori Nishizawa and Naohiro Takahara bagging five apiece, including hat-tricks in an 8-1 first-round win over Uzbekistan. A single goal by Shigeyoshi Mochizuki was enough to settle the final against Saudi Arabia.

2018

Japan's fans and players impressed many at the 2018 FIFA World Cup with their displays – and their manners. Japanese fans were filmed meticulously tidying up after themselves in the stands at full time of their games, and the support staff took a similar approach to their dressing rooms, even after seeing a 2-0 lead slip away in their 3-2 defeat by Belgium in the round of 16.

NATIONAL LEGEND
THE ENDO

Midfielder **Yasuhito Endo** scored the opening goal of Japan's defence of their AFC Asian Cup crown in 2015 as they began their campaign with a 4-0 win over debutants Palestine. However, after winning their three group matches without conceding a goal, Japan promptly lost in the quarter-finals to the United Arab Emirates, bowing out on penalties after a 1-1 draw. It was their worst showing at the AFC Asian Cup for 19 years. Endo had the consolation of becoming the first Japanese player to win 150 caps, but he left the international stage after the finals, having scored 15 times in 152 games.

NATIONAL LEGEND
YOU TOO, YUTO

Full-back Yuto Nagatomo, a 2011 AFC Asian Cup winner and later captain of Italian giants Internazionale, skippered Japan when he became the seventh man to win 100 Samurai Blue caps in a 3-1 friendly defeat to Brazil in November 2017. Two years later, he equalled the 122 appearances of Masami Ihara – Japan's captain for their first AFC Asian Cup triumph in 1992 – when Japan beat Kyrgyzstan 2-0. A month earlier, Nagatomo had scored his fifth international goal, but his first for ten years, in a 6-0 victory over Mongolia. Nagatamo also starred at the 2018 FIFA World Cup when Japan reached the second round despite replacing manager Vahid Halilhodžić with former midfielder Akira Nishino just two months before the finals.

11

After making his international debut in the 2011 AFC Asian Cup group-stage match against Jordan, striker Tadanari Lee could not have picked a better time to score his first goal for his country, finding the back of the net with just 11 minutes of extra time left in the final against Australia.

LEE

117

KOREA REPUBLIC

"Be the Reds!" was the rallying cry of Korea Republic's fervent fans during their country's co-hosting of the 2002 FIFA World Cup – and they saw their energetic team become the first Asian side to reach the semi-finals, ultimately finishing fourth.

Joined FIFA: 1948
Biggest win:
v. Nepal, 16-0, 2003
Highest FIFA ranking: 17th
Home stadium: Seoul World Cup Stadium
Major honours: 2 AFC Asian Cups (1956, 1960)

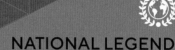

NATIONAL LEGEND
HONG SETS FIFA WORLD CUP RECORD

Defender **Hong Myung-bo** captained Korea Republic to fourth place in the 2002 FIFA World Cup on home soil and was voted third-best player of the tournament to boot. Ten years later, as coach of the U-23 squad, Hong led his side to Olympic bronze at the 2012 Summer Games after a 2-0 victory over Japan in the bronze medal match. Hong became Korea Republic's national team coach in June 2013, and he was still in charge at the 2014 FIFA World Cup, where one group game pitted him against Belgium and their coach Marc Wilmots – the pair having played against each other at the 1998 finals.

HONG

22M
Son Heung-min became Asia's most expensive footballer when English club Tottenham Hotspur bought him for GBP 22m from Germany's Bayer Leverkusen in 2015.

56
Since the FIFA/Coca-Cola World Ranking was introduced in 1992, no top-ranked team had ever lost to a country as many as 56 places below them until defending champions Germany were beaten 2-0 by Korea Republic at the 2018 FIFA World Cup.

4
Korea Republic defender Hong Myung-bo was the first Asian footballer to appear in four consecutive FIFA World Cup finals tournaments, from 1990 to 2002.

NATIONAL LEGEND
PARK LIFE

Park Ji-sung can claim to be the most successful Asian footballer of all time. He became the first Asian player to claim a UEFA Champions League winner's medal when Manchester United beat Chelsea in 2008, despite missing the final. Park shares the Korean record for the most FIFA World Cup goals – three – with Ahn Jung-hwan, and Son Heung-min. Park became the eighth South Korean to reach a century of caps when he captained the side in their 2011 AFC Asian Cup semi-final defeat to Japan, before announcing his international retirement to allow a younger generation to emerge.

PARK

TOP SCORERS:
1   Cha Bum-kun, 58
2   Hwang Sun-hong, 50
3   Park Lee-chun, 36
4   Kim Jae-han, 33
    = Lee Dong-gook, 33

STAR PLAYER
HERE COMES THE SON

At the 2018 FIFA World Cup, Korea Republic's latest hero **Son Heung-min** scored his side's consolation goal in a 2-1 defeat by Mexico, and he later sealed their 2-0 win over Germany, just three minutes after Kim Young-gwon's injury-time opener, Son tapping the ball into an empty net after German goalkeeper Manuel Neuer was left stranded at the other end of the pitch. That lifted Son to 23 goals in 70 internationals and put him level with Park Ji-sung and Ahn Jung-hwan on three FIFA World Cup goals for his country. He was picked for the 2014 FIFA World Cup despite his former international footballer father Son Woong-jung believing he needed more time to develop as a player.

SON

NATIONAL LEGEND
SPIDER CATCHER

Goalkeeper Lee Woon-jae – nicknamed "Spider Hands" – made himself a national hero by making the crucial penalty save that took co-hosts Korea Republic into the semi-finals of the 2002 FIFA World Cup. He blocked Spain's fourth spot kick, taken by winger Joaquin, in a quarter-final shoot-out. Lee, who also played in the 1994, 2006 and 2010 FIFA World Cups, pulled off more penalty saves at the 2007 AFC Asian Cup – stopping three spot kicks in shoot-outs on his side's march to third place. Lee's form restricted his frequent back-up, Kim Byung-ji, to just 62 international appearances.

LEE

NATIONAL LEGEND
CHA BOOM AND BUST

Even before Korea Republic made their FIFA World Cup breakthrough under Guus Hiddink in 2002, the country had a homegrown hero of world renown – thunderous striker **Cha Bum-kun**, known for his fierce shots and suitable nickname "Cha Boom". He helped pave the way for more Asian players to make their name in Europe by signing for German club Eintracht Frankfurt in 1979 and later played for *Bundesliga* rivals Bayer Leverkusen. His achievements in Germany included two UEFA Cup triumphs – with Frankfurt in 1980 and with Leverkusen eight years later – while his performances helped make him a childhood idol for future German internationals such as Jürgen Klinsmann and Michael Ballack.

TOURNAMENT TRIVIA
MILITARY GAMES

Although the Korea Republic players who won the 2018 Asian Games were given lifelong immunity from national military service as a reward, captain Son Heung-min returned home from London to do his service during the COVID-19 pandemic. Son had been one of the three permitted overage players at the U-23 tournament, but the star of the show was fellow striker Hwang Ui-jo, who scored nine times in seven games to finish as top scorer. Korea Republic beat Japan 2-1 after extra time in the final thanks to strikes from left winger Lee Seung-woo and striker Hwang Hee-chan. Hwang was also named Korean Footballer of the Year in 2018; Son took the award in 2017 and 2019.

MOST APPEARANCES:

1 Hong Myung-bo, 136

2 Cha Bun-kun, 134

3 Lee Woon-jae, 133

4 Lee Young-pyo, 127

5 Kim Ho-kon, 124
= Yoo Sang-chu, 124

BUM-KUN

34

Korea Republic have played more FIFA World Cup games than any other Asian country, taking their tally to 34 with three first-round matches in 2018.

ASIA : SELECTED TEAMS

13

Though many of Asia's other nations have had limited footballing success on the world stage, their achievements in and passion and for the game are no less vibrant or impressive.

Country: Iraq
Joined FIFA: 1950
Most appearances:
Younis Mahmoud, 148
Top scorer: Hussein Saeed, 78
Major honours: 1 AFC Asian Cup (2007)

Country: IR Iran
Joined FIFA: 1948
Most appearances:
Javad Nekounam, 151
Top scorer: Ali Daei, 109
Major honours: 3 AFC Asian Cups (1968, 1972, 1976)

Country: China PR
Joined FIFA: 1931
Most appearances:
Li Weifeng, 112
Top scorer:
Hao Haidong, 41
Major honours: -

Country: Uzbekistan
Joined FIFA: 1994
Most appearances:
Server Djeparov, 128
Top scorer:
Maksim Shatskikh, 34
Major honours: -

Country: Qatar
Joined FIFA: 1970
Most appearances:
Hassan Al-Haydos, 131
Top scorer: Sebastián Soria, 40
Major honours: 1 AFC Asian Cup (2019)

Country: Syria
Joined FIFA: 1937
Most appearances:
Mosab Balhous, 88
Top scorer:
Firas Al Khatib, 36
Major honours: -

Country: Saudi Arabia
Joined FIFA: 1956
Most appearances:
Mohamed Al-Deayea, 175
Top scorer:
Majed Abdullah, 71
Major honours: 3 AFC Asian Cups (1984, 1988, 1996)

TOURNAMENT TRIVIA
IRAQ AND ROLL

One of the greatest – and most heart-warming – surprises in international football in recent years was Iraq's unexpected triumph at the AFC Asian Cup in 2007, barely a year after the end of the war that had ravaged the country and forced them to play "home" games elsewhere. Despite disrupted preparations, they eliminated Vietnam and Korea Republic en route to the 2007 final in which captain **Younis Mahmoud**'s goal proved decisive against Saudi Arabia. They were unable to retain their title four years later, losing to Australia in the quarter-finals.

MAHMOUD

TOURNAMENT TRIVIA
AHMED'S CONSOLATION

Qatar, the FIFA World Cup 2022 hosts, enjoyed their finest football triumph in 2019 when they lifted their first AFC Asian Cup. The team coached by Spaniard Félix Sánchez scored 19 goals and conceded only one – to Japan in their 3-1 final victory in Abu Dhabi – along the way. Their three goals in the final came from Almoez Ali, Abdulaziz Hatem and Akram Hassan Afif. Ali scored four goals in 51 minutes in a 6-0 defeat of Korea DPR, and ended with a tournament record of nine goals. Uruguayan-born striker Sebastián Soria holds Qatar's all-time record for most goals (40), but his total of 123 caps was passed by Hassan Al-Haydos (131) in late 2019.

XU

SCORING RECORD
SAUDIS LEAVE IT LATE

Saudi Arabia ended a run of 12 matches in the FIFA World Cup finals without a victory when they defeated Egypt 2-1 in their final group match in 2018. It was the first time they had celebrated a victory on the game's biggest stage since defeating Belgium 1-0 in June 1994. Egypt scored first, but the Saudis equalised with a penalty by midfielder Salman Al-Faraj five minutes and 50 seconds into first-half stoppage time – the latest goal in the first half of a finals tie since 1966. Their winner also came late on – winger **Salem Al-Dawsari** striking five minutes into second-half stoppage time.

CUP RECORDS
AFC FIGUREHEADS

IR Iran dominate AFC Asian Cup records. They have played the most games (68), celebrated the most wins (41), had the most draws (19) and scored the most goals (131). South Yemen and Yemen both failed to score in their only appearance, and China PR have conceded the most goals (65) – and have suffered the most defeats (20) – while Myanmar and Singapore have conceded the fewest goals (four), but in only one appearance. Japan have won a record four championships; IR Iran and Saudi Arabia have three apiece.

130,000
The highest attendance for an Asian team in a home FIFA World Cup qualifier was the 130,000 who watched IR Iran draw 1-1 with Australia at the Azadi Stadium, Tehran, on 22 November 1997.

26
The 2015 AFC Asian Cup set a remarkable international tournament record for consecutive matches without a draw. All 24 matches in the group stage and then the first two quarter-finals turned up positive results after 90 minutes.

TOURNAMENT TRIVIA
CHINA PR YET TO REALISE POTENTIAL

China PR may be the world's most populous country but the national team has qualified just once for the FIFA World Cup – even though recent national coaches have included Italy's 2006 FIFA World Cup-winning manager Marcello Lippi and captain Fabio Cannavaro. Lippi's second spell in charge ended in November 2019 when the job went to Li Tie. The midfielder had been in China PR's 2002 FIFA World Cup squad, alongside record caps-holder Li Weifeng (112) and leading scorer Hao Haidong (41) – although the Chinese failed to score in defeats by Costa Rica, Brazil and Turkey. Hope springs eternal, however, and their FIFA World Cup 2022 qualifying campaign included a 7-0 victory over Guam in October 2019, including five goals by striker **Yang Xu** – the first man in 18 years, since Australia's Archie Thompson and David Zdrilic against American Samoa, to score four goals in the first half of a FIFA World Cup qualifier. The game took Yang to second in China PR's scoring ranks, with 29.

NATIONAL LEGEND
PRIDE OF SYRIA

In 2017, **Omar Kharbin** became the first Syrian to be named AFC Player of the Year. The free-scoring winger helped his Saudi Arabian club Al-Hilal to their first domestic league title in six years, and they also finished as AFC Champions League runners-up behind Japan's Urawa Red Diamonds. Kharbin, who made his debut as a 15-year-old for Al-Wahda in his home city of Damascus, also equalised for Syria in a 2019 AFC Asian Cup first-round defeat by defending champions Australia. Players from 2019 AFC Asian Cup winners Qatar claimed the AFC Player of the Year awards in 2018 and 2019, with winger Akram Afif, who set a tournament record with ten assists, succeeding defender Abdelkarim Hassan.

KHARBIN

NATIONAL LEGEND
HAPPY DAEI

IR Iran striker **Ali Daei** ended his career having scored 109 times for IR Iran in 149 internationals between 1993 and 2006 – although none of his goals came during FIFA World Cup finals appearances in 1998 and 2006. He is, however, the all-time leading scorer in the AFC Asian Cup, with 14 goals, despite never winning the tournament. His time as national team coach was less auspicious – he lasted only a year from March 2008 to March 2009 before being fired as the Iranians struggled in qualifiers for the 2010 FIFA World Cup.

37

China PR reached an all-time high of 37 in the FIFA/Coca-Cola World Ranking in 1998, however they failed to maintain that position. They dropped as low as 100 in 2008, before rising again to 76 in 2020.

1938

The first Asian country to play in a FIFA World Cup finals was Indonesia, who played in France in 1938 as the Dutch East Indies. The tournament was a straight knockout and Hungary beat them 6-0 in Reims on 5 June.

DAEI

TOURNAMENT TRIVIA
BHUTAN DO THE BEATING

Bhutan enjoyed an unprecedented winning streak in March 2015. The world's then-lowest-ranked nation had won only two official internationals in 34 years before they beat Sri Lanka twice in a two-legged 2018 FIFA World Cup qualifier. Tshering Dorji scored the only goal of the first leg, and the nation's only professional footballer – Chencho Gyeltshen – struck both goals in a 2-1 victory a week later. The Himalayan nation reached the second round of AFC qualification for the first time, but lost all eight matches with a goal difference of –52.

4-0

On the same day that Brazil and Germany contested the FIFA World Cup final on 30 June 2002, the two lowest-ranked FIFA countries were also taking each other on. Asian side Bhutan ran out 4-0 winners over Concacaf's Montserrat.

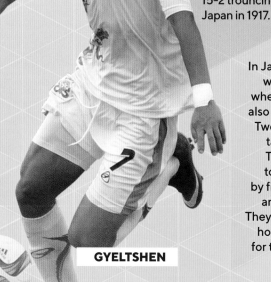

GYELTSHEN

NATIONAL LEGEND
ONE OF BARCA'S BEST

The first Asian footballer to play for a European club was also, for almost a century, the all-time leading scorer for Spanish giants FC Barcelona, before being finally overtaken by Lionel Messi in March 2014. Paulino Alcántara, from the Philippines, scored 369 goals in 357 matches for the Catalan club between 1912 and 1927. He made his debut aged just 15, and remains Barcelona's youngest-ever first-team player. Alcántara was born in the Philippines, but had a Spanish father, and appeared in internationals for Catalonia, Spain and the Philippines, for whom he featured in a record 15-2 trouncing of Japan in 1917.

TOURNAMENT TRIVIA
FIRST-ROUND FIRSTS

In January 2019, India finally ended a 55-year wait for victory in the AFC Asian Cup finals when they defeated Thailand 4-1 in what was also their biggest ever win in the competition. Two goals from Sunil Chhetri took his overall tally for his country to a national record 67. Those proved to be their only points of the tournament, however. Thailand responded by firing their Serbian coach Milovan Rajevac and replacing him with Sirisak Yodyardthai. They recovered to beat Bahrain and draw with hosts UAE, and reached the knockout stage for the first time in 47 years, before falling 2-1 to China PR in the round of 16.

102

IR Iran's Ali Daei became the first men's footballer to score a century of international goals, when his four strikes in a 7-0 defeat of Laos on 17 November 2004 took him to 102.

SHATSKIKH

NATIONAL LEGEND
FAB MABKHOUT

No man scored more international goals in 2019 than the United Arab Emirates' **Ali Mabkhout**, whose 19 strikes in 13 appearances put him ahead of Qatar's Almoez Ali (15), Portugal's Cristiano Ronaldo (14), Uzbekistan's Eldor Shomurodov (13) and England's Harry Kane (12). A double against Malaysia in September took him past 52-goal Adnan Al Talyani as his country's leading scorer and he now has 63 goals from 83 appearances. Mabkhout also scored the fastest goal in Asian Nations Cup history, finding the net just 14 seconds into his side's 2-1 first-round victory over Bahrain in 2015. He ended the tournament with the Golden Boot as the UAE finished third. The UAE's only FIFA World Cup appearance came in 1990 – when Poland's Bernard Blaut replaced Brazilian great Mário Zagallo as coach on the eve of the finals.

NATIONAL LEGEND
MAXIMUM MAKSIM

Uzbekistan's record marksman **Maksim Shatskikh** retired from international football after winning his 61st cap in a friendly against Oman in 2014. He had equalled previous top scorer Mirjalol Qosimov's 31-goal tally in a 7-3 defeat of Singapore in June 2008. Shatskikh also holds the Uzbek single-game record with five goals against Taiwan in 2007. While playing for Dynamo Kiev in Ukraine, Shatskikh joined ex-Alania Vladikavkaz striker Qosimov as the only Uzbeks to score in a UEFA club competition. Qosimov has been national coach twice, leading them to the AFC Asian Cup quarter-finals in 2015. The nation's most-capped player, however, is still forward Server Djeparov, who retired in 2017 on 128 caps.

1934
Palestine, then under British rule, were the first Asian team to enter the FIFA World Cup qualifiers. They lost 7-1 away to Egypt on 16 March 1934.

NATIONAL LEGEND
WORTH HIS KUWAIT IN GOLD

Bader Al-Mutawa is both Kuwait's most-capped player and leading goalscorer. When international football was suspended in 2020, he had scored 56 goals in 178 appearances. Together with Ahmed Mubarak of Oman (179 matches), he is closing in on the world caps record of Egypt's Ahmed Hassan (184). Al-Mutawa also finished as runner-up in the 2006 AFC Asian Footballer of the Year awards – having mistakenly been named third initially.

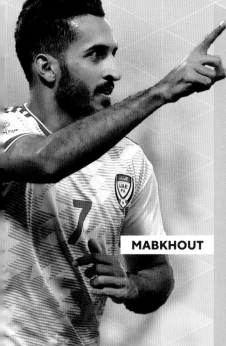
MABKHOUT

STAR PLAYER
SAMI TO THE FORE

Sami Al-Jaber is undoubtedly one of Saudi Arabia's greatest-ever players. Not only is he the country's second-top scorer with 46 goals, but he became only the second Asian player to appear at four FIFA World Cups when he started against Tunisia in Munich in 2006. He marked the occasion with his third FIFA World Cup goal, after previously netting in the 1994 and 1998 tournaments. Al-Jaber was also a key man as the Saudis won their third AFC Asian Cup title in 1996, beating the hosts UAE on penalties in the final.

AL-MUTAWA

OCEANIA

Football in Oceania can claim some of the most eye-catching football statistics – although not necessarily in a way that many there would welcome, especially the long-suffering goalkeepers from minnow islands on the end of cricket-style scorelines.

Country: New Zealand
Joined FIFA: 1948
Most appearances: Ivan Vicelich, 88
Top scorer: Vauhan Coveny, 28
Major honours: 5 OFC Nations Cups (1973, 1998, 2002, 2008, 2016)

Country: Fiji
Joined FIFA: 1964
Most appearances: Esala Masi, 52
Top scorer: Esala Masi, 32
Major honours: -

Country: Tahiti
Joined FIFA: 1989
Most appearances: Angelo Tchen, 34
Top scorer: Teaonui Tehau, 24
Major honours: 1 OFC Nations Cup (2012)

STAR PLAYER
THE WOOD LIFE

Chris Wood scored four goals at the 2016 OFC Nations Cup, only one less than the tournament's top scorer Raymond Gunemba of Papua New Guinea – as New Zealand lifted the trophy for a record fifth time. Wood scored his first international goal in October 2010 in a 1-1 draw with Honduras – although he received an instant yellow card for his celebration, which involved revealing underpants bearing his nickname "Woodzee". On 14 November 2014, in a friendly against China PR, he became New Zealand's second-youngest captain, aged 22 years and 343 days.

WOOD

3

Ricki Herbert is one of only three New Zealand-born men to be national coach, along with Barrie Truman who was in charge between 1970 and 1976, and Danny Hay, who took over in 2019.

NATIONAL LEGEND
RETURNING RICKI

Ricki Herbert is the only New Zealander to have featured in two FIFA World Cups. A left back at the 1982 tournament in Spain, he then coached the country in their second World Cup appearance, in 2010. Their second qualification came after a play-off defeat of AFC representatives Bahrain. Herbert resigned in November 2013, and then briefly took charge of the Maldives. In August 2019, former Leeds United defender Danny Hay – a winner of 31 caps between 1996 and 2007 – became All Whites coach. Hay and Herbert are the only men to have both captained and managed the side.

HERBERT

TOURNAMENT TRIVIA
TEHAU ABOUT THAT

Pacific Island underdogs Tahiti finally broke the stranglehold that Australia and New Zealand had over the OFC Nations Cup by winning the tournament when it was held for the ninth time in 2012, following four previous triumphs for Australia and four for New Zealand. Tahiti scored 20 goals in their five games at the event in the Solomon Islands – 15 of which came from the Tehau family: brothers Lorenzo (five), Alvin and Jonathan (four each) and their cousin Teaonui (two). Steevy Chong Hue scored the only goal of the final, against New Caledonia, to give the team the trophy and a place at the FIFA Confederations Cup in 2013.

34

Commins Menapi is the Solomon Islands' all-time top scorer, with 34 goals in 37 games between 2000 and 2009.

MENAPI

24

Tahiti conceded a whopping 24 goals in their three games at the FIFA Confederations Cup in 2013. Ten came against Spain in one match.

31-0
American Samoa set an unwanted international record by losing 31-0 to Australia in April 2001 – two days after the Australians had crushed Tonga 22-0.

TOURNAMENT TRIVIA
BAD LUCK OF THE DRAW

Despite featuring at only their second-ever FIFA World Cup – and their first since 1982 – New Zealand did not lose a game in South Africa in 2010. They drew all three first-round matches, against Slovakia, Italy and Paraguay. The three points were not enough to secure a top-two spot in Group F, but their third-placed finish did see the Kiwis finish above defending world champions Italy. The only other three teams to have gone out despite going unbeaten in their three first-round group games were Scotland (1974), Cameroon (1982) and Belgium (1998).

STAR PLAYER
FIJI FIREPOWER

Esala Masi holds Fiji's record for most appearances and goals, scoring 32 times in 52 games between 1997 and 2005 – including a brace to help his side beat Tahiti 4-2 and clinch third place at the 1998 OFC Nations Cup, his country's best performance and one that they would match a decade later. Fiji also came close to becoming the first Oceania team other than Australia or New Zealand to qualify for the men's football tournament at the summer Olympic Games but they slipped to a 1-0 defeat at the hands of the All Whites in a final play-off for London 2012.

MASI

NATIONAL LEGEND
RIGHT VAN MEN

Vanuatu's best performance at an OFC Nations Cup was their fourth-place finish in 2007, but three years earlier they also pulled off one of the tournament's biggest surprises, beating New Zealand 4-2 in a first-round clash. Recent star players have included most-capped Etienne Mermer, who played 31 times as a striker and was briefly national manager in 2017/2018, and leading scorer Richard Iwai, who struck 19 international goals and later took over as U-23 coach. Vanuatu's biggest victory saw them defeat Kiribati 18-0 in July 2003, although one of Mermer's first games in charge was a December 2017 10-0 away win over Tuvalu.

17

Chris Wood was just 17 when he made his New Zealand debut against Tanzania in June 2009 – the same year in which he became the fifth and youngest New Zealander to play in England's Premier League, for West Bromwich Albion.

CONCACAF

Football history will be made three times over in 2026 when the Concacaf trio of Canada, Mexico and the USA host the FIFA World Cup. This will be the first time three nations have shared the excitement, Mexico will become the first three-time host or co-host, and this will be the first finals to feature 48 teams, up from 32.

Founded: 1961

Number of associations: 35 (+6 non-FIFA members)

Headquarters: Miami, USA

Most continental championship wins: Mexico, 11

2026 FIFA WORLD CUP™

The Member Associations of

CANADA, MEXICO, USA

have been selected by the FIFA Congress to host the 2026 FIFA World Cup™

WILMAR VALDEZ   LUIS HERNANDEZ   FERNANDO SARNEY   KOHZO TASHIMA   CONSTANT OMARI

3

Come 2026, Mexico will have hosted or co-hosted the FIFA World Cup three times, more than any other nation.

4

There are four Concacaf zones: North America, Central America, the Caribbean, and South America.

2000

Between them, Mexico and the USA have won all but one Concacaf Gold Cup. The other was won in 2000 by Canada.

The best performance from a Concacaf team in the FIFA World Cup was in 1930, when the USA finished third.

The Mexican national team is the only Concacaf team to have won a senior FIFA men's tournament, the FIFA Confederations Cup in 1999.

MEXICO

SÁNCHEZ

Mexico may well be the powerhouse of the Concacaf region – they have missed out on the FIFA World Cup final tournament only five times (in 1934, 1938, 1974, 1982 and 1990) – but they have struggled to impose themselves on the international stage.

Joined FIFA: 1927

Biggest win:
13-0 v. Bahamas, 1987

Highest FIFA Ranking: 4

Home stadium: Estadio Azteca, Mexico City

Honours: 11 Concacaf championships (1965, 1971, 1977, 1993, 1996, 1998, 2003, 2009, 2011, 2015, 2019), 1 FIFA Confederations Cup (1999)

NATIONAL LEGEND
VICTOR HUGO

Javier Hernández may have overtaken Jared Borghetti as Mexico's all-time leading goalscorer, but perhaps the country's most inspirational striker remains **Hugo Sánchez**, famed for his acrobatic bicycle-kick finishes and somersault celebrations. During spells in Spain with Atlético Madrid and Real Madrid, he finished as *La Liga*'s top scorer five years out of six between 1985 and 1990. He was less successful as Mexico coach from 2006 to 2008, his best result being third in the 2007 *Copa América*.

NATIONAL LEGEND
INSPIRATIONAL IGNACIO

Mexican football mourned the country's longest-serving national coach **Ignacio Trelles** when he died at the age of 103 following a heart attack in April 2020. Trelles holds the record for most matches as Mexico coach – overseeing 50 victories in 106 games during three spells between 1958 and 1976. These included Mexico's first victory at a FIFA World Cup, beating Czechoslovakia 3–1 in 1962, although they departed Chile at the end of the first round as well as England at the same stage four years later. Trelles – known as "Don Nacho" – also oversaw a record 1,083 games as top-flight coach in Mexico, while only he and Victor Manuel Vucetich (Mexico manager for just 35 days in 2013) have won the country's league at the helm of four different clubs. Bora Milutinović was coach for 104 games over two stints (1983–86 and 1995–97), including Mexico's run to the quarter-finals as hosts in 1986.

16

Only four countries – Argentina, Brazil, Germany and Italy – have more FIFA World Cup finals appearances than Mexico's 16.

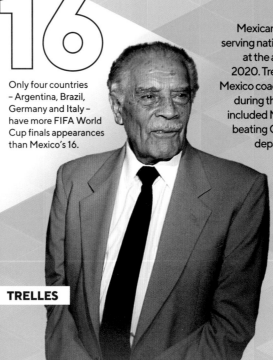

TRELLES

TOP SCORERS:

1 Javier Hernández, 52

2 Jared Borghetti, 46

3 Cuauhtémoc Blanco, 39

4 Carlos Hermosillo, 35
= Luis Hernández, 35

NATIONAL LEGEND
MAKING HIS MÁRQUEZ

Centre-back Rafael Márquez holds many of Mexico's records in the FIFA World Cup. His 19 matches in the finals are seven more than Javier Hernández. He – along with Cuauhtémoc Blanco and Hernández – are the only Mexican players to have scored in three World Cup final tournaments. Also, at the age of 39 years and 139 days, Márquez is – by six days – the second-oldest outfielder to start a FIFA World Cup knock-out match; the only person who was older was England winger Stanley Matthews when he played against Uruguay in 1954.

MOST APPEARANCES:

1 **Claudio Suárez**, 177

2 **Andrés Guardado**, 162

3 **Rafael Márquez**, 147

4 **Pável Pardo**, 146
  = **Gerardo Torrado**, 146

HERNANDEZ

3

Hugo Sánchez played for Mexico at three FIFA World Cups – 1978, 1986 and 1994 – and would surely have featured had they qualified in 1982 and 1990.

NATIONAL LEGEND
EMPEROR SUÁREZ

For a long time, only Egypt's Ahmed Hassan (184) had played more internationals than Mexico defender Claudio Suárez, who made 177 appearances between 1992 and 2006. Suárez – nicknamed "The Emperor" – played in all four of Mexico's games at the 1994 and 1998 FIFA World Cups, but had to miss the 2002 finals after suffering a broken leg. He was a member of the squad for the 2006 tournament in Germany, but did not play and retired after the finals.

SUÁREZ

STAR PLAYER
LITTLE PEA FROM A POD

Javier Hernández's goal against Costa Rica on 24 March 2017 saw him join Jared Borghetti as Mexico's leading scorer – both men with 46 goals from 89 games. Further goals have followed – as has Hernández's 100-cap milestone – and he reached 50 goals with a strike against Korea Republic at the 2018 FIFA World Cup. In June 2010, playing against South Africa in the opening match, he became the third generation of his family to play at a FIFA World Cup.

42

Mexico's Manuel Rosas scored the first penalty ever awarded in the FIFA World Cup finals when he converted a 42nd-minute spot-kick in his country's match against Argentina in 1930.

5

In 2014, commanding centre-back Rafael Márquez became the first player to captain his country at four consecutive FIFA World Cups – a record he extended to five in Mexico's second-round tie against Brazil in 2018. He, along with compatriot Antonio Carbajal and Germany's Lothar Matthäus, are the only men to have played at five FIFA World Cup finals.

TOURNAMENT TRIVIA
SECOND ROUNDS OUT

Mexico have yet to go beyond the quarter-finals of the FIFA World Cup, and their two last-eight visits, in 1970 and 1986, were only achieved when they hosted the tournament. Mexico's place at the 2018 FIFA World Cup in Russia owed plenty to winger **Hirving Lozano**, who top-scored with five goals in their qualifying campaign, including the only goal in a win over Panama in September 2017 that booked their place in Russia. He then got Mexico's challenge off to the ideal start with the only goal of their opening game, defeating defending champions Germany and winning himself the Man of the Match prize.

LOZANO

22

Mexico's shock 7-0 trouncing by Chile in the quarter-finals of the 2016 *Copa América Centenario* was their heaviest defeat in an official competition – and it brought to an end a 22-match unbeaten run, a Mexican international record.

USA

Over the year, football has steadily grown in both popularity and quality in the USA, which remains one of only 17 nations to have hosted the FIFA World Cup.

Joined FIFA: 1913

Biggest win: 8-0 v. Barbados, 2008

Highest FIFA ranking: 4th

Home stadium: (rotation)

Honours: 6 Concacaf Championships (1991, 2002, 2005, 2007, 2013, 2017)

NATIONAL LEGEND
LANDON HOPE AND GLORY

The USA's joint all-time leading scorer **Landon Donovan** was the star of their 2010 FIFA World Cup campaign, scoring three goals in four matches, including a stoppage-time winner against Algeria to help his team top Group C. . His four games at the tournament meant he featured in 13 FIFA World Cup matches for the USA, two ahead of Earnie Stewart, Cobi Jones and DaMarcus Beasley. Donovan's goal in the second-round loss to Ghana also made him the USA's all-time top scorer in the finals, with five – one more than 1930 hat-trick hero Bert Patenaude and Clint Dempsey, who scored twice in 2014.

DONOVAN

TOP SCORERS:
1. Landon Donovan, 57
= Clint Dempsey, 57
3. Jozy Altidore, 42
4. Eric Wynalda, 34
5. Brian McBride, 30

3

Landon Donovan was the first man to score more than one hat-trick for the United States, with four goals against Cuba in July 2003 and trebles versus Ecuador in March 2007 and Scotland in May 2012.

NATIONAL LEGENDS
GLOVE STORIES

Five goalkeepers have been on the winning team in United States internationals more than 25 times. **Tim Howard** leads the way with 62, followed by the 53 of Kasey Keller, 37 of Tony Meola, 34 of Brad Guzan, and 27 of Brad Friedel. Keller, however, kept a team-record 47 clean sheets, five more than Howard and ten more than Meola, while Friedel, 24, and Guzan, 20, round out the top five. Keller has the most Concacaf Gold Cup winners' medals as a USA goalkeeper with three.

HOWARD

148
No one has been coach of the USA men's team more times than Bruce Arena, who had two spells, concluding in October 2017, after 148 matches. He stepped down following the team's shock failure to qualify for the 2018 FIFA World Cup.

19

Jozy Altidore became the USA's youngest scorer of an international hat-trick in a 3-0 victory over Trinidad and Tobago on 1 April 2009, aged 19 years and 146 days.

STAR PLAYER
MAGIC CHRISTIAN

Philadelphia native **Christian Pulisic** moved to Germany as a 16-year-old in 2015 to sign for Borussia Dortmund. He was joined there a year later by his cousin Will, a goalkeeper who has played for the USA's U-17s. In March 2017, Christian scored the USA's fastest second-half goal, taking just 12 seconds after the restart to find the net in a 6-0 victory over Honduras. He became his country's youngest captain, aged 20 years and 63 days, against Italy in November 2018, and two months later he became the most expensive US footballer when it was announced that he would be joining English club Chelsea in the summer for USD 73 million or GBP 58 million.

PULISIC

17

Christian Pulisic became the USA's youngest international goalscorer when he netted against Bolivia, aged 17 years and 253 days, in May 2016.

2

The United States became the first Concacaf nation to have two players reach a half-century of goals. Clint Dempsey equalled Landon Donovan's national record after scoring his 57th goal for his country in a 2-0 win over Costa Rica in July 2017.

NATIONAL LEGEND
ALL IN THE FAMILY

In July 2019, midfielder **Michael Bradley** 2019 Concacaf Gold Cup final – his celebrations were muted by Mexico's 1-0 victory in Chicago – but he, fellow midfielder Christian Pulisic and defender Aaron Long were voted into the team of the tournament. Bradley made his debut in May 2006, and established himself as a regular after his father Bob Bradley was appointed national coach later that year. German legend Jürgen Klinsmann, USA manager between 2011 and 2016, made Bradley permanent captain in 2015. He continued in the role under Klinsmann's successors Bruce Arena (who returned for a second spell in charge after leading the USA to the 2002 and 2006 FIFA World Cups) and then Gregg Berhalter.

BRADLEY

MOST APPEARANCES:

1 Cobi Jones, 164
2 Landon Donovan, 157
3 Michael Bradley, 151
4 Clint Dempsey, 141
5 Jeff Agoos, 134

DEMPSEY

TOURNAMENT TRIVIA
ENGLAND STUNNED BY GAETJENS

USA's 1-0 win over England on 29 June 1950 ranks among the biggest surprises in FIFA World Cup history. England, along with hosts Brazil, were joint favourites to win the trophy. The USA had lost their last seven matches, scoring just two goals. Joe Gaetjens scored the only goal, in the 37th minute, diving to head Walter Bahr's cross past goalkeeper Bert Williams. England dominated the game, but USA keeper Frank Borghi made save after save. Defeats by Chile and Spain eliminated the USA at the end of the group stage, but their victory over England remains the greatest result in the country's football history.

STAR PLAYER
WEAH ON THE WAY

In March 2018, striker **Tim Weah** became the first man born in the 21st century to appear in a full international for the USA when he made his bow as an 86th-minute substitute in a 1-0 friendly victory over Paraguay. Weah – the son of former World Footballer of the Year and now Liberian President George Weah – was born in New York City on 22 February 2000, but moved to Paris Saint-Germain in 2014.

In November 2017, one of Weah's U-17 team-mates, Werder Bremen forward Josh Sargent, became the first man to be selected for US squads at U-17, U-20 and senior level in the same calendar year. On 28 May 2018, Sargent became the USA's fourth - youngest scorer - for seven minutes. He scored in the 52nd minute against Bolivia only for Weah, two days younger, to net in the 59th.

WEAH

CONCACAF : OTHER TEAMS

Mexico and the USA have dominated the Concacaf region down the years, but with recent standout performances from Costa Rica in FIFA World Cup competition, and Panama making the 2018 tournament, the region is starting to boast more and more talent.

Country: Costa Rica
Joined FIFA: 1927
Most appearances: Wálter Centeno, 137
Top scorer: Rolando Fonseca, 47
Honours: 3 Concacaf championships (1963, 1969, 1989)

Country: Honduras
Joined FIFA: 1946
Most appearances: Maynor Figueroa, 162
Top scorer: Carlos Pavón, 57
Honours: 1 Concacaf championships (1981)

Country: Canada
Joined FIFA: 1912
Most appearances: Julian de Guzman, 89
Top scorer: Dwayne De Rosario, 22
Honours: 2 Concacaf Gold Cups (1985, 2000)

Country: El Salvador
Joined FIFA: 1938
Most appearances: Alfredo Pacheco, 85
Top scorer: Raúl Díaz Arce, 39
Honours: -

Country: Trinidad & Tobago
Joined FIFA: 1964
Most appearances: Angus Eve, 117
Top scorer: Stern John, 70
Honours: -

Country: Panama
Joined FIFA: 1938
Most appearances: Gabriel Gómez, 149
Top scorer: Luis Tejada /Blas Pérez, 43
Honours: -

NATIONAL LEGEND
PAN-TASTIC TORRES

Panama made their FIFA World Cup finals debut in Russia in 2018, captained by mighty centre-back **Róman Torres**, whose goal three minutes from time sealed a 2-1 win over Costa Rica and secured their place at the expense of the USA, who lost by the same scoreline to Trinidad & Tobago that night. Panama President Juan Carlos Valera declared a national holiday to celebrate. Panama lost all three games in Russia – 3-0 to Tunisia, 6-1 to England and 2-1 to Tunisia – but their fans celebrated exuberantly in Nizhny Novgorod when substitute Felipe Baloy scored their first-ever FIFA World Cup goal, against England.

TORRES

99
Weighing 99kg, Panama's Róman Torres was the heaviest player at the 2018 FIFA World Cup, and he announced his international retirement after the tournament, having scored ten goals in 114 appearances.

TOURNAMENT TRIVIA
ALL FOR EL SALVADOR

El Salvador can claim to be the first Central American country – other than Mexico or the USA – to have qualified for the FIFA World Cup twice, doing so in 1970 and 1982. Recent years have brought more struggles, however, although left-back Alfredo Pacheco became his country's most-capped player with 86 appearances between 2002 and 2013.

JOHN

70
Only 14 men have netted more than the 70 international goals – in 115 matches – scored by Trinidad & Tobago's Stern John between his debut in 1995 and his final game in 2011.

STAR PLAYER
KEYLOR IS THE KEY

Costa Rica made their FIFA World Cup finals debut in 1990, and goalkeeper Luis Gabelo Conejo shared the best goalkeeper award with Argentina's Sergio Goycochea as his displays helped his team reach the knockout stages. *Los Ticos* did even better in 2014 and while goalscorers Joel Campbell and Bryan Ruiz impressed, again a goalkeeper was crucial: **Keylor Navas** was named Man of the Match four times in five games. At the other end of the pitch, the first man to score twice for Costa Rica at the FIFA World Cup was charismatic striker Paulo Wanchope, who found the net both times for his country when they lost the 2006 tournament's opening match 4-2 to hosts Germany. His record tally of 45 for Costa Rica was later passed by 47-goal striker Rolando Fonseca.

NAVAS

NATIONAL LEGEND
TEEN PHENOMENON ALPHONSO

Left-winger **Alphonso Davies** became Canada's youngest international when he made his debut against Curaçao on 13 June 2017, aged just 16 years and 225 days, Twenty-three days later, he became not only Canada's youngest international scorer – he scored twice – in a Concacaf Gold Cup 4-2 victory over French Guyana, but also the tournament's youngest-ever scorer. His three strikes earned him the Golden Boot despite Canada's second-round elimination. Davies, who joined Germany giants Bayern Munich in 2018, was born in a Ghana refugee camp to Liberian parents who were fleeing civil war before the family moved to Canada with Alphonso aged five. He received Canadian citizenship in seven days before his international debut. Davies was also on the scoresheet, along with Lucas Cavallani, in a 2-0 victory over the USA in October 2019 – Canada's first win over their neighbours in 19 encounters across the previous 34 years. Canada's all-time scorer remains Dwayne De Rosario, whose 22 goals included helping his country to a Concacaf Gold Cup triumph in 2000.

DAVIES

NATIONAL LEGEND
CELSO LIKE HIS FATHER

Costa Rica playmaker Celso Borges was delighted, in 2014, to emulate his father by reaching the knockout stages of the FIFA World Cup. He actually went one better as he scored the first penalty of Los Ticos' 5-3 shoot-out defeat of Greece in the round of 16. His Brazilian-born father, Alexandre Borges Guimães, played at the 1990 FIFA World Cup and set up Hernán Medford's late winner against Sweden to take the FIFA World Cup finals debutants beyond the first round. The man affectionately known as "Guima" was Costa Rica's coach at both the 2002 and 2006 FIFA World Cup finals.

3 Canada, Haiti, Jamaica, Panama and Trinidad & Tobago all played three matches in their only World Cup finals appearances. Jamaica won once and Trinidad & Tobago drew once; all their other games were lost.

9 The number of players from Costa Rica with 100 caps. In Concacaf, only the USA – with 17 – and Mexico – 15 – have more.

2 In 2014, Costa Rica became only the second Concacaf side, after Mexico in 1986, to go out of a FIFA World Cup without losing a game in normal time.

TOURNAMENT TRIVIA
BROTHERS IN ARMS

One of three brothers, defensive midfielder **Wilson Palacios** was perhaps the most famous and acclaimed player in the first Honduras side to reach a FIFA World Cup in 28 years. Like the 1982 side, though, Reinaldo Rueda's men went three games without a win. An older brother, Milton Palacios, played 14 times as a defender for Honduras between 2003 and 2006. Both Jerry and Wilson made it into the 2014 FIFA World Cup squad, but it was not a happy time, especially for Wilson, who was sent off in the opener against France, and Honduras lost all three matches, but did at least score in the defeat against Ecuador.

PALACIOS

FIFA WORLD CUP™

France triumphed at the 2018 FIFA World Cup for the second time when *Les Bleus* climaxed a thrilling tournament in Russia by defeating surprise outsiders Croatia 4-2 in the final at Luzhniki Stadium in Moscow.

First held:
1930

Current champions:
France

Most wins:
Brazil, 5

Next edition:
Qatar, 2022

210

210 teams entered qualification for the 2018 FIFA World Cup. The first in 1930 was the only one not to feature qualification.

The **2018 FIFA World Cup** saw stadiums at 98 per cent capacity, the Fan Fests drew 7.7m visitors, Russia recorded more than 1m tourists and the tournament attracted more than three billion television viewers as well as record numbers to FIFA's digital channels.

FIFA WORLD CUP
RUSSIA 2018

180

MBAPPÉ

Kylian Mbappé was named Best Young Player at the 2018 FIFA World Cup finals after his explosive performances for France. Mbappé, 19, had cost Paris Saint-Germain EUR 180m from Monaco the previous year and he justified the fee in Russia.

169

There were 169 goals at the FIFA World Cup in 2018, an average of 2.64 a game.

The **Azteca Stadium** in Mexico is the only stadium to have hosted the FIFA World Cup final twice. Brazil's Maracanã has hosted the deciding game twice, but in 1950, the tournament was held in a round-robin format with no set final.

FIFA WORLD CUP QUALIFIERS

To get to the greatest show on Earth, first countries must fight it out in regional confederations.

BIGGEST-EVER QUALIFYING WINS:

1 Australia 31–0 American Samoa, 11 April 2001

2 Australia 22–0 Tonga, 9 April 2001

3 Maldives 0–17 IR Iran, 2 June 1997

4 Australia 13–0 Solomon Islands, 11 June 1997

= New Zealand 13–0 Fiji, 16 August 1981

= Fiji 13–0 American Samoa, 7 April 2001

NATIONAL QUALIFICATION RECORD
GERMANY IN A HURRY

2014 world champions Germany were the only European team to complete their 2018 qualifying campaign with a 100 per cent record, winning all ten group-stage matches. Coach Joachim Löw's team scored 43 goals and conceded only four. Remarkably, Germany's goals were shared among 22 players (including one own goal). Their top marksmen, Thomas Müller and Sandro Wagner, scored a modest five goals apiece. In between qualification, they won the FIFA Confederations Cup in 2017.

OFF THE MARK

Norjmoogiin Tsedenbal of Mongolia scored the first goal of the 2022 FIFA World Cup qualification campaign in a 2–0 defeat of Brunei Darussalam on 6 June 2019.

SCORING RECORD
LEWANDOWSKI IN POLE POSITION

Poland's **Robert Lewandowski** was the 16-goal joint-leading marksman in the qualifying campaign for the 2018 finals, level with Mohammad Al-Sahlawi from Saudi Arabia and Ahmed Khalil from the United Arab Emirates. The trio scored one more than Portugal captain Cristiano Ronaldo, the Best FIFA Men's Player in both 2016 and 2017. Both Lewandowski and Ronaldo – now the all-time leading goalscorer in European qualification history with 30 – beat the 14-goal European record set by Yugoslavia's Predrag Mijatović in the 1998 preliminaries.

32

Just 32 countries entered qualification for the 1934 FIFA World Cup. Sweden and Estonia played the first match on 11 June 1933.

39

With 39 goals, Guatemala's Carlos Ruiz is the all-time top scorer in FIFA World Cup qualifiers, despite never reaching the finals.

41

At 41, Zambia's Kalusha Bwalya is the oldest player to have scored a match-winning goal in a FIFA World Cup qualifying match.

117 SECONDS

Abdel Hamid Bassiouny of Egypt scored the fastest-ever qualification hat-trick in their 8-2 win over Namibia on 13 July 2001.

NATIONAL LEGEND
THIERRY'S TRICKERY

France qualified for the 2010 FIFA World Cup finals thanks to one of the most controversial international goals of recent history. The second leg of their play-off against the Republic of Ireland in November 2009 was 14 minutes into extra time when striker **Thierry Henry** controlled the ball with his hand before crossing to William Gallas, who gave his side a decisive 2-1 aggregate lead. After Swedish referee Martin Hansson allowed the goal to stand, the Football Association of Ireland first called for the game to be replayed, then asked to be allowed into the finals as a 33rd country – but both requests proved in vain.

HENRY

NATIONAL QUALIFICATION RECORD
ORANJE AND *AZZURRI* OFF COLOUR

Among the notable European absentees from the party in Russia were 2006 champions Italy, and the Netherlands, who were runners-up in 2010 and third in Brazil in 2014. The *Oranje* were eliminated after finishing third in Group A, behind Sweden on goal difference. Italy lost 1-0 on aggregate to Sweden in the play-offs. The Swedes won 1-0 at home, then withstood everything the *Azzurri* could throw at them at the "San Siro" in Milan. In 1934, Italy were the only hosts ever to go through the qualifying competition, but this was to be only their third-ever absence from the finals: they did not enter in 1930, and failed to qualify in 1958.

NATIONAL QUALIFICATION RECORD
WELCOME NEWCOMERS

Panama and Iceland qualified for their first FIFA World Cup finals in Russia. The Icelanders followed up their historic quarter-finals run at UEFA EURO 2016 by becoming the smallest nation (population 335,000) to qualify for the FIFA World Cup finals. Panama left it late to make their own little bit of history. A goal two minutes from time by defender Róman Torres earned a 2-1 win over Costa Rica in their last game to clinch an all-important third place in the final Concacaf group.

ALL-TIME QUALIFICATIONS BY REGIONAL CONFEDERATION:

1 Europe – 246

2 South America – 85

3 Africa – 44

4 North/Central America & Caribbean – 42

5 Asia – 37

6 Oceania – 4

NATIONAL QUALIFICATION RECORD
THE "FOOTBALL WAR"

War broke out between El Salvador and Honduras after El Salvador beat Honduras 3-2 in a play-off on 26 June 1969 to qualify for the 1970 finals. Tensions had been running high between the neighbours over a border dispute and there had been rioting at the match. El Salvador lost all three matches at the 1970 FIFA World Cup, and left without scoring a single goal.

FIFA WORLD CUP TEAM RECORDS

From the most decorated nations in world football to those that have only played a single game, and every team in-between.

138

TOURNAMENT TRIVIA
CHAMPIONS' CURSE

At the 2018 FIFA World Cup finals, Germany became the fourth holders since 2000 to be eliminated at the group stage. France were eliminated in the group stage in 2002, Italy went out in the first round in 2010 in South Africa and Spain followed their unfortunate example in Brazil four years later. In 2018, the Germans never recovered from an opening 1-0 defeat by Mexico. They beat Sweden 2-1, only thanks to a stoppage-time goal from **Toni Kroos**, before losing 2-0 to Korea Republic.

KROOS

TOURNAMENT TRIVIA
ONE-TIME WONDERS

Indonesia, then known as the Dutch East Indies, made one appearance in the finals, in the days when the tournament was a strictly knockout affair. On 5 June 1938, they lost 6-0 to Hungary in the first round, and have never qualified for the tournament since. This is the fewest number of FIFA World Cup games ever played by a country, though El Salvador have the worst-ever World Cup record; in six matches across two tournaments they have lost all six, scored one goal and conceded 22.

7

Brazil's record of seven wins in the 2002 FIFA World Cup – a 100 per cent record – is the most by any country at any tournament ever.

NATIONAL LEGEND
BRAZIL OFF COLOUR

Brazil's yellow shirts are famous around the world, but the team wore white shirts at the first four FIFA World Cup finals. Their 2-1 loss to Uruguay in the 1950 tournament's final match – when a draw would have given them the cup – was such a shock that they switched to yellow. The Brazilian FA insisted no further colour change would follow the shock of the 7-1 semi-final defeat by Germany and 3-0 third-place play-off loss to the Netherlands in 2014.

SOUTH AFRICA
South Africa is the only host country to fail to progress from the first round of a FIFA World Cup.

MOST APPEARANCES IN A FIFA WORLD CUP FINAL:

1. Germany/West Germany – 8
2. Brazil – 7* (*includes 1950)
3. Italy – 6
4. Argentina – 5
5. France – 3
   = Netherlands – 3

MOST APPEARANCES IN FINALS TOURNAMENTS:

1 Brazil – 21

2 Germany/West Germany – 19

3 Italy – 18

4 Argentina – 17

5 Mexico – 16

FRANCE
France hold the record for the worst performance by defending champions: they scored no goals and managed a single draw in 2002.

KIT TRIVIA
EVER RED

England's victory in 1966 remains the only time the FIFA World Cup final has been won by a team wearing red. Spain, who usually wear red, changed into blue for their 2010 victory over the Netherlands to avoid a colour-clash. **Luka Modrić** and his Croatia teammates did wear their unique red-and-white checks in the 2018 final but lost to France. Wearing red also proved unlucky for losing finalists Czechoslovakia in 1934 and then Hungary in both 1938 and 1954.

MODRIĆ

NATIONAL RECORD
SAFE EUROPEAN HOME

Germany's 1-0 victory over Argentina in the 2014 FIFA World Cup final meant they became the first European nation to win the FIFA World Cup in any of the eight tournaments staged in North, Central or South America, going back to 1930. Spain, winners of the 2010 FIFA World Cup in South Africa, were the first European side to triumph outside their home continent, and only since 2010 has a team other than Brazil won the trophy in a foreign continent; Brazil achieved it in 1958 (Sweden), 1970 (Mexico), 1994 (USA) and 2002 (Japan/Korea Republic).

NATIONAL LEGEND
TODAY EUROPE, TOMORROW THE WORLD

Spain's 2010 trophy-lifting coach **Vicente del Bosque** became only the second manager to have won both the FIFA World Cup and the UEFA Champions League or its previous incarnation, the European Champions' Cup. Marcello Lippi won the UEFA prize with Juventus in 1996, ten years before his Italy team became world champions. Del Bosque won the UEFA Champions League twice with Real Madrid, in 2000 and 2002, though he was sacked in summer 2003 for "only" winning the Spanish league title the previous season.

DEL BOSQUE

0

Switzerland hold the record for the least number of goals conceded in one tournament (2006), despite losing in the round of 16 on penalties to Ukraine.

18

Brazil (1930-58) and West Germany/Germany (1934-58, 1986-98) share the record for the most consecutive games scoring a goal at the FIFA World Cup.

CHAMPIONS
2014 FIFA World Cup

🏆 TOURNAMENT TRIVIA
EXTRA SPECIAL GERMANS

Germany, in beating Argentina 1-0 in the Maracanã Stadium in 2014, became the fifth team to win the FIFA World Cup final in extra time after Italy (1934), England (1966), Argentina (1978) and Spain (2010). In both 2010 and 2014, the final had finished goalless after 90 minutes. Andrés Iniesta, for Spain in 2010, and Mario Götze, for Germany in Rio de Janeiro, both struck their lone winning goals in the second period of the additional 30 minutes. Extra time was not enough in 1994 and 2006, when Brazil and Italy, respectively, won on penalties.

ZENGA

🥅 DEFENSIVE RECORD
ITALY KEEP IT TIGHT

Italy set the record for the longest run without conceding a goal at the FIFA World Cup finals. They went five games without conceding at the 1990 finals, starting with their 1-0 group win over Austria. Goalkeeper **Walter Zenga** was unbeaten until Claudio Caniggia scored Argentina's equaliser in the semi-final. However, a watertight defence did not bring Italy the glory it craved: Argentina reached the final by winning the penalty shoot-out 4-3.

2

There were two nations making their FIFA World Cup debut in 2018 – Iceland and Panama.

HALLGRÍMSSON

TOURNAMENT TRIVIA
TWICE AS ICE

Minnows Iceland caused trouble for the giants at the 2018 FIFA World Cup, just as they had in the 2016 UEFA European Championship. In France in 2016, Iceland, newcomers to the big stage, defeated England in the round of 16. They followed up in Russia by holding Lionel Messi's Argentina 1-1 on their debut in the World Cup finals. But they kept their feet firmly on the ground. Part-time manager **Heimir Hallgrímsson** said: "I am still a dentist and I will never stop being a dentist."

DEFENSIVE RECORD
THE FEWEST GOALS CONCEDED

FIFA World Cup winners France (1998), Italy (2006) and Spain (2010) hold the record for the fewest goals conceded on their way to victory. All three conceded just two. Spain also hold the record for fewest goals scored by FIFA World Cup winners. They netted just eight in 2010, below the 11 scored by Italy in 1938, England in 1966 or Brazil in 1994.

70

Brazil have won more FIFA World Cup matches than any other nation, with 70.

TOURNAMENT TRIVIA
STUBBORN SCOTS

England and Scotland may be where international football began but none of the home nations, including Wales and Northern Ireland, entered the FIFA World Cup until 1950, as they were not members of FIFA in the 1930s. England and Scotland both qualified for the 1950 finals but the Scots refused to go to Brazil out of principle, because they "only" finished second in the British qualifying group.

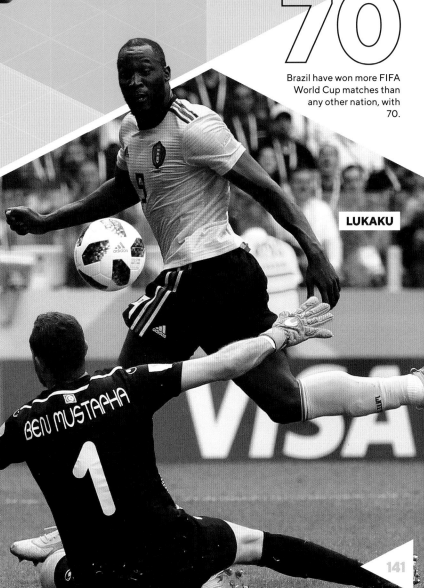

LUKAKU

SCORING RECORD
SHARING THE GOALS

France in 1982, winners Italy in 2006 and third-placed Belgium in 2018 supplied the most individual goalscorers during a FIFA World Cup finals tournament – ten. Germany's 17 goals were shared among seven players on their way to ultimate success in Brazil in 2014: Thomas Müller (five), André Schürrle (three), Mats Hummels (two), Miroslav Klose (two), Toni Kroos (two), Mario Götze (two) and Mesut Özil (one). Belgium's top scorer in 2018 was **Romelu Lukaku,** who finished joint second overall with four.

141

5

Germany, in beating Argentina 1–0 in 2014, became the fifth team to win the FIFA World Cup final in extra time.

TOURNAMENT TRIVIA
HOME DISCOMFORT

South Africa became the first host nation to fail to reach the second round of a FIFA World Cup, when staging the 2010 tournament – though their first-round record of one win, one draw and one defeat was only inferior on goal difference to the opening three games played by hosts Spain, in 1982, and the USA, in 1994, both of whom reached the second round. Uruguay's 3–0 victory over South Africa in Pretoria on 16 June 2010 equalled the highest losing margin suffered by a FIFA World Cup host, following Brazil's 5–2 win over Sweden in the 1958 final and Italy's 4–1 trouncing of Mexico in their 1970 quarter-final.

DEFENSIVE RECORD
BRAZIL'S GOAL GLOOM

The 14 goals conceded by Brazil in the 2014 FIFA World Cup finals are the most ever conceded by the host nation. The overall record was 16 goals shipped by Korea Republic in Switzerland in 1954. In those finals, West Germany let in 14 but still won the tournament for the first time. That included conceding eight in a group match against beaten finalists Hungary.

 ## TOURNAMENT TRIVIA
BRAZIL PROFIT FROM RIMET'S VISION

Jules Rimet, President of FIFA from 1921 to 54, was the driving force behind the first FIFA World Cup, in 1930. The tournament, in Uruguay, was not high-profile, with only 13 nations taking part. The long sea journey kept most European teams away, and only Belgium, France, Romania and Yugoslavia made the trip. Rimet's dream of a truly global competition has long since been realised and the FIFA World Cup has grown enormously in popularity. Brazil have been the competition's most successful team, winning five times. The only ever-presents at FIFA World Cup finals, they have more wins (70) than any other country, though Germany (66 wins) have played more matches: 106 to Brazil's 104. Germany and Italy are the most successful European nations with four World Cup wins apiece. The original finalists, Uruguay and Argentina, are both two-time champions alongside France, though Argentina have also lost two finals. England (1966) have won once as hosts. Spain failed as hosts in 1982 but won in South Africa in 2010.

RIMET

TOURNAMENT TRIVIA
COLOUR-FAST JAPAN

Japan and Poland were the only teams in 2018 to play in their first-choice kit in all their first-round ties. Japan's blue shirts incorporated the national flag and a crest to mark the 20th anniversary of their first appearance in the finals.

TOURNAMENT TRIVIA
TIGHTEST OF MARGINS

Before 2010, no country had won five consecutive FIFA World Cup matches by a one-goal margin – but the Netherlands became the first, thanks to their 3-2 semi-final victory over Uruguay. Before then, the record rested with Italy, who managed four single-goal wins in a row across the 1934 and 1938 FIFA World Cups. Spain's 1-0 defeat of the Dutch in the 2010 FIFA World Cup was also their fifth consecutive single-goal victory and fourth in the knockout stages.

HONDA

13

Only 13 nations participated in the first FIFA World Cup. Pioneered by Jules Rimet, it was held in Uruguay in 1930.

TOURNAMENT TRIVIA
SMALL IS BEAUTIFUL

Croatia, coached by **Zlatko Dalić**, became the second-smallest nation (population 4m) to appear in the FIFA World Cup final when they lost to France in Moscow in 2018. They were also the youngest, having an average age of just 27 years old. The only smaller finalist nation was Uruguay (population 3m), who had last reached the showdown back in 1950.

DALIĆ

FIFA WORLD CUP GOALSCORING

The goals are what everyone remembers from the FIFA World Cup. Over the years, some of the world's greatest strikers have showcased their talents on the world stage.

11
Hakan Şükür of Turkey holds the record for the fastest-ever FIFA World Cup goal, scored after 11 seconds against Korea Republic in 2002.

9
Brazil have scored more goals than any other nation in opening matches of the FIFA World Cup: 9.

7-5
The highest-scoring game in the FIFA World Cup finals was the quarter-final between Austria and Switzerland on 26 June 1954, which ended 7-5 to Austria.

2,500
Tunisia's Fakhreddine Ben Youssef scored the 2,500th FIFA World Cup finals goal, against Panama in 2018.

TOURNAMENT TRIVIA
FINAL FLURRY

France's 4-2 victory over Croatia in the 2018 FIFA World Cup final was the highest 90-minute aggregate in the showdown since Brazil defeated hosts Sweden by 5-2 in 1958 in Stockholm. England and West Germany tallied six goals in the hosts' 4-2 victory in 1966, but the score was 2-2 after 90 minutes. The overall goals total at the 2018 tournament was 169, two short of the 171 in both 1998 and 2014, which is the record for the 32-team, 64-match finals.

TOURNAMENT TRIVIA
PENALTY PROGRESS

The 2018 FIFA World Cup finals in Russia equalled the number of shoot-outs in the knockout stage, with four matches decided from the penalty spot, matching the number in 1990, 2006 and 2014. Croatia became only the second team, after Argentina in 1990, to win consecutive shoot-outs, against Denmark and Russia. They were also the first team to be taken to extra time in all three knockout ties on their way to the final, meaning that they played 90 minutes more than final opponents France.

TOURNAMENT TRIVIA
GENEROUS OPPONENTS

Chile were the first team to benefit from an opponent's own goal at the FIFA World Cup. Mexico's Manuel Rosas put the ball into his own net during the Chileans' 3-0 win at the inaugural 1930 finals in Uruguay. France, courtesy of two in both 2014 and 2018, are out on their own as recipients of the most own goals with six; Germany and Italy have four apiece. In 2018, **Mario Mandžukić** of Croatia scored the first own goal in a FIFA World Cup final, while the other own goal to benefit France came from Australia's Aziz Behich in the group stage.

MANDŽUKIĆ

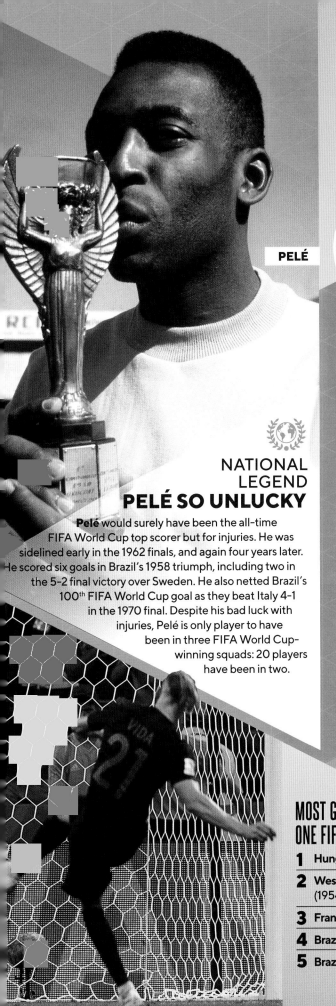

PELÉ

1 Miroslav Klose, Germany – 16 (2002, 2006, 2010, 2014)

2 Ronaldo, Brazil – 15 (1998, 2002, 2006)

3 Gerd Müller, West Germany – 14 (1970, 1974)

4 Just Fontaine, France – 13 (1958)

5 Pelé, Brazil – 12 (1958, 1962, 1966, 1970)

MESSI'S ASSISTS
Lionel Messi is the only player to have recorded an assist in each of the last four FIFA World Cups.

KLOSE

NATIONAL LEGEND
PELÉ SO UNLUCKY

Pelé would surely have been the all-time FIFA World Cup top scorer but for injuries. He was sidelined early in the 1962 finals, and again four years later. He scored six goals in Brazil's 1958 triumph, including two in the 5-2 final victory over Sweden. He also netted Brazil's 100th FIFA World Cup goal as they beat Italy 4-1 in the 1970 final. Despite his bad luck with injuries, Pelé is only player to have been in three FIFA World Cup-winning squads: 20 players have been in two.

NATIONAL LEGEND
KLOSE ENCOUNTERS

Eight players have scored at FIFA World Cups 12 years apart: the most notable was **Miroslav Klose**. The Polish-born centre-forward opened with a hat-trick when Germany beat Saudi Arabia 8-0 in Japan in 2002 and scored his 16th goal in the 7-1 destruction of hosts Brazil in the 2014 semi-finals. That established Klose as the finals' all-time record marksman with one more goal than Brazil's Ronaldo. The other seven men to have scored in FIFA World Cups 12 years apart are: Pelé (Brazil), Uwe Seeler (West Germany), Diego Maradona (Argentina), Michael Laudrup (Denmark), Henrik Larsson (Sweden), Sami Al-Jaber (Saudi Arabia) and Cuauhtémoc Blanco (Mexico).

SCORING RECORD
NO GUARANTEE FOR TOP SCORERS

Topping the FIFA World Cup finals scoring chart is a great honour for all strikers, but few have been leading scorer and won the tournament. Argentina's Guillermo Stábile started the luckless trend in 1930, topping the scoring charts but finishing up on the losing side in the final. The list of top scorers who have played in the winning side is small: Garrincha and Vavá (joint-top scorers in 1962), Mario Kempes (top scorer in 1978), Paolo Rossi (1982) and Ronaldo (2002). Gerd Müller, top scorer in 1970, gained his reward as West Germany's trophy-winner four years later.

MOST GOALS IN ONE FIFA WORLD CUP:

1 Hungary – 27 (1954)

2 West Germany – 25 (1954)

3 France – 23 (1958)

4 Brazil – 22 (1950)

5 Brazil – 19 (1970)

FIFA WORLD CUP APPEARANCES

Since the dawn of the FIFA World Cup, many players have left their mark on the competition. But some have left bigger legacies than others...

MARADONA

NATIONAL LEGEND
LEADING CAPTAINS

Three players have been team captain in the FIFA World Cup final on two occasions – Diego Maradona of Argentina, Dunga of Brazil and West Germany's Karl-Heinz Rummenigge. Maradona lifted the trophy in 1986, but was on the losing side four years later. Dunga was the winning skipper in 1994, but lost out in 1998. Rummenigge was a beaten finalist on both occasions, in 1982 and 1986. Rafael Márquez has made the most appearances in the FIFA World Cup finals as captain, leading out Mexico 17 times.

TOURNAMENT TRIVIA
THE "DOUBLE" CHAMPIONS

Didier Deschamps joined Franz Beckenbauer and Mário Zagallo in the history books at the 2018 FIFA World Cup finals. Until France's victory in Russia under Deschamps, their 1998 winning captain, Zagallo and Beckenbauer had been the only men to win the World Cup as both player and manager. Zagallo won the World Cup in 1958 and 1962 on the wing; he took over at short notice from João Saldanha as Brazil manager and secured his third triumph at the 1970 final. Beckenbauer played in 1970 too for West Germany, whom he captained to victory on home soil in 1974. Beckenbauer was appointed national coach in 1984, and won the FIFA World Cup in 1990.

NATIONAL LEGEND
PROSINEČKI'S SCORING RECORD

Robert Prosinečki is the only player to have scored for different countries in FIFA World Cup finals tournaments. He netted for Yugoslavia in their 4–1 win over the United Arab Emirates in the 1990 tournament. Eight years later, following the break-up of the old Yugoslavia, he scored for Croatia in their 3–0 group-game win over Jamaica, and then netted the first goal in his side's 2–1 third-place play-off victory over the Netherlands.

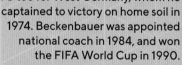

PROSINEČKI

DESCHAMPS

MOST APPEARANCES IN FIFA WORLD CUP FINALS:

1 Lothar Matthäus (West Germany/Germany) – 25
2 Miroslav Klose (Germany) – 24
3 Paolo Maldini (Italy) – 23
4 Diego Maradona (Argentina) – 21
= Uwe Seeler (West Germany) – 21
= Władysław Żmuda (Poland) – 21

GRANQVIST

DELPH

TOURNAMENT TRIVIA
BABY LOVE

Sweden's **Andreas Granqvist** and England's **Fabian Delph** took different approaches to fatherhood during the 2018 FIFA World Cup. Manchester City midfielder Delph flew home to welcome his new daughter before flying back to Russia to rejoin the England squad. Granqvist stayed at the finals while his wife Sofia gave birth to a daughter. She had insisted her husband stay with the team because "it's these World Cup moments that he dreamed about as a little boy."

EXTRA-TIME HISTORY

Russia's Aleksandr Erokhin became the first-ever fourth substitute at a FIFA World Cup in 2018, a rule amendment by the law-making International Football Association Board to the effect that teams could make a fourth substitution, but only in extra time.

FEDERATION HISTORY
GERMANY UNITED

Germany and West Germany are counted together in FIFA World Cup records because the Deutscher Fussball-Bund, founded in 1900, Germany's governing body, was in charge of the national game before World War II, during the East–West split and post-reunification. German sides have won the World Cup four times and appeared in the final a record eight times. In 2014, match-deciding substitutes André Schürrle and Mario Götze were the first players born in Germany since reunification to win the World Cup, while team-mate Toni Kroos was the only 2014 squad member to have been born in what was East Germany. Kroos was also the first player from the former East Germany to win the World Cup.

4

The three fastest substitutions in the history of the FIFA World Cup have been made in the fourth minute: Steve Hodge (England, 1986), Giuseppe Bergomi (Italy, 1998) and Peter Crouch (England, 2006).

17

Northern Ireland's Norman Whiteside is the youngest player in FIFA World Cup finals history, being just 17 years and 41 days old when he started against Yugoslavia in 1982.

16

Manchester City sent more players than any other club to the 2018 FIFA World Cup. Their 16 included one who collected a winner's medal, defender Benjamin Mendy.

4

The most players sent off in one FIFA World Cup finals game is four during a match between Portugal and the Netherlands, refereed by Russian official Valentin Ivanov in 2006.

VARANE

NATIONAL LEGEND
VARANE AT THE DOUBLE

Raphaël Varane became the 11th player to clinch the double of success in the UEFA Champions League and FIFA World Cup when he anchored France's defence at the 2018 finals in Russia. Varane, born in Lille and a youth prodigy at Lens, joined Real Madrid in 2011, two years before making his senior debut for France. By the time he lined up at the 2018 FIFA World Cup, he had won 15 major club honours with Madrid. At the FIFA World Cup, he played every minute in all seven of France's games, including the final victory over Croatia.

FASTEST SENDINGS-OFF IN FIFA WORLD CUP FINALS:

1 José Batista (Uruguay) v. Scotland, 1986 – 1 min
2 Carlos Sánchez (Colombia) v. Japan, 2018 – 4 min
3 Giorgio Ferrini (Italy) v. Chile, 1962 – 8 min
4 Zezé Procópio (Brazil) v. Czechoslovakia, 1938 – 14 min
5 Mohammed Al Khlaiwi (Saudi Arabia) v. France 1998 – 19 min
= Miguel Bossio (Uruguay) v. Denmark, 1986 – 19 min

FIFA WORLD CUP GOALKEEPING

The FIFA World Cup has produced a fair few legends between the sticks. From the old dependables to the crazy keepers, many have written their names in the history books.

MEOLA

CABALLERO

RIGHT WAY FOR RICARDO

Spain's Ricardo Zamora became the first man to save a penalty in a FIFA World Cup finals match, stopping Waldemar de Brito's spot-kick for Brazil in 1934. Spain went on to win 3-1.

NATIONAL LEGEND
TONY AWARD

USA goalkeeper **Tony Meola** left the national team after the 1994 FIFA World Cup because he wanted to switch sports and take up American football instead. He failed to make it in gridiron and returned to soccer, but did not play for his country again until 1999. He retired for a second time after reaching a century of international appearances and still holds the record for being the youngest FIFA World Cup captain, having worn the armband for the USA's 5-1 defeat to Czechoslovakia in 1990, aged 21 years and 316 days.

RECENT HISTORY
KEEPERS CAUGHT OUT

The 2018 FIFA World Cup proved a testing tournament for goalkeepers. Mistakes by **Willy Caballero** cost goals in Argentina's opening 1-1 draw against Iceland and the next game, a 3-0 defeat by Croatia. Uruguay's Fernando Muslera began well with three clean sheets but then misjudged a goal-bound shot from Antoine Griezmann in their quarter-final defeat by France. Even Germany's goalkeeper-captain Manuel Neuer had a tough time on returning to duty after a long injury lay-off. In the last group game, as Germany chased an equaliser against Korea Republic, Neuer was caught in the opposition half by a high-speed counter-attack, which provided the South Koreans' second goal.

NATIONAL LEGEND
KING HUGO THE FOURTH

Hugo Lloris became the fourth goalkeeper to captain his country to FIFA World Cup glory when France became champions for the second time in Russia in 2018. Lloris joined Italians Gianpiero Combi (1934) and Dino Zoff (1982) as well as Spain's Iker Casillas (2010). A mistake by Lloris on a back-pass in the final cost France their second goal, but they went on to beat Croatia 4-2. The final was Loris's 104th appearance in ten years for France. The former Nice and Lyon keeper had been appointed national team captain in 2012.

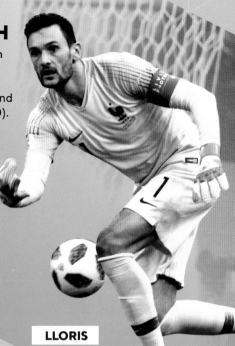

LLORIS

1 There was just a single shot from a goalkeeper in the 2014 FIFA World Cup: Switzerland's Diego Benaglio was the only goalkeeper who swung at the target.

6 Spain goalkeeper David de Gea had a terrible time at the 2018 FIFA World Cup, conceding six goals despite facing just seven shots.

16 Tim Howard famously made an incredible 16 saves in the USA's round-of-16 clash with Belgium in 2014.

OLIVER'S ARMS
Germany's Oliver Kahn is the only goalkeeper to have received the adidas Golden Ball as the tournament's best player, winning the award at the 2002 FIFA World Cup – despite taking a share of the blame for Brazil's winning goals in the final

NEUER

TOURNAMENT TRIVIA
END-TO-END STUFF

When Miroslav Klose raced on to a long ball from German team-mate **Manuel Neuer** to score against England in their 2010 FIFA World Cup round-of-16 tie, it made Neuer the first goalkeeper to directly set up a finals goal for 44 years. The last before then had been the Soviet Union's Anzor Kavazashvili, providing an assist for Valeriy Porkuyan's late winner against Chile in the 1966 group stage.

NATIONAL LEGEND
BATTERING RAMÓN

Argentina's 6-0 win over Peru at the 1978 FIFA World Cup aroused suspicion because the hosts needed to win by four goals to reach the final at the expense of arch-rivals Brazil – and Peruvian goalkeeper Ramón Quiroga had been born in Argentina. He insisted, though, that his saves prevented the defeat from being even more embarrassingly emphatic. Earlier in the same tournament, Quiroga had been booked for a foul on Grzegorz Lato after running into the Polish half of the field.

NATIONAL LEGEND
ITALY'S ELDER STATESMEN

Dino Zoff became both the oldest player and oldest captain to win the FIFA World Cup when Italy lifted the trophy in Spain in 1982. He was 40 years and 133 days old. A predecessor as goalkeeper and captain of both Italy and Juventus, Gianpiero Combi, had led Italy to World Cup glory in 1934. Zoff also holds the record (1,142 minutes) for the longest stretch without conceding in international football, set between 1972 and 1974.

ZOFF

FIFA WORLD CUP MANAGERS

Behind every great team is a tactical mastermind, and the FIFA World Cup has introduced the world to some of the greatest minds football has ever seen.

NATIONAL LEGEND
WAISTCOAT WONDER

England manager **Gareth Southgate** became an unlikely style icon at the 2018 FIFA World Cup by eschewing a suit or tracksuit and wearing a waistcoat during matches. Southgate was the first man to have represented England in semi-finals as both a player (UEFA EURO '96) and a manager (Russia 2018). After missing the decisive penalty that sent England out of UEFA EURO '96, Southgate earned some redemption when he became the first England manager to win a penalty shoot-out at a FIFA World Cup.

DALIĆ

NATIONAL LEGEND
BETTER LATE THAN NEVER

Zlatko Dalić proved at the 2018 FIFA World Cup that a pedigree of club success is not essential to succeed in the national team sphere. Dalić had been working in club football in Saudi Arabia and the United Arab Emirates before being selected to replace Ante Čačić when Croatia struggled in qualifying. Under Dalić, they finished second in the group behind Iceland and reached Russia by defeating Greece in the play-offs. Dalić then varied his tactics masterfully to achieve three wins in the group stage of the finals plus two nerve-jangling victories on penalties and one in extra time to take Croatia to their first final.

27

Juan José Tramutola was the youngest-ever FIFA World Cup finals coach, leading Argentina to the 1930 final at the age of 27 years and 267 days.

TOURNAMENT TRIVIA
DIVIDED LOYALTIES

No coach has won the FIFA World Cup in charge of a foreign team, but several have faced their homeland. These include Jürgen Klinsmann, who played for West Germany when they won the World Cup in 1990 and then managed them to third place in 2006. Klinsmann, who had been in charge of Germany from 2004 to 2006, had already made his home in California, was then appointed coach of the USA in 2011. In the 2014 FIFA World Cup, "Klinsi" and the USA lost 1–0 in a group match to Germany, now led by his former assistant, Joachim Löw, whom he had appointed in 2004.

NATIONAL LEGEND
CRASHING BORA

Only one tournament behind record-holder Carlos Alberto Parreira, **Bora Milutinović** has coached at five different FIFA World Cups – with a different country each time, two of them being the hosts. As well as Mexico in 1986 and the USA in 1994, he led Costa Rica in 1990, Nigeria in 1998 and China PR in 2002. He reached the knockout stages with every country except China PR – who failed to score a single goal.

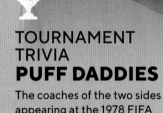

MILUTINOVIC

SCOLARI

71

The oldest manager in the finals was German Otto Rehhagel, aged 71 years and 307 days, when he led Greece in South Africa in 2010.

25

West Germany's Helmut Schön was coach for more FIFA World Cup matches than any other man – 25, across the 1966, 1970, 1974 and 1978 tournaments.

6

Carlos Alberto Parreira holds the record for most FIFA World Cups attended as a coach. Parreira won with Brazil in 1994 and fell at the quarter-finals with them in 2006, but also led Kuwait (1982), the United Arab Emirates (1990), Saudi Arabia (1998) and hosts South Africa (2010).

1

There's only ever been one FIFA World Cup-winning manager who's won the trophy twice: Vittorio Pozzo of Italy, in 1934 and 1938.

TOURNAMENT TRIVIA
PUFF DADDIES

The coaches of the two sides appearing at the 1978 FIFA World Cup final were such prolific smokers that an oversized ashtray was produced for Argentina's César Luis Menotti and the Netherlands's Ernst Happel so they could share it on the touchline. Menotti, the triumphant coach that day, also managed Barcelona and Atlético Madrid in an illustrious managerial career.

NATIONAL LEGEND
DREAM TO NIGHTMARE

Luiz Felipe Scolari quit as Brazil coach after the 2014 FIFA World Cup brought the worst defeat in their history, by 7–1 against Germany in the semi-finals, and then a 3–0 defeat to the Netherlands in the third-place play-off. However, he had won the FIFA World Cup with Brazil in 2002 and went on, with Portugal in 2006, to set an individual record of 11 successive wins at the finals.

LAST TEN COACHES TO WIN FIFA WORLD CUP:

2018: Didier Deschamps, France

2014: Joachim Löw, Germany

2010: Vicente del Bosque, Spain

2006: Marcello Lippi, Italy

2002: Luiz Felipe Scolari, Brazil

1998: Aimé Jacquet, France

1994: Carlos Alberto Parreira, Brazil

1990: Franz Beckenbauer, Germany

1986: Carlos Bilardo, Argentina

1982: Enzo Bearzot, Italy

FIFA WORLD CUP ATTENDANCES

From the modest hundreds of 1930 to the hundreds of thousands who watch these days, FIFA World Cups are all about the fans. Every four years, millions pack into the stadiums to watch the greatest show on Earth.

ATTENDANCE RECORD
RUSHING TO RUSSIA

FIFA claimed a near-perfect attendance rate at the FIFA World Cup 2018 Russia after concern over empty seats at low-profile matches in some of the early group-stage matches. Colin Smith, FIFA's Chief Tournaments & Events Officer, reported an average 98 per cent capacity in the 12 stadiums in the 11 Russian cities. The largest slice of the 2.4m tickets were bought by Russian fans (872,000), with the USA recording the greatest number of foreign sales (88,825). Ticket sales to England supporters, normally amongst the highest in visiting nations, were a disappointing 10th overall – around 33,000 were sold.

7,000,000
More than 7m fans visited Fan Fest sites over the 31 days of the 2018 finals in Russia – an increase of 2m on the totals in Brazil in 2014.

ATTENDANCE RECORD
MORBID MARACANÃ

The largest attendance for a FIFA World Cup match was at Rio de Janeiro's Maracanã for the last clash of the 1950 tournament – though no one is quite sure how many were there. The final tally was officially given as 173,850, though some estimates suggest as many as 210,000 witnessed the host country's traumatic defeat. Tensions were so high at the final whistle; FIFA president Jules Rimet described the crowd's overwhelming silence as "morbid, almost too difficult to bear". Uruguay's triumphant players barricaded themselves inside their dressing room for several hours before they judged it safe enough to emerge.

NATIONAL STADIUM
LUZHNIKI'S NEW LIFE

Moscow's Luzhniki Stadium, which staged seven matches at the 2018 FIFA World Cup, including the opening match and final, is one of sport's historic venues. Originally the Lenin Stadium, it was opened in 1956 as a multi-sport venue with a 100,000 capacity. Major events included the 1980 Olympic Games and it also hosted the finals of the UEFA Champions League in 2008 and the UEFA Cup in 1999. Recent redevelopment meant a 78,011 capacity in a football-specific stadium for the World Cup.

3,587,538
The highest attendance of a FIFA World Cup came in 1994, in the USA, where over 3.5 million people attended matches.

363,000
Only 363,000 people attended the 1934 FIFA World Cup in Italy. At 21,352, it's the lowest average attendance for any tournament.

ATTENDANCE RECORD
CAPACITY PLANNING

The Lusail National Stadium in Qatar, which will host the 2022 FIFA World Cup final, could record the biggest attendance for the competition climax since 1994. The planned capacity for Lusail is 86,250, which would exceed the final attendances recorded at Saint-Denis (1998), Yokohama (2002), Berlin (2006), Johannesburg (2010), Rio de Janeiro's Maracanã (2014) and Moscow (2018) – but not the 94,194 who attended in Pasadena in 1994. Initially Qatar's Supreme Committee for Delivery & Legacy proposed 12 new stadiums, but this was later scaled back to eight. A number of these stadiums will be reduced in size or even dismantled altogether after the finals.

300

The 300 people who were recorded as watching Romania beat Peru 3-1 in 1930 formed the FIFA World Cup finals' smallest attendance, at the Estadio Pocitos in Montevideo. A day earlier, ten times as many people are thought to have been there for France's 4-1 win over Mexico.

ATTENDANCE RECORD
ABSENT FRIENDS

Only 2,823 spectators turned up at the Råsunda Stadium in Stockholm to see Wales play Hungary in a first-round play-off match during the 1958 FIFA World Cup. More than 15,000 had attended the first game between the two sides, but boycotted the replay in tribute to executed Hungarian uprising leader Imre Nagy. It's not the lowest-ever attendance at a FIFA World Cup match, though: that honour goes to Romania v. Peru at Estadio Pocitos in Montevideo, Uruguay, in 1930. Just 300 fans showed their faces.

TOP TEN
FIFA WORLD CUP ATTENDANCES:

1 173,850 – **Maracanã Stadium,**
Rio De Janeiro, Brazil, 1950

2 114,600 – **Azteca Stadium,**
Mexico City, Mexico, 1986

3 107,412 – **Azteca Stadium,**
Mexico City, Mexico, 1970

4 98,000 – **Wembley Stadium,**
London, England, 1966

5 94,194 – **Rose Bowl,**
Pasadena, USA, 1994

6 93,000 – **Estadio Centenario,**
Montevideo, Uruguay, 1930

7 90,000 – **Estadio Santiago Bernabéu,**
Madrid, Spain, 1982

8 84,490 – **Soccer City,**
Johannesburg, South Africa, 2010

9 80,000 – **Stade de France,**
Paris, France, 1998

10 78,011 – **Luzhniki Stadium,**
Moscow, Russia, 2018

107,160

Yet another FIFA World Cup attendance record was set in the Azteca Stadium in 1970, when 107,160 people watched Mexico draw 0-0 with the Soviet Union – the largest ever crowd at a FIFA World Cup opening match. The lowest-attended opening match also included Mexico – a 4-1 loss to France in 1930.

TOURNAMENT TRIVIA
GENDER EQUALITY

Only two stadiums have hosted the finals of the FIFA World Cup for both men and women. The Rose Bowl, in Pasadena, California, was the venue for the men's final in 1994 – when Brazil beat Italy – and the women's showdown between the victorious USA and China PR five years later, which was watched by 90,185 people. But Sweden's Råsunda Stadium, near Stockholm, just about got there first – though it endured a long wait between the men's final in 1958 and the women's in 1995.

FIFA WORLD CUP STADIUMS AND HOSTS

From the hosts with the most to the stadiums where so many classic tournament moments have occurred, the FIFA World Cup has visited almost every corner of the Earth.

INFANTINO

TERRITORIAL GAINS
In 2022, Qatar will become the smallest country ever to host a FIFA World Cup.

FUTURE TOURNAMENT
FUTURE PERFECT

The future of the FIFA World Cup depends more and more on neighbouring countries banding together to play host. **Gianni Infantino**, elected as FIFA President in 2016, has declared himself in favour of co-hosting as a means both to encourage more countries to share organisation of the finals and to guard against the building of "white elephant" stadiums. The USA, Mexico and Canada will host the 2026 tournament and a co-hosting bid for 2030 is planned by Uruguay, Argentina and Paraguay.

FUTURE TOURNAMENTS
THREE-WAY WINNERS

The FIFA World Cup finals in 2026 will make history twice over. Firstly, they will feature 48 teams – playing 80 matches – after world football's governing body decided to open up the finals to more national teams than the current 32 that competed in Russia in 2018. Secondly, staging the finals will be shared between three countries after the USA, Canada and Mexico were awarded hosting rights by the FIFA Congress in Moscow in June 2018. Canada and Mexico will host ten matches each with the USA the other 60, including all ties from the quarter-finals onwards.

HOST HISTORY
ARCHITECTS' PREROGATIVE

Distinctive and creative elements were added to the stadiums built especially for the 2010 FIFA World Cup in South Africa, including the giraffe-shaped towers at Nelspruit's Mbombela Stadium, the 350-metre-long arch with its mobile viewing platform soaring above Durban's main arena, and the white "petals" shrouding the Nelson Mandela Bay Stadium in Port Elizabeth. 2002's Sapporo Dome turned heads for being an indoor arena with a retractable pitch: it was the second stadium to host a FIFA World Cup match "indoors" after the Pontiac Silverdome in 1994.

MOSCOW

HOST HISTORY
RATIONAL IN RUSSIA

Organisers of the 2018 FIFA World Cup in Russia tried to return to the "cluster" system of adjacent venues to ease travel, accommodation and logistical problems around the 11 host cities, thus reducing costs for fans. Two stadiums were used in Moscow – Luzhniki and Spartak. The system was compromised, however, by the use of Ekaterinburg in the far eastern region of European Russia. The "cluster" concept had been abandoned by the French hosts for 1998. Michel Platini, president of the local organising committee, preferred a rotation schedule so the top teams' matches could be spread all around the country.

HOST HISTORY
BERLIN CALL

Despite later becoming the capital of a united Germany, then-divided Berlin only hosted three group games at the 1974 FIFA World Cup in West Germany – the host country's surprise loss to East Germany took place in Hamburg. An unexploded World War II bomb was discovered beneath the seats at Berlin's Olympiastadion in 2002, by workers preparing the ground for the 2006 tournament. Germany, along with Brazil, had applied to host the tournament in 1942, before it was cancelled due to the outbreak of World War II.

HOST HISTORY
MEXICAN SAVE

Mexico was not the original choice to host the 1986 FIFA World Cup, but it stepped in when Colombia withdrew in 1982 due to venue problems. Mexico held on to the staging rights despite suffering from an earthquake in September 1985 that left approximately 10,000 people dead, but which left the stadiums unscathed. The Azteca Stadium went on to become the first venue to host two FIFA World Cup final matches – and Mexico the first country to stage two FIFA World Cups.

23

With 19 games at Azteca Stadium and 4 at Estadio Olimpico Universitario, Mexico City has hosted more FIFA World Cup games than any other city on Earth.

7

Seven stadiums have staged both the final of a FIFA World Cup and the Summer Olympics athletics: Berlin's Olympiastadion, Paris's Stade Colombes, London's Wembley Stadium, Rome's Stadio Olimpico, Munich's Olympiastadion and Moscow's Luzhniki Stadium.

5

Morocco have failed on five attempts to lure the FIFA World Cup to their country, with failed bids in 1994, 1998, 2006, 2010 and 2026. This is a record high.

14

In 1982, Spain spread the FIFA World Cup across 14 venues, still a record for single country hosting the finals.

155

FIFA WORLD CUP PENALTIES

A quick-draw battle of nerves from 12 yards, the penalty shoot-out is either one of the most anticipated moments of a FIFA World Cup, or one of the most dreaded: it often depends on your history...

SCORING RECORD
GERMAN EFFICIENCY

Germany, or West Germany, have won all four of their FIFA World Cup penalty shoot-outs, more than any other team. The run began with a semi-final victory over France in 1982, when goalkeeper Harald Schumacher was the match-winner. West Germany also reached the 1990 final thanks to their shoot-out expertise, this time proving superior to England. In the 2006 quarter-final, Germany's goalkeeper Jens Lehmann consulted a note predicting the direction the Argentinian players were likely to shoot towards. The only German national team to lose a major tournament penalty shoot-out were the West Germans, who contested the 1976 UEFA European Championship final against Czechoslovakia.

8
England and Italy share the record for most players to miss in FIFA World Cup shoot-outs. Notable "missers" include Franco Baresi, Roberto Baggio, Stuart Pearce, Steven Gerrard, and Frank Lampard, the last of whom never scored a FIFA World Cup finals goal.

POULSEN

18
Spain have been awarded the most tournament penalties during regulation time. Of the 18 given, they've converted 15.

TOURNAMENT TRIVIA
WOE FOR ASAMOAH

Ghana striker Asamoah Gyan is the only player to have missed two penalties during match time at FIFA World Cups. He hit the post from a spot kick against the Czech Republic during a group game at the 2006 tournament, then struck a shot against the bar with the final kick of extra time in Ghana's 2010 quarter-final versus Uruguay. Had he scored then, Gyan would have given Ghana a 2-1 win – following Luis Suárez's goal-stopping handball on the goal line – and a first African place in a FIFA World Cup semi-final. Despite such a traumatic miss, Gyan scored Ghana's first penalty in the shoot-out. His team still lost 4-2, though.

TOURNAMENT TRIVIA
DOUBLE TROUBLE

Denmark's **Yussuf Poulsen**, at the 2018 FIFA World Cup, became the first player to concede two penalties in a single tournament since Serbia's Milan Dudić in 2006. In the team's opening game, Poulsen fouled Christian Cueva, but the Peruvian fired his spot kick over the bar and Poulsen made amends by scoring Denmark's winner, then received a yellow card in additional time. In the next game, he not only gave away a penalty against Australia but also collected another yellow card that ruled him out of the final group game, against France. Mile Jedinak scored the equaliser in a 1-1 draw.

LAST FIVE FIFA WORLD CUP PENALTY SHOOT-OUTS:

1 Croatia 4-3 Russia, quarter-final, 2018 (2-2 AET)

2 England 4-3 Colombia, round of 16, 2018 (2-2 AET)

3 Croatia 3-2 Denmark, round of 16, 2018 (1-1 AET)

4 Russia 4-3 Spain, round of 16, 2018 (1-1 AET)

5 Argentina 4-2 Netherlands, semi-final, 2014 (0-0 AET)

SUBAŠIĆ

5
No team has ever scored more than five penalties in a FIFA World Cup shoot-out.

RECENT HISTORY
DANIJEL THE LION

At the 2018 FIFA World Cup in Russia, **Danijel Subašić** of Croatia became the second goalkeeper to save four penalties in shoot-outs in one tournament. The Monaco man saved three against Denmark in a round-of-16 shoot-out and then another in Croatia's quarter-final victory over hosts Russia. Before Subašić, the only other goalkeeper to have saved four kicks in shoot-outs in the same tournament had been Sergio Goycochea of Argentina in the 1990 finals. Goycochea saved two against Yugoslavia in the quarter-final and another two against Italy in the last four to book Argentina's final place.

29

A record 29 penalties were awarded at the 2018 FIFA World Cup in Russia. The sharp rise, from 13 in 2014, was down to the introduction of video assistant referees (VARs).

3-0

The biggest-ever margin in a FIFA World Cup shoot-out came in 2006, when Ukraine defeated Switzerland 3-0 in the round of 16 of the competition.

TOURNAMENT TRIVIA
FRENCH KICKS

The first penalty shoot-out at a FIFA World Cup finals tournament came in the 1982 semi-final in Seville between West Germany and France, when French takers Didier Six and **Maxime Bossis** were the unfortunate players to miss. The same two countries met in the semi-final four years later – and West Germany again won, though in normal time, 2-0. The record for most shoot-outs is shared by the 1990, 2006 and 2018 tournaments, with four each. Both semi-finals in 1990 went to penalties, while the 2006 final was the second to be settled that manner – Italy beating France 5-3, the only miss coming from David Trezeguet, who struck the crossbar.

BOSSIS

BAGGIO

TOURNAMENT TRIVIA
BAGGIO OF DISHONOUR

Pity poor **Roberto Baggio**: the Italian maestro stepped up in three FIFA World Cup penalty shoot-outs, more than any other player – and was a loser in every one. Most painfully, it was his shot over the bar that gifted Brazil the trophy at the end of the 1994 final. He had also ended on the losing side against Argentina in a 1990 semi-final and would do so again, against France in a 1998 quarter-final. At least, in 1990 and 1998, his own attempts were successful.

UEFA EUROPEAN CHAMPIONSHIP

The UEFA European Championship finals have gone from being a four-team curiosity, snubbed by major nations, to perhaps the third-biggest sporting event on earth, behind only the FIFA World Cup and the Summer Olympic Games.

First held: 1960

Current champions: Portugal

Most wins: Germany/ West Germany, Spain, 3

Next edition: various, 2021

1968

The 1968 finals in Italy were used as a backdrop to a famous English-language film – **The Italian Job**, starring Michael Caine – about a British gang who use the cover of the finals to stage a daring gold robbery in Turin.

108

The expanded, 24-team UEFA European Championship in 2016 may have boasted **more goals** than any previous UEFA EUROs – 108 in all. But these came at a rate of just 2.12 per game – the lowest since the 1996 UEFA European Championship's 2.06.

9

In 1984, **Michel Platini** scored more goals than any player in a single UEFA European Championship finals.

PLATINI

3

France have **hosted the tournament three times**, more than any other nation.

BIERHOFF

Germany's **Oliver Bierhoff** scored the first golden goal in the history of the tournament when he hit the winner against the Czech Republic in the UEFA Euro '96 final at Wembley on 30 June.

UEFA EUROPEAN CHAMPIONSHIP QUALIFIERS

The UEFA European Championship qualifying competition is a major event in its own right. For EURO 2020 – now in 2021 – 55 countries entered the group stage. Times had changed dramatically since the inaugural 1960 competition, which featured only 17 nations. For EURO 2020 the top two in all ten groups qualified automatically. The remaining four spots were to be decided by play-offs among the best other finishers.

UEFA EURO 2020 QUALIFYING TOP SCORERS:

1. Harry Kane, England, 12
2. Cristiano Ronaldo, Portugal, 11
   = Eran Zahavi, Israel, 11
4. Teemu Pukki, 10
   = Aleksandar Mitrović, 10

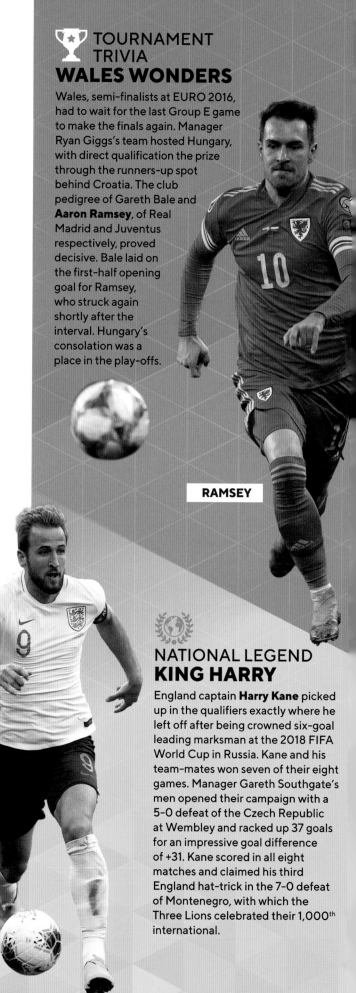

KANE

TOURNAMENT TRIVIA
WALES WONDERS

Wales, semi-finalists at EURO 2016, had to wait for the last Group E game to make the finals again. Manager Ryan Giggs's team hosted Hungary, with direct qualification the prize through the runners-up spot behind Croatia. The club pedigree of Gareth Bale and **Aaron Ramsey**, of Real Madrid and Juventus respectively, proved decisive. Bale laid on the first-half opening goal for Ramsey, who struck again shortly after the interval. Hungary's consolation was a place in the play-offs.

RAMSEY

NATIONAL LEGEND
KING HARRY

England captain **Harry Kane** picked up in the qualifiers exactly where he left off after being crowned six-goal leading marksman at the 2018 FIFA World Cup in Russia. Kane and his team-mates won seven of their eight games. Manager Gareth Southgate's men opened their campaign with a 5-0 defeat of the Czech Republic at Wembley and racked up 37 goals for an impressive goal difference of +31. Kane scored in all eight matches and claimed his third England hat-trick in the 7-0 defeat of Montenegro, with which the Three Lions celebrated their 1,000th international.

TOURNAMENT TRIVIA
MAKING A MARC

Andorra made history by ending their 21-year wait for a first UEFA EURO victory. They defeated Moldova 1-0 at the Estadi Nacional in October 2019 despite playing the last 35 minutes with ten men after a red card for Radu Gînsari. Andorra had lost all 56 of their previous qualifying ties, since starting out against Armenia in September 1998. **Marc Vales** was their match-winning hero.

LUKAKU

TOURNAMENT TRIVIA
RECORD ROM

Belgium's *Red Devils* became the first country to secure a place in the finals when **Romelu Lukaku** scored twice in a 9-0 defeat of San Marino. Lukaku's double took his international tally to 51 and made him the first player to score 50 goals for the *Red Devils*. They wrapped up the campaign with a 100 per cent record of ten victories from ten, having scored 40 goals and conceded a mere three.

VALES

NATIONAL LEGEND
IRRESISTIBLE RONALDO

Cristiano Ronaldo proved he had lost none of his magic touch in the 2020 qualifiers. Captain Cristiano, who had inspired Portugal's triumph in 2016, was on target in the 2-0 victory over Luxembourg which secured their return to the finals. The goal was Ronaldo's 99th for his country and established him as the group's 11-goal leading scorer.

TOURNAMENT TRIVIA
FINALLY FINLAND

Finland reached the finals of a major tournament for the first time after finishing as Group J runners-up behind Italy. Their hero was striker **Teemu Pukki** of England's Norwich City. His ten goals lifted him to third place in Finland's all-time ranking as they ended a run of 32 unsuccessful qualifying campaigns.

PUKKI

UEFA EUROPEAN CHAMPIONSHIP TEAM RECORDS

Over the past 60 years, the UEFA European Championship has grown to become arguably the most important international football tournament after the FIFA World Cup.

TOURNAMENT RECORD
FRANCE BOAST PERFECT RECORD

France, on home soil in 1984, were the first team to win all their matches since the finals expanded beyond four teams. They won them without any shoot-outs too (unlike Spain in 2000), beating Denmark 1-0, Belgium 5-0 and Yugoslavia 3-2 in their group, Portugal 3-2 after extra time in the semi-finals and Spain 2-0 in the final. Michel Platini was the star of the tournament for the French, netting nine goals; Platini went on to pick up his second Ballon d'Or that year.

6-1

The biggest winning margin in a finals tournament was the co-hosts Netherlands' 6-1 victory over Yugoslavia in Rotterdam at UEFA EURO 2000.

17

Just 17 teams entered the first four-team tournament, won by the Soviet Union in 1960 – yet 53 took part in qualifying for the right to join hosts France in a newly expanded 24-team event in 2016.

ALBA

TOURNAMENT TRIVIA
FANCY SEEING YOU AGAIN

When Spain beat Italy 4-0 in the 2012 final, it was the fourth time that UEFA European Championship opponents had faced each other twice in the same tournament. Each time, it followed a first-round encounter. The Netherlands lost to the Soviet Union, then beat them in the 1988 final; Germany beat the Czech Republic twice at UEFA EURO '96, including the final; and Greece did the same to Portugal in 2004. Spain and Italy drew in UEFA EURO 2012's Group C, with Cesc Fàbregas cancelling out Antonio Di Natale's opener for Italy. Their second showdown was rather less even.

TOSS FAVOURS THE HOSTS

Italy reached the 1968 final on home soil thanks to the toss of a coin: the only game in finals history decided in such fashion. Italy drew 0-0 against the Soviet Union after extra time in Naples on 5 June 1968.

TOURNAMENT TRIVIA
SAME OLD SPAIN

Spain not only cruised to the largest winning margin of any UEFA European Championship final by trouncing Italy 4-0 in the climax to 2012 – they also became the first country to successfully defend the title. David Silva, **Jordi Alba** – with his first international goal – and substitutes Fernando Torres and Juan Mata got the goals at Kyiv's Olympic Stadium on 1 July. Spain thus landed their third major trophy in a row, having also won UEFA EURO 2008 and the 2010 FIFA World Cup.

VOGTS

TOURNAMENT TRIVIA
GERMANY IN THE ASCENDANCY

Germany (as West Germany) and Spain have each won the UEFA European Championship three times, although the Germans have played and won the most matches (49 and 26, respectively), as well as scoring and conceding more goals (72 and 48) than any other nation. **Berti Vogts** is the only man to have won the tournament as both a player (1972) and coach (1996), both with the (West) Germans. Portugal's 2016 triumph, in their 35th UEFA European Championship finals match, means England are now the team that has played the most tournament games (31) without ever lifting the trophy.

DELLAS

SCORING RECORD
DELLAS TIMES IT RIGHT FOR GREECE

Greece secured the only "silver goal" victory in EURO history in their 2004 semi-final. (The silver goal rule meant that a team leading after the first period of extra time won the match.) **Traianos Dellas** headed Greece's winner seconds before the end of the first period of extra time against the Czech Republic in Porto on 1 July. Both golden goals and silver goals were abandoned for UEFA EURO 2008, and drawn knockout ties reverted to being decided over the full 30 minutes of extra time, and penalties if necessary.

UEFA EUROPEAN CHAMPIONSHIP WINNERS:

1 3 – West Germany/ Germany
= 3 – Spain

3 2 – France

4 1 – Soviet Union
= 1 – Italy
= 1 – Czechoslovakia
= 1 – Netherlands
= 1 – Denmark
= 1 – Greece
= 1 – Portugal

3

Czechoslovakia's 3-1 semi-final win over the Netherlands in Zagreb, on 16 June 1976, featured a record three red cards.

14

France scored 14 goals at their own EURO in 1984: more than any other nation in a tournament ever.

TOURNAMENT TRIVIA
DENMARK'S UNEXPECTED TRIUMPH

Denmark were unlikely winners of UEFA EURO '92. They had not even expected to take part after finishing behind Yugoslavia in their qualifying group, but they were invited to complete the final eight when Yugoslavia were excluded. Goalkeeper **Peter Schmeichel** was their hero – in the semi-final shoot-out win over the Netherlands and again in the final against Germany, when goals by John Jensen and Kim Vilfort earned the Danes a 2-0 win.

SCHMEICHEL

UEFA EUROPEAN CHAMPIONSHIP PLAYER RECORDS

The UEFA European Championship has played host to some of the continent's greatest footballers over the past 60 years.

SCORING RECORD
KIRICHENKO NETS QUICKEST GOAL

The fastest goal in the history of the finals was scored by Russia forward **Dmitri Kirichenko**. who netted after just 67 seconds to give his side the lead against Greece on 20 June 2004. Russia won 2-1, but Greece still qualified for the quarter-finals – and went on to become shock winners. The fastest goal in the final was Spain midfielder Jesús Pereda's sixth-minute strike in 1964, when Spain beat the Soviet Union 2-1. The latest opening goal was Eder's 109th-minute winner for Portugal against France in the 2016 final.

KIRICHENKO

38

The oldest scorer in finals history is Austria's Ivica Vastić. He was 38 years and 257 days old when he equalised in the 1-1 draw with Poland at UEFA EURO 2008.

TOURNAMENT RECORD
GOLDEN ONE-TOUC

Spain striker Fernando Torres claimed the UEFA EURO 2012 Golden Boot, despite scoring the same number of goals – three – as Italy's Mario Balotelli, Russia's Alan Dzagoev, Germany's Mario Gómez, Croatia's Mario Mandžukić and Portugal's Cristiano Ronaldo. The decision came down to number of assists – with Torres and Gómez level on one apiece – and then the amount of time played. The 92 fewer minutes spent on the pitch by Torres, compared to Gómez, meant his contributions were deemed better value for the prize.

SHEARER

NATIONAL LEGEND
SHEARER TALLY BOOSTS ENGLAND

Alan Shearer is the only Englishman to have topped the finals scoring chart, leading the way with five goals as England lost on penalties to Germany in the UEFA EURO '96 semi-final at Wembley. He netted against Switzerland, Scotland and the Netherlands (two) in the group and gave England a third-minute lead against the Germans. He added two more goals at UEFA EURO 2000 and is behind only Michel Platini and Cristiano Ronaldo in the all-time list.

6

Antoine Griezmann bagged six goals at UEFA EURO 2016 in France, the most since fellow Frenchman Michel Platini scored nine in 1984. Both tournaments were on home soil.

10

The most red cards were shown at EURO 2000, when the ten dismissals included Romania's Gheorghe Hagi, Portugal's Nuno Gomes, Italy's Gianluca Zambrotta and the Czech Republic's Radoslav Látal who, having been sent off at EURO 96, is the only man to be dismissed in two tournaments.

SCORING RECORD
VONLANTHEN BEATS ROONEY RECORD

The youngest scorer in finals history is Switzerland midfielder **Johan Vonlanthen**. He was 18 years and 141 days old when he netted in the Swiss' 3–1 defeat by France on 21 June 2004, beating the record set by England forward Wayne Rooney four days earlier. Rooney was 18 years and 229 days old when he scored the first goal in England's 3–0 win over the Swiss. Vonlanthen retired at the age of 26 in May 2012 due to a knee injury.

VONLANTHEN

SCORING RECORD
PONEDELNIK'S MONDAY MORNING FEELING

Striker Viktor Ponedelnik headed the Soviet Union's extra-time winner to beat Yugoslavia 2–1 in the first final on 10 July 1960 – and sparked some famous headlines in the Soviet media. The game in Paris kicked off at 10pm Moscow time on Sunday, so it was Monday morning when Ponedelnik – whose name means "Monday" in Russian – scored. He said: "When I scored, all the journalists wrote the headline '*Ponedelnik zabivayet v Ponedelnik*' – 'Monday scores on Monday'." This goal, in the 113th minute, remains the latest ever in a European Championship/Nations Cup final.

ILYIN MAKES HISTORY
Anatoli Ilyin of the Soviet Union scored the first-ever goal in the UEFA European Championship when he netted after four minutes in a first-round tie against Hungary on 29 September 1958.

1

Only one man has been sent off in a UEFA European Championship final: France defender Yvon Le Roux, who received a second yellow card with five minutes remaining of his team's 2–0 triumph over Spain in 1984.

NATIONAL LEGEND
BIERHOFF NETS FIRST GOLDEN GOAL

Germany's **Oliver Bierhoff** scored the first golden goal in the history of the tournament when he hit the winner against the Czech Republic in the UEFA EURO '96 final at Wembley on 30 June. (The golden goal rule meant the first team to score in extra time won the match.) Bierhoff netted in the fifth minute of extra time, his shot from 20 yards deflecting off defender Michal Horňák and slipping through goalkeeper Petr Kouba's fingers.

BIERHOFF

TOP SCORERS IN UEFA EURO FINALS HISTORY:

1 Michel Platini, France, 9

= Cristiano Ronaldo, Portugal, 9

3 Alan Shearer, England, 7

4 Nuno Gomes, Portugal, 6

= Antoine Griezmann, France, 6

= Thierry Henry, France, 6

= Zlatan Ibrahimović, Sweden, 6

= Patrick Kluivert, Netherlands, 6

= Wayne Rooney, England, 6

= Ruud van Nistelrooy, Netherlands, 6

UEFA EUROPEAN CHAMPIONSHIP OTHER RECORDS

SAEVARSSON

The UEFA European Championship has provided tons of trivia over the years, from the goal droughts to the host countries and everything in between.

RECENT HISTORY
GOALS AREN'T EVERYTHING

UEFA EURO 2016 was the first edition of the tournament to feature 24 teams competing, and it duly delivered a best-ever return of 108 total goals. The goals per game rate of 2.12, however, fell well short of the UEFA European Championship record – 4.75 at EURO 1976. UEFA EURO 2016's three own goals was another competition record – the unlucky players putting into their own nets were the Republic of Ireland's Ciaran Clark, Northern Ireland's Gareth McAuley and Iceland's **Birkir Már Sævarsson**.

3

Only three red cards were shown at UEFA EURO 2016: the same tally as at each of the 2008 and 2012 UEFA European Championships. In contrast, twice as many players were sent off at the 2004 tournament.

TOURNAMENT RECORD
RECORD UEFA EURO GOAL DROUGHT

Between **Xabi Alonso**'s added-time penalty in Spain's 2-0 quarter-final defeat of France, and Mario Balotelli's 20th-minute semi-final strike for Italy in their 2-1 victory against Germany, UEFA EURO 2012's goalless spell lasted 260 minutes – a UEFA European Championship record. In the goalless interim, Italy drew 0-0 with England before beating them on penalties, and Spain drew 0-0 with Portugal before beating them on penalties, both after extra time.

LAST TEN UEFA EUROPEAN CHAMPIONSHIP FINAL REFEREES:

2016 – **Mark Clattenburg** (England)

2012 – **Pedro Proença** (Portugal)

2008 – **Roberto Rosetti** (Italy)

2004 – **Markus Merk** (Germany)

2000 – **Anders Frisk** (Sweden)

1996 – **Pierluigi Palretto** (Italy)

1992 – **Bruno Galler** (Switzerland)

1988 – **Michel Vautrot** (France)

1984 – **Vojtech Christob** (Czechoslovakia)

1980 – **Nicolae Rainea** (Romania)

ALONSO

3-0

When Greece were drawn against Albania in the first round of the 1964 tournament, the Greeks immediately withdrew, handing Albania a 3-0 walkover win. The countries had technically been at war since 1940.

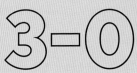

REFEREE TRIVIA
TAKE CLATT

In 2012, Pedro Proença from Portugal achieved the double feat of refereeing the UEFA Champions League final between Chelsea and Bayern Munich and that summer's UEFA European Championship final between Spain and Italy. English referee **Mark Clattenburg** went one better in 2016: he took charge of his homeland's FA Cup final between Manchester United and Crystal Palace, the UEFA Champions League final between Real Madrid and Atlético Madrid in May, and the UEFA European Championship final between France and Portugal in July.

CLATTENBURG

NATIONAL LEGEND
LÖW CONQUERS ALMOST ALL

Germany coach **Joachim Löw** holds the record for the most UEFA European Championship matches and victories in charge. His side's shoot-out victory over Italy in a UEFA EURO 2016 quarter-final took him to 12 victories, before their 2-0 defeat to France in the semi-finals put him on 17 games across the 2008, 2012 and 2016 tournaments. Despite this, Löw has never won the competition; he has however won the FIFA World Cup and FIFA Confederations Cup.

LÖW

2016

The 2016 UEFA European Championship final between hosts France and eventual champions Portugal was the sixth to go to extra time but the first to be goalless after 90 minutes, before Eder's 109th minute winner.

HOST HISTORY
SHARE AND SHARE ALIKE

Ten venues across France were used for the 2016 UEFA European Championship. This equalled the record set by Portugal in 2004, and was two more than the eight stadiums that were used in the three shared tournaments (four in each country): Belgium and the Netherlands in 2000; Austria and Switzerland in 2008; and Poland and Ukraine in 2012. It will be all change for the finals in 2021, however, as, for the first time, the first-round group stage and first two knock-out rounds will be played across 12 cities in 12 different countries. England will have the honour of hosting both semi-finals and the final, with all three to be played at London's Wembley Stadium.

HOST HISTORY
HOSTS WITH THE ALMOST

In 2000, Belgium and the Netherlands began the trend for co-hosting the UEFA European Championship finals – the first time the tournament had been staged in more than one country. The opening game was Belgium's 2-1 win over Sweden in Brussels on 10 June, with the final taking place in Rotterdam. Austria and Switzerland co-hosted UEFA EURO 2008, starting in Basel and climaxing in Vienna, before Poland and Ukraine teamed up in 2012. Warsaw staged the opening match and Kyiv was the host city for the final.

76,833

The EURO 2016 final between France and Portugal could not claim the event's biggest crowd. Instead, that honour went to the French hosts' 5-2 victory over Iceland in the quarter-finals, watched at the Stade de France by 76,833 spectators.

1992

Players wore their names as well as their numbers on the back of their shirts for the first time at UEFA EURO '92. They had previously been identified only by numbers.

UEFA NATIONS LEAGUE

LÖW

The UEFA Nations League was devised as a competition to replace increasingly unpopular friendly matches. Mooted first in 2011, it was finally unveiled in 2017. Europe's 55 national teams were ranked according to a coefficient and distributed among across four divisions. Promotion and relegation would decide the divisions' make-up for the event's second edition in the autumn of 2020.

NATIONAL LEGEND
LÖW'S HIGH EXPECTATIONS

Germany coach **Joachim Löw** emerged as an early advocate for the UEFA Nations League after his team were drawn in the top group of League A against France and the Netherlands. Löw said: "I like these kind of games against big nations with very good players. It's interesting for us, for our players and of course for our fans. It's better than the friendly games we have sometimes. I'm really happy." Löw was not so happy, however, after Germany lost a 2-0 lead in their last game against the Dutch and were relegated after a 2-2 draw. The Netherlands went on to the finals.

16

The UEFA Nations League consists of 16 groups in total, spread across four divisions, with each containing either three or four teams.

STAR PLAYER
PICK THAT ONE OUT

Jordan Pickford was England's penalty shoot-out hero in the third-place victory over Switzerland. The Everton goalkeeper not only saved from Josip Drmić in the shootout but converted his own spot-kick as the Three Lions won 6-5 on penalties. This was England's second shootout success in a year after victory over Colombia in the second round of the 2018 FIFA World Cup. England thus finished third in a senior tournament for the first time since the 1968 UEFA European Championship. They had reached the finals when late goals from Jesse Lingard and Harry Kane earned a 2-1 win over Croatia, which sent them top of Group A4 and relegated the FIFA World Cup runners-up.

PICKFORD

TOURNAMENT TRIVIA
GIBRALTAR ROCKS

Some of the primary beneficiaries of the UEFA Nations League were smaller nations, who were given opportunities to play more competitive matches against opposition of a similar standard. One such country was Gibraltar who managed to notch their first ever competitive wins in their League D matches against Armenia and then Liechtenstein. Joseph Chipolina was the hero in both games, nabbing the winning goal in each.

TOURNAMENT TRIVIA
AN UNEXPECTED SUCCESS

UEFA was so happy with the initial reaction of broadcasters and sponsors that it increased the UEFA Nations League prize money. The overall winning country was promised EUR 10.5m, up from the original EUR 7.5m. UEFA said the pay rise had been enabled by its own "solid financial situation" and "earnings from UEFA EURO 2016".

UEFA NATIONS LEAGUE A

	PLAYED	WON	DRAWS	LOST	FOR	AGAINST	POINTS
GROUP 1							
Netherlands	4	2	1	1	8	4	7
France	4	2	1	1	4	4	7
Germany	4	0	2	2	3	7	2
GROUP 2							
Switzerland	4	3	0	1	14	5	9
Belgium	4	3	0	1	9	6	9
Iceland	4	0	0	4	1	13	0
GROUP 3							
Portugal	4	2	2	0	5	3	8
Italy	4	1	2	1	2	2	5
Poland	4	0	2	2	4	6	2
GROUP 4							
England	4	2	1	1	6	5	7
Spain	4	2	0	2	12	7	6
Croatia	4	1	1	2	4	10	4

SEMI-FINALS

Portugal 3–1 Switzerland
Netherlands 3–1 England (AET)

THIRD PLACE PLAY-OFF

England 0–0 Switzerland
(6-5 on pens, aet)

FINAL

Portugal 1–0 Netherlands

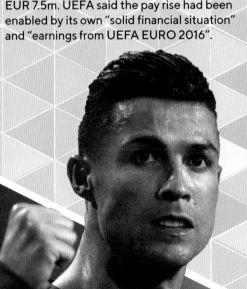

53

Cristiano Ronaldo's 53rd career hat-trick fired Portugal into the UEFA Nations League final with a 3-1 win over Switzerland. It was his seventh treble for his country.

RONALDO

GUEDES

TOURNAMENT TRIVIA
PORTUGUESE PREMIERE

Hosts Portugal won the inaugural UEFA Nations League in June 2019 to make eventual amends for defeat in front of their own fans in the UEFA EURO 2004 final. Back then, a teenaged Cristiano Ronaldo was among the tearful runners-up. Some 15 years later he was captain and three-goal leading scorer as his Portuguese team defeated the Netherlands 1-0 in the final in Porto. **Gonçalo Guedes** scored the goal.

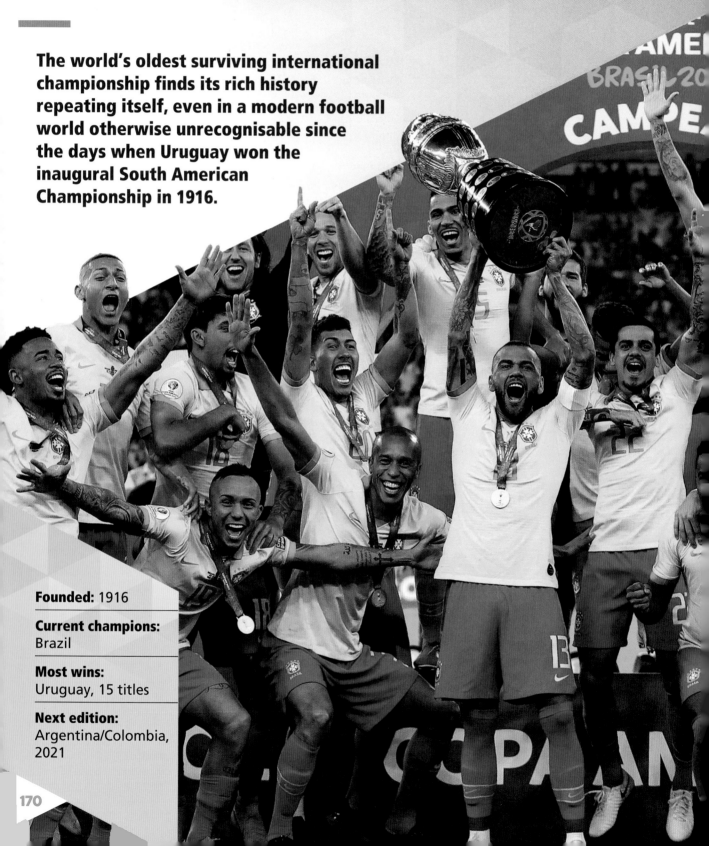

COPA AMÉRICA

The world's oldest surviving international championship finds its rich history repeating itself, even in a modern football world otherwise unrecognisable since the days when Uruguay won the inaugural South American Championship in 1916.

Founded: 1916

Current champions:
Brazil

Most wins:
Uruguay, 15 titles

Next edition:
Argentina/Colombia, 2021

2

Colombia and Argentina will stage the *Copa América* in 2021, rescheduled from 2020. This will be the first multi-nation hosting since the home-and-away mini-league system was dropped in 1983.

In 1984, CONMEBOL adopted the policy of rotating the right to host the *Copa América* among the ten member associations.

3

The *Copa América* has been hosted across the whole continent three times (1975, 1979, 1983).

In 1916, the current *Copa América* trophy was purchased from Casa Escasany, a jewellery shop in Buenos Aires, at the cost of 3,000 Swiss francs.

Across more than 100 years of the *Copa América*, there have been only three editions in which neither Argentina nor Brazil finished in the top four (1939, 2001, 2011).

COPA AMÉRICA TEAM RECORDS

South America was the first region to organise its own confederation, which led to the creation, in 1916, of the South American Championship. Four countries contested that opening tournament – hosts Argentina as well as Brazil, Chile and Uruguay, who were the inaugural winners.

NATIONAL LEGEND
HOW IT STARTED

The first South American "Championship of Nations", as it was then known, was held in Argentina from 2 to 17 July 1916 during the country's independence centenary commemorations. The tournament was won by Uruguay, who drew with Argentina in the last match of the tournament. It was an inauspicious beginning. The 16 July encounter had to be abandoned at 0–0 when fans invaded the pitch and set the wooden stands on fire. The match was continued at a different stadium the following day and still ended goalless ... but Uruguay ended up topping the mini-league table and were hailed as the first champions.

GRADÍN

3

19-year-old Uruguayan **Isabelino Gradín** was the inaugural tournament's top scorer with three goals. The event also saw the foundation of the South American confederation CONMEBOL, which took place a week into the competition on 9 July 1916.

150

The longest match in the history of the *Copa América* was the 1919 final between Brazil and Uruguay. It lasted 150 minutes, 90 minutes of regular time plus two extra-time periods of 30 minutes each.

DYBALA

COPA AMÉRICA TITLES:

1 **Uruguay, 15** (1916, 1917, 1920, 1923, 1924, 1926, 1935, 1942, 1956, 1959, 1967, 1983, 1987, 1995, 2011)

2 **Argentina, 14** (1921, 1925, 1927, 1929, 1937, 1941, 1945, 1946, 1947, 1955, 1957, 1959, 1991, 1993)

3 **Brazil, 9** (1919, 1922, 1949, 1989, 1997, 1999, 2004, 2007, 2019)

4 **Peru, 2** (1939, 1975)
= **Paraguay, 2** (1939, 1979)
= **Chile, 2** (2015, 2016)

7 **Bolivia, 1** (1963)
= **Colombia, 1** (2001)

TOURNAMENT TRIVIA
RECORD-BREAKERS

Argentina, despite finishing only third in the 2019 *Copa América*, maintained their proud record of having achieved the most victories in the history of the tournament: 122. The Argentinians have also scored the most goals with 462, the last of which was claimed by **Paulo Dybala** in the 2-1 victory over Chile in the third-place play-off in Brazil. Less happily, Argentina also share with Uruguay the record of five defeats in penalty shoot-outs. Lionel Messi & Co lost to Chile on penalties in the finals of the both the 2015 *Copa* and the 2016 *Copa Centenario*.

TOURNAMENT TRIVIA
SUB-STANDARD

During the 1953 *Copa América*, Peru were awarded a walkover win when Paraguay tried to make one more substitution than they were allowed. Would-be substitute Milner Ayala was so incensed that he kicked English referee Richard Maddison and was banned from football for three years. Yet Paraguay remained in the tournament and went on to beat Brazil in the final – minus, of course, the disgraced Ayala. The entire tournament was staged at the Estadio Nacional de Perú.

TOURNAMENT TRIVIA
HISTORY MEN

Four nations entered the inaugural *Copa América* when it launched in 1916: Argentina, Brazil, Chile and Uruguay. Bolivia, Colombia, Ecuador, Paraguay, Peru and Venezuela had all joined by 1967. In 1910, an unofficial South American championship was won by Argentina, who beat Uruguay 4-1 in the decider – although the final match had been delayed a day after rioting fans burnt down a stand at the Gimnasia stadium in Buenos Aires.

TOURNAMENT TRIVIA
WELCOME VISITORS

Nine guest nations have appeared in the *Copa América*. **Mexico**, from Central America, have not only been the most frequent guests with ten appearances but they nearly achieved what would have been embarrassing victories in 1993 and 2001, when they reached the final before losing 2-1 to Argentina and 1-0 to Colombia respectively. Four guests have appeared only once: Honduras (2001), Haiti and Panama (both in 2016), and Australia (2020).

0

Paraguay reached the 2011 final despite not winning a single game in normal play. Instead, they drew all three matches in the first-round group stage, then needed penalties to win their quarter-final against Brazil and semi-final versus Venezuela after both games ended goalless.

HOSTING RIGHTS BY COUNTRY:

1 **Argentina, 10** (1916, 1921, 1925, 1929, 1937, 1946, 1959, 1987, 2011, 2021)

2 **Chile, 7** (1920, 1926, 1941, 1945, 1955, 1991, 2015)

= Uruguay, 7 (1917, 1923, 1924, 1942, 1956, 1967, 1995)

3 **Peru, 6** (1927, 1935, 1939, 1953, 1957, 2004)

4 **Brazil, 5** (1919, 1922, 1949, 1989, 2019)

TOURNAMENT TRIVIA
MORE FROM MORENO

Argentina were not only responsible for the *Copa América*'s biggest win, but also the tournament's highest-scoring game, when they put 12 past Ecuador in 1942 – to no reply. José Manuel Moreno's five strikes in that game included the 500th goal in the competition's history. Moreno, born in Buenos Aires on 3 August 1916, ended that tournament as joint top scorer with team-mate Herminio Masantonio – hitting seven goals. Both men ended their international careers with 19 goals for their country, although Moreno did so in 34 appearances – compared to Masantonio's 21. Masantonio scored four in the defeat of Ecuador.

31

In 1942, Ecuador and their goalkeeper Napoléon Medina conceded more goals in one tournament than any other team, when they let in 31 goals across six games – and six defeats.

ARISTIZÁBAL

11

In 2001, Colombia, who went on to win the trophy for the first and only time in their history, became the only country to go through an entire *Copa América* campaign without conceding a single goal. They scored 11 themselves, more than half of them from six-goal tournament top scorer **Victor Aristizábal**.

COPA AMÉRICA PLAYER RECORDS

For more than a century, the *Copa América* has showcased the very best of South America's football talent on the pitch. Unsurprisingly, its goalscoring and appearance records read as a who's who of the continent's most enduring footballing superstars.

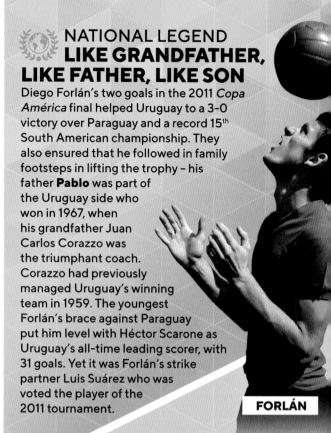

NATIONAL LEGEND
LIKE GRANDFATHER, LIKE FATHER, LIKE SON

Diego Forlán's two goals in the 2011 *Copa América* final helped Uruguay to a 3-0 victory over Paraguay and a record 15th South American championship. They also ensured that he followed in family footsteps in lifting the trophy – his father **Pablo** was part of the Uruguay side who won in 1967, when his grandfather Juan Carlos Corazzo was the triumphant coach. Corazzo had previously managed Uruguay's winning team in 1959. The youngest Forlán's brace against Paraguay put him level with Héctor Scarone as Uruguay's all-time leading scorer, with 31 goals. Yet it was Forlán's strike partner Luis Suárez who was voted the player of the 2011 tournament.

FORLÁN

NATIONAL LEGEND
FROG PRINCE

Chilean goalkeeper Sergio Livingstone holds the record for the most *Copa América* appearances, with 34 games from 1941 to 1953. Livingstone, nicknamed "The Frog", was voted the player of the tournament in 1941 – becoming the first goalkeeper to win the award – and he might have played even more *Copa América* matches had he not missed out on the 1946 competition. Livingstone, born in Santiago on 26 March 1920, spent almost his entire career in his home country – save for a season with Argentina's Racing Club in 1943–44. Overall, he made 52 appearances for Chile between 1941 and 1954 before retiring and becoming a popular TV journalist and commentator.

NATIONAL LEGEND
MAGIC ÁLEX

Ecuador's Álex Aguinaga, a midfielder born in Ibarra on 9 July 1969, played a total of 109 times for his country – 25 of them in the *Copa América*, a competition that yielded four of his 23 international goals. His *Copa América* career certainly began well: Ecuador went undefeated for his first four appearances, at the 1987 and 1989 events, but his luck had ran out by the time his Ecuador career was coming to an end: he lost his final seven *Copa América* matches.

MÉNDEZ

OVERALL TOP SCORERS:

1 **Norberto Méndez** (Argentina), 17
= **Zizinho** (Brazil), 17
3 **Teodoro Fernández** (Peru), 15
= **Severino Varela** (Uruguay), 15
5 **Paolo Guerrero** (Peru), 14

1917
The first *Copa América* own goal was scored by Chile's Luis García, giving Argentina a 1-0 win in 1917, the second edition of the tournament.

8

When Álex Aguinaga lined up for Ecuador against Uruguay in his country's opening game at the 2004 event, he became only the second man to take part in eight different *Copa Américas* – joining legendary Uruguayan goalscorer Ángel Romano.

MOST GAMES PLAYED:

1 **Sergio Livingstone** (Chile), 34

2 **Zizinho** (Brazil), 33

3 **Leonel Álvarez** (Colombia), 27

= **Carlos Valderrama** (Colombia), 27

= **Lionel Messi** (Argentina), 27

NATIONAL LEGEND
START TO FINISH

Colombia playmaker Carlos Valderrama and defensive midfielder **Leonel Álvarez** played in all 27 of their country's *Copa América* matches between 1987 and 1995, winning ten, drawing ten and losing seven – including third-place finishes in 1987, 1993 and 1995. Valderrama's two *Copa América* goals came in his first and final appearances in the competition – in a 2-0 victory over Bolivia in 1987 and a 4-1 defeat of the USA eight years later.

17

Brazilian forward Zizinho jointly holds the all-time goalscoring record for the *Copa América*, along with Argentina's Norberto Méndez. Both men struck 17 goals, Zizinho across six tournaments and Méndez three.

4-0
The first-ever *Copa América* goal, in 1916, was scored by José Piendibene – setting Uruguay on the way to a 4-0 triumph over Chile.

ÁLVAREZ

NATIONAL LEGEND
REPEATING THE FEAT

Gabriel Batistuta is the only Argentinian to have twice won the award for leading marksman at the *Copa América*. He made his *Albiceleste* debut only days before the 1991 event in which his six goals – including a crucial strike in the concluding match (it was a mini group as opposed to a final) victory over Colombia – earned a transfer from Boca Juniors to Fiorentina. Nicknamed "Batigol" in Italy, he was joint top scorer in 1995, with four goals, along with Mexico's Luis García.

BATISTUTA

5

Four players have scored five goals in one *Copa América* game: Héctor Scarone was the first in Uruguay's 6-0 win over Bolivia in 1926.

NATIONAL LEGEND
PELÉ'S INSPIRATION

Brazilian forward **Zizinho** shares the all-time goalscoring record in the *Copa América*, along with Argentina's Norberto Méndez. Méndez was top scorer once and runner-up twice and won championship medals on all three occasions, while Zizinho's 17 goals helped Brazil take the title once, in 1949. Zizinho, Pelé's footballing idol, would emerge from the 1950 FIFA World Cup as Brazil's top scorer and he was also voted the tournament's best player – but was forever traumatised by the hosts' surprise defeat to Uruguay that cost Brazil the title.

ZIZINHO

OTHER *COPA AMÉRICA* RECORDS

Format changes, guest teams and a highly competitive field have meant that the *Copa América* rarely looks the same from one edition to the next. Nevertheless, a number of records have stood the test of time.

NASAZZI

38

Uruguay have a unique record in remaining unbeaten in 38 *Copa América* games on home turf, all played in the country's capital Montevideo – comprising 31 wins and seven draws.

TROPHY-WINNING COACHES:

1 **Guillermo Stábile**, 6 (Argentina 1941, 1945, 1946, 1947, 1955, 1957)

2 **Alfio Basile**, 2 (Argentina 1991, 1993)

= **Juan Carlos Corazzo**, 2 (Uruguay 1959, 1967)

= **Ernesto Fígoli**, 2 (Uruguay 1920, 1926)

3 (34 coaches on 1 title each)

NATIONAL LEGEND
KEEP COMING BACK

Hérnan Dario Gómez coached Panama at the 2016 *Copa América Centenario*, making him only the third man to manage at six different *Copa América* tournaments. He was joined three years later by Óscar Washington Tabárez, who took charge of Uruguay at a sixth *Copa América* in 2019, having been in charge in 1989, 2007, 2011, 2015 and 2016. Dario Gómez previously led his native Colombia in 1995, 1997 and 2011, and Ecuador in 2001 and 2004.

GÓMEZ

44

Guillermo Stábile solely holds the record for managing most *Copa América* matches (44), followed by Chile's Luis Tirado (35), Paraguay's Manuel Fleitas Solich (33), and Uruguay's Óscar Tabárez (30).

STÁBILE

NATIONAL LEGEND
MULTI-TASKING

Argentina's **Guillermo Stábile** coached Argentina from 1939 to 1960, having been appointed at the age of just 34. He was in charge for 123 games, winning 83 of them – and still managed to coach three clubs on the side at different times throughout his reign. He remained as Red Star Paris manager during his first year in the Argentina role, then led Argentine club Huracán for the next nine years – before leading domestic rivals Racing Club from 1949 to 1960. Stábile's Argentina missed out on *Copa América* success in 1949, but that year brought the first of three Argentina league championships in a row for Stábile's Racing Club.

SCORING RECORD
GOALS AT A PREMIUM

In terms of goals per game, the 2011 *Copa América* was the second tightest of all time – with only 54 strikes hitting the back of the net in 26 matches, at an average of 2.08 per game. The 1922 tournament, in Brazil, saw even fewer – 22 goals in 11 games, an average of two per game. Both competitions were a far cry from the prolific 1927 event in Peru, where 37 goals across six games averaged out at 6.17. The 91 goals in 2016 came at an average of 2.84 per match.

6

Argentina's Guillermo Stábile not only holds the record for most *Copa América* triumphs as a coach – he trounces all opposition. He led his country to the title on no fewer than six occasions – in 1941, 1945, 1946, 1947, 1955 and 1957. No other coach has lifted the trophy more than twice.

6

Six overseas "guests" were invited to play in the special *Copa América* Centenario tournament in 2016: Costa Rica, Haiti, Jamaica, Mexico, Panama and the USA, who were also the hosts.

TOURNAMENT TRIVIA
AWAY WINNERS

Only four men have coached a country other than their native one to *Copa América* glory. The first was Englishman Jack Greenwell, with Peru in 1939. Brazilian Danilo Alvim was the second to do it, with Bolivia in 1963 – against Brazil. History repeated itself in 2015 and 2016, when Argentina-born Jorge Sampaoli and then Juan Antonio Pizzi took Chile to *Copa* glory, both times beating Argentina in final penalty shoot-outs.

TOURNAMENT TRIVIA
SEEING RED

Brazil may have the worst FIFA World Cup disciplinary record, but neighbours Uruguay assume that unenviable position in the *Copa América*. Uruguayan players have been sent off 32 times – the latest being **Matías Vecino** against Mexico in 2016 – followed by Argentina on 25 dismissals, Peru (24), Brazil and Venezuela (21 each), Chile (19), Paraguay (15), Bolivia and Ecuador (13 apiece), Colombia (11), Mexico (ten), the United States (three), Costa Rica (two), and Honduras, Jamaica, Japan and Panama (one each).

VECINO

INVITED GUESTS:

1 **Mexico**, 10

2 **Costa Rica**, 5

3 **USA**, 4

4 **Jamaica**, 2
= **Japan**, 2
= **Qatar**, 2

7 **Honduras**, 1
= **Haiti**, 1
= **Panama**, 1
= **Australia**, 1

21

It took 21 years, but Uruguay's Juan Emilio Piríz became the first *Copa América* player to be sent off, against Chile in 1937.

CAF AFRICA CUP OF NATIONS

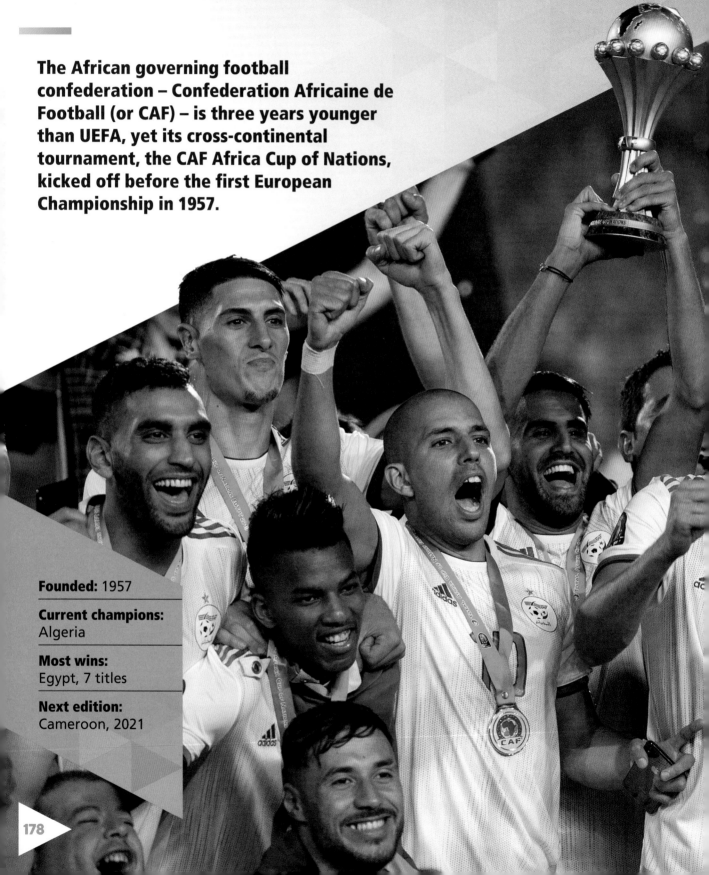

The African governing football confederation – Confederation Africaine de Football (or CAF) – is three years younger than UEFA, yet its cross-continental tournament, the CAF Africa Cup of Nations, kicked off before the first European Championship in 1957.

Founded: 1957

Current champions:
Algeria

Most wins:
Egypt, 7 titles

Next edition:
Cameroon, 2021

6

Six different nations won titles from 1970 to 1980: Sudan, Congo DR, Zaire, Morocco, Ghana, and Nigeria.

As of 2013, the CAF Africa Cup of Nations was switched to being held in odd-numbered years so as not to clash with the FIFA World Cup.

11

The UNAF (North Africa) regional federation has won more titles than any other in Africa.

24

24 teams competed in the 2019 tournament, an increase from 16 in 2017.

The original CAF Africa Cup of Nations trophy was the Abdelaziz Abdallah Salem Trophy, named after the first CAF President, Egyptian Abdelaziz Abdallah Salem.

AFRICA CUP OF NATIONS TEAM RECORDS

Only three nations competed in the inaugural 1957 Africa Cup of Nations, while while 51 vied for the 24 slots at the 2019 event. Egypt were late replacements as hosts, so participated in qualifying. The three countries not to play were Chad, Eritrea and Somalia.

TOURNAMENT TRIUMPHS:

1 **7 – Egypt** (1957, 1959, 1986, 1998, 2006, 2008, 2010)

2 **5 – Cameroon** (1984, 1988, 2000, 2002, 2017)

3 **4 – Ghana** (1963, 1965, 1978, 1982)

4 **3 – Nigeria** (1980, 1994, 2013)

5 **2 – Côte d'Ivoire** (1992, 2015)

= **Zaire/Congo DR, 2** (1968, 1974)

= **Algeria, 2** (1990, 2019)

⭐ TOURNAMENT TRIVIA
FROM TRAGEDY TO TRIUMPH

Zambia's unexpected glory at the 2012 CAF Africa Cup of Nations was fitting and poignant as the setting for their glory was just a few hundred metres from the scene of earlier tragedy. The 2012 players spent the day before the final against Côte d'Ivoire laying flowers in the sea in tribute to the 30 people who died when a plane crashed off the coast of Gabonese city Libreville on 27 April 1993. The victims that day included 18 Zambian internationals flying to Senegal for a FIFA World Cup qualifier. After the 2012 final, in which Zambia beat Côte d'Ivoire on penalties following a goalless draw after extra time, coach Hervé Renard dedicated the victory to those who lost their lives in 1993.

2

The 2012 event was only the second to be shared between two host nation – Equatorial Guinea and Gabon – after Ghana and Nigeria shared duties in 2000.

⭐ TOURNAMENT TRIVIA
REIGNING PHARAOHS

Egypt dominate the CAF Africa Cup of Nations records. They won the first tournament, in 1957, having been helped by a bye to the final when semi-final opponents South Africa were disqualified, and they have emerged as champions another six times since – more than any other country. Their victories in 2006, 2008 and 2010 make them the only country to have lifted the trophy three times in a row. They have also appeared in a record 24 tournaments, one more than Côte d'Ivoire and two more than Ghana.

4

Ghana's *Black Stars* are still the only team to reach the final of four consecutive Africa Cup of Nations, lifting the trophy in 1963 and 1965 and finishing as runners-up in 1968 and 1970.

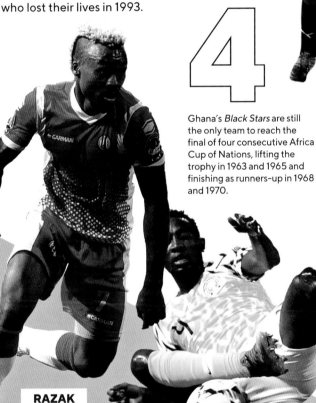

RAZAK

⭐ TOURNAMENT TRIVIA
FOUR SHAME

Hosts Angola were responsible for perhaps the most dramatic collapse in Africa Cup of Nations history, when they threw away a four-goal lead in the opening match of the 2010 tournament. Even more embarrassingly, they were leading 4-0 against Mali with just 11 minutes left, in the capital Luanda's Estadio 11 de Novembro. Mali's final two goals, by Barcelona's Seydou Keita and Boulogne's Mustapha Yatabaré, were scored deep into stoppage time. Mali failed to make it past the first round, while Angola went out in the quarter-finals.

⭐ TOURNAMENT TRIVIA
THE WAITING IS THE HARDEST PART

Some 12 of the 54 full members of CAF have yet to appear in the finals of the Cup of Nations. The latest newcomers to join the party were Burundi, Madagascar and Mauritania in 2019 – with Madagascar especially causing a stir by reaching the quarter-finals. Mauritania made it there thanks to a 2-1 victory over Botswana in November 2018, with both their goals scored by forward Ismaël Diakité – while Burundi were spearheaded by striker **Fiston Abdul Razak** who struck four times that month in their 5-2 defeat of South Sudan. Still waiting to make their first finals are Central African Republic, Chad, Comoros, Djibouti, Eritrea, Gambia, Lesotho, São Tomé and Príncipe, Seychelles, Somalia, Eswatini (Swaziland) and South Sudan. The latter only made their qualifying debut in 2015.

24

Côte d'Ivoire have won two of the highest-scoring penalty shoot-outs in full international history – they defeated Ghana 11-10 over 24 penalties in the 1992 Africa Cup of Nations final, and Cameroon 12-11, over the same number of kicks, in the quarter-finals of the 2006 Africa Cup of Nations.

3

In 2012, both Côte d'Ivoire and Zambia were competing in their third Africa Cup of Nations final, Côte d'Ivoire having won in 1992 and lost in 2006, while Zambia had finished as runners-up in 1974 and 1994.

CAF AFRICA CUP OF NATIONS PLAYER RECORDS

The global prominence of the CAF Africa Cup of Nations has also grown, especially when the spotlight fell on major African stars taking time off from European club duties every other January. Now, more than ever, the tournament is a showcase for many of the most talented and successful players in the sport.

8

Ghana striker Asamoah Gyan became the third man to appear at eight different CAF Africa Cup of Nations tournaments when he captained the side in 2019, following Cameroon's Rigobert Song and Egypt's Ahmed Hassan.

🏆 TOURNAMENT TRIVIA
SIBLING HARMONY

Both teams in the final of the 2015 CAF Africa Cup of Nations called upon a pair of brothers. Runners-up Ghana included Jordan and André Ayew, while Côte d'Ivoire's champions were spearheaded by captain **Yaya Touré** and his centre-back brother Kolo. . All four brothers took penalties in the 2015 final and scored, unlike in 2012, when Côte d'Ivoire were beaten in another penalty shoot-out, this time by Zambia. Yaya had been substituted in extra time, but Kolo missed in the 8-7 loss. Zambia's triumphant captain in 2012, player of the tournament Christian Katongo, had his brother Felix among his team-mates – he came off the bench – and they both scored in that shoot-out.

TOURÉ

1957
The first CAF Africa Cup of Nations goal was a penalty scored by Egypt's Raafat Ateya in the 21st minute of their 2-1 semi-final win over Sudan in 1957.

ETO'O

ALL-TIME TOP SCORERS:

1 **Samuel Eto'o** (Cameroon), 18
2 **Laurent Pokou** (Côte d'Ivoire), 14
3 **Rashidi Yekini** (Nigeria), 13
4 **Hassan El-Shazly** (Egypt), 12
5 **André Ayew** (Ghana), 11
  = **Didier Drogba** (Côte d'Ivoire), 11
  = **Hossam Hassan** (Egypt), 11
  = **Patrick Mboma** (Cameroon), 11

NATIONAL LEGEND 🏅
SAM THE MAN

Cameroon's Samuel Eto'o, who made his full international debut – away to Costa Rica on 9 March 1997 – one day short of his 16th birthday, is the CAF Africa Cup of Nations' all-time leading goalscorer. He was part of Cameroon's victorious teams in 2000 and 2002, but had to wait until 2008 to pass Laurent Pokou's 14-goal CAF Africa Cup of Nations record. That year's competition took his overall tally to 16 goals – only for the former Real Madrid and Barcelona striker, to add another two in 2010. In 2005, Eto'o became the first player to be named African Footballer of the Year three years running.

⚝◎ STAR PLAYER
MANÉ MAKES HIS MARK

The timing of the CAF Africa Cup of Nations has often fallen during the middle of European club season, as it did when Senegal's **Sadio Mané** left Liverpool to play at the finals in Gabon in January 2017. Liverpool bought Mané for GBP 30m in 2016, making him, at the time, the most expensive African player. Mané won the 2019 UEFA Champions League final with Liverpool in June 2019 but said he would happily trade that for victory in the CAF Africa Cup of Nations final in Egypt the following month, only to end the game forlorn as Senegal were beaten 1-0 by Algeria. This was their second runners-up finish after losing the 2002 final on penalties to Cameroon.

MANÉ

SINGLE TOURNAMENT TOP SCORERS:

1 **Ndaye Mulamba** (Zaire), 9 – 1974

2 **Laurent Pokou** (Côte d'Ivoire), 8 – 1970

3 **Hossam Hassan** (Egypt), 8 – 1998

= **Benni McCarthy** (South Africa), 8 – 1998

5 **Hassan El Shazly** (Egypt), 6 – 1963

= **Laurent Pokou** (Côte d'Ivoire), 6 – 1968

🏵 NATIONAL LEGEND
NO HASSLE FOR HASSAN

Egypt's **Ahmed Hassan** not only became the first footballer to play in the final of four different CAF Africa Cup of Nations in 2010 – he also became the first to collect his fourth winners' medal. Earlier in the same tournament, his appearance in the quarter-final against Cameroon gave him his 170th cap – an Egyptian record. Hassan marked the game with three goals – one in his own net and two past Cameroon goalkeeper Carlos Kameni – although one appeared not to cross the line.

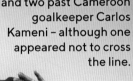

POKOU

Côte d'Ivoire striker Laurent Pokou scored a record five goals in one CAF Africa Cup of Nations match as his side trounced Ethiopia 6-1 in the first round of the 1968 tournament. He finished top scorer at that tournament, and the following one – although he ended both without a winner's medal.

HASSAN

🏵 NATIONAL LEGEND
YO, YOBO

Nigeria's **Joseph Yobo** was brought on as a late substitute to the fans' acclaim in the closing minutes of the *Super Eagles'* victory over Burkina Faso in the 2013 CAF Africa Cup of Nations final in Johannesburg, South Africa. As captain, the one-time Marseille and Everton defender then had the honour of lifting the trophy. Yobo retired from international football in 2014, having made a record 101 appearances in his 13-year career.

No player has scored more goals in one CAF Africa Cup of Nations than Zaire's Ndaye Mulamba's nine during the 1974 tournament.

YOBO

OTHER CAF AFRICA CUP OF NATIONS RECORDS

Stephen Keshi – known to admiring fans as "Big Boss" – became only the second man to win the CAF Africa Cup of Nations as both player and manager when he led Nigeria to the title in 2013. He had previously lifted the trophy as captain in 1994. He tragically passed away in 2016, aged just 54.

KESHI

More different countries have won the African Cup of Nations than any other continental championship, with glory being shared among 14 separate nations – including Africa's three largest countries, Sudan, Algeria and Congo DR.

TOURNAMENT TRIVIA
ATAK ATTACKS

South Sudan won an international for the first time on 5 September 2015 when midfielder Atak Lual notched the only goal of a 2017 CAF Africa Cup of Nations qualifier against Equatorial Guinea. The game was played at South Sudan's national stadium in Juba. South Sudan had initially gained independence as a country in 2011, receiving CAF admission in February 2012 and FIFA status three months later. They drew their first official international, 2–2 against Uganda on 10 July 2012, but their winless run continued with one more draw and ten defeats before that success against Equatorial Guinea.

1.96
The 2019 tournament in Egypt was the second-lowest-scoring Cup of Nations ever, with an average of a mere 1.96 goals per game.

NATIONAL LEGEND
RENARD REDEEMED

In 2015, Frenchman **Hervé Renard** became the first coach to win the CAF Africa Cup of Nations with two different countries. This time he was in charge of Côte d'Ivoire as they defeated Ghana on penalties. Three years earlier, Renard's Zambia had defeated the Ivorians, also on spot kicks, in what was his second spell as national coach. He had resigned in 2010 to become Angola's coach, and his return was not universally welcomed in Zambia. All was forgiven when his team won their first CAF Africa Cup of Nations though. Renard's celebrations included carrying on to the pitch injured defender Joseph Musonda, who had limped off after ten minutes of the final.

LAST FIVE CAF AFRICA CUP OF NATIONS-WINNING COACHES:

2019 – Djamel Belmadi (Algeria)

2017 – Hugo Broos (Cameroon)

2015 – Hervé Renard (Côte d'Ivoire)

2013 – Stephen Keshi (Nigeria)

2012 – Hervé Renard (Zambia)

RENARD

TOURNAMENT TRIVIA
TOGO'S TRAGIC FATE

Togo were the victims of tragedy shortly before the 2010 CAF Africa Cup of Nations kicked off – followed by expulsion from the event. The team's bus was fired on by Angolan militants three days before their first scheduled match, killing three people: the team's assistant coach, press officer and bus driver. The team returned home to Togo for three days of national mourning, and were then thrown out of the competition by the CAF as punishment for missing their opening game against Ghana. Togo were later expelled from the 2012 and 2014 competitions, but this sanction was overturned on appeal in May 2010.

5

Mauritania made unwanted CAF Africa Cup of Nations history by having five players sent off during a qualifier away to Cabo Verde in June 2003, forcing the match to be abandoned. The hosts were leading 3–0 at the time and that stood as the final result.

LAST FIVE CAF AFRICA CUP OF NATIONS FINALS:

2019 – Algeria 1–0 Senegal

2017 – Cameroon 2–1 Egypt

2015 – Côte d'Ivoire 0–0 Ghana
(aet; Côte d'Ivoire 9–8 on pens)

2013 – Nigeria 1–0 Burkina Faso

2012 – Zambia 0–0 Côte d'Ivoire
(aet; Zambia 8–7 on pens)

The most recent CAF Africa Cup of Nations' 15 hat-tricks was scored back in 2008, by **Soufiane Alloudi** in the opening half-hour of Morocco's 5–1 first-round win over Namibia.

15

ALLOUDI

NAGY

NATIONAL LEGEND
GEDO BLASTER

Egypt's hero in 2010 was **Mohamed Nagy**, better known by his nickname "Gedo" – Egyptian Arabic for "Grandpa". He scored the only goal of the final, against Ghana, his fifth of the tournament, giving him the CAF Africa Cup of Nations Golden Boot. Yet he did all this without starting a single game. He had to settle for coming on as a substitute in all six of Egypt's matches, playing a total of 135 minutes. Gedo – born in Damanhur on 3 October 1984 – had made his international debut only two months earlier, and had played only two friendlies for Egypt before the tournament proper.

TOURNAMENT TRIVIA
UNFINISHED BUSINESS

Beware – if you go to see Nigeria play Tunisia, you may not get the full 90 minutes. Nigeria were awarded third place at the 1978 CAF Africa Cup of Nations after Tunisia walked off after 42 minutes of their play-off, with the score at 1–1. . They were protesting about refereeing decisions, but Nigeria were thus granted a 2–0 victory by default. Oddly enough, it had been Nigeria who had walked off when the two teams met in the second leg of a qualifier for the 1962 tournament. Their action came when Tunisia equalised after 65 minutes. The punishment was a 2–0 win for Tunisia – putting them 3–2 ahead on aggregate.

TOURNAMENT TRIVIA
MISSING THE POINT

The absences of Cameroon, Nigeria and reigning champions Egypt from the 2012 African Cup of Nations were surprising – although each could at least comfort themselves on not missing out in quite such embarrassing circumstances as South Africa. They appeared happy to play out a goalless draw with Sierra Leone in their final qualifier, believing that would be enough to go through – and greeted the final whistle with celebrations on the pitch. But they were mistaken in thinking goal difference would be used to separate teams level on points in their group, with Niger qualifying instead thanks to a better head-to-head record.

2

Only Egypt's Hassan El-Shazly has hit two CAF Africa Cup of Nations hat-tricks: his first came in a 6–3 victory over Nigeria in 1963, and he repeated the feat six years later in a 3–1 victory over Côte d'Ivoire.

OTHER FIFA TOURNAMENTS

More than three billion people are involved in football in one way or another. This passion and ambition explains why the international game's competitive structure has expanded to meet demand.

Liverpool celebrate their FIFA Club World Cup victory in 2019.

Innovations in world competition have been introduced down to a local level, and increasingly imaginative concepts for tournament hosting have allowed more and more nations to enjoy the excitement of welcoming the world. One legacy benefit is the development and upgrading of stadiums and training facilities, which assist local football long after the various tournaments have concluded. In 2016, Jordan became the first Muslim country in the Middle East to host a FIFA women's tournament – the FIFA U-17 Women's World Cup. The following year, more new ground was broken when India hosted the men's FIFA U-17 World Cup.

Tournament development has also evolved to meet demand. The FIFA World Youth Championship (now the FIFA U-20 World Cup) was launched in 1977, followed eight years later by the FIFA U-16 World Championship (now the FIFA U-17 World Cup). Simultaneously, the Men's Olympic Football Tournament became an under-23 event, although three over-age players are allowed to play in the finals. In 2000, FIFA initiated the FIFA Club World Cup. All of these world-class events have encouraged regional confederations to create their own tournaments so that their teams can take to the world stage and test themselves against elite opponents.

FIFA U-20 WORLD CUP

First staged in 1977 in Tunisia and known as the FIFA World Youth Championship until 2005, the FIFA U-20 World Cup was claimed by first-time winners Ukraine in 2019 following a 3-1 win over Korea Republic in Poland.

🏆 TOURNAMENT TRIVIA
SUPER SUB

In 1977, the Soviet Union became the first winners of the event when they beat hosts Mexico 9-8 on penalties after a 2-2 draw in the final. Their shoot-out hero was substitute goalkeeper Yuri Sivuha, who had replaced Aleksandre Novikov during extra-time. This was the Soviet Union's only triumph, although their striker **Oleg Salenko**, a future 1994 FIFA World Cup Golden Boot winner, took the top scorer award in 1989 with five goals.

SALENKO

NATIONAL LEGENDS
CAPTAIN MARVELS

Only two men have lifted both the FIFA U-20 World Cup and the FIFA World Cup as captain: Brazil's Dunga (in 1983 and 1994) and Argentina's Diego Maradona (in 1979 and 1986). Many had expected Maradona to make Argentina's full squad for the 1978 FIFA World Cup but he missed out on selection. He underlined his potential, however, by being voted best player at the 1979 youth tournament in Japan.

3

Only three players have won the tournament twice: Fernando Brassard (Portugal; 1989, 1991), João Pinto (Portugal; 1989, 1991) and Sergio Agüero (Argentina; 2005, 2007).

🕐 RECENT HISTORY
HISTORY BOYS

England celebrated their first world crown since 1966 in 2017 when the U-20s triumphed in Korea Republic. They defeated Venezuela 1-0 in the final in Suwon thanks to a 34th-minute goal from Everton's Dominic Calvert-Lewin. Both teams hit the post during the game and Newcastle United goalkeeper Freddie Woodman was England's other hero, saving a 75th-minute penalty from Adalberto Peñaranda, who, ironically, was on the books of English Premier League club Watford. Woodman took the award as the tournament's top keeper while Dominic Solanke was voted best player. England manager Paul Simpson was born on 26 July 1966, four days before England's FIFA World Cup victory.

SCORING RECORD
SAVIOUR SAVIOLA

Javier Saviola holds the record for the most goals in a single FIFA U-20 World Cup – 11 in seven games at the 2001 competition as his Argentina side went on to beat Ghana in the final, with Saviola scoring his team's three unanswered goals. Saviola, born in Buenos Aires on 11 December 1981, was playing for River Plate at the time but joined Barcelona for GBP 15 million not long afterwards – before later signing for their arch-rivals Real Madrid. When Pelé picked his 125 "greatest living footballers" for FIFA in March 2004, 22-year-old Saviola was the youngest player to make the list.

SAVIOLA

1991
In 1991, Portugal became the first hosts to win the tournament with a team that became known as the country's "Golden Generation", featuring Luís Figo, Rui Costa, João Pinto, Abel Xavier and Jorge Costa.

4-0
The joint-highest scoring in a tournament final – West Germany beat Qatar 4-0 in 1981, and Spain beat Japan by the same margin in 1999.

18
Brazil have appeared in the most editions of the tournament – 18 – and they have managed 16 of those in a row, also a record.

NATIONAL LEGEND
WHAT A MESSI

Lionel Messi was the star of the show for Argentina in 2005, and not just because he scored both of his country's goals in the final – both from the penalty spot. He achieved a hat-trick by not only winning the Golden Boot for top scorer and Golden Ball for best player, but also by captaining his side to the title. His feat was emulated two years later by compatriot Sergio Agüero, who scored once in the final against the Czech Republic, before team-mate Mauro Zárate struck a late winner.

MESSI

TOURNAMENT TRIVIA
DOMINANT DOMINIC

Ghana became the first African country to lift the trophy in 2009 when they upset Brazil in the final – despite playing 83 of the 120 minutes with just ten men following Daniel Addo's red card. The final finished goalless, one of only two games in which **Dominic Adiyiah** failed to score. He still ended the tournament as top scorer with eight goals and also won the Golden Ball for best player. The Silver Ball went to Brazil's Alex Teixeira, even though it was his missed penalty, when the final shoot-out went to sudden death, which handed Ghana victory.

1
Only one player has scored a hat-trick in the final of a FIFA U-20 World Cup: Brazilian midfielder Oscar, who hit all of his side's goals in their 3-2 triumph over Portugal to claim the trophy in August 2011.

ADIYIAH

189

FIFA U-17 WORLD CUP

First staged in China PR in 1985 as the FIFA U-16 World Championship, the age limit was adjusted from 16 to 17 in 1991. The tournament has been known as the FIFA U-17 World Cup since 2007.

5-2

The highest-scoring final was in 2017, when England beat Spain 5-2 in India.

TOURNAMENT TRIVIA
HOPE AND GLORY

England won their first U-17 world title in the most thrilling way possible by hitting back from two goals down to beat Spain 5-2 in the 2017 final in Kolkata, India. They were the second successive England age-group team, after the U-20s' victory in Korea Republic, to become world champions. Liverpool's Rhian Brewster led the recovery with a goal just before half-time, after Spain had hit England twice on the break through Sergio Gómez. Brewster ended the tournament as the Golden Boot winner with hat-tricks in the quarter- and semi-finals.

HOST HISTORY
BRAZILIAN LATE SHOW

Hosts Brazil clinched the 2019 crown with one of the most dramatic recoveries in even their own illustrious history. Home fans in the central city of Gama, including legends Ronaldo and Cafu, were losing hope after seeing Mexico take a 66th-minute lead through Bryan González. But then Kaio Jorge equalised with an 84th-minute penalty before **Lázaro Vinicius Marques** volleyed Brazil's winning goal deep into stoppage time. Brazil have now won the title four times, one fewer than Nigeria. The young *Seleção* had further success to celebrate when forward Gabriel Veron was hailed as the tournament's best player. Dutch teenager Sontje Hansen was its six-goal leading marksman.

SEOUL WORLDCUP STADIUM

LÁZARO

HOST HISTORY
SEOUL SURVIVOR

The final of the 2007 tournament was the first to be hosted by a former FIFA World Cup venue – the 68,476-capacity Seoul FIFA World Cup Stadium in Korea Republic's capital, which had been built for the 2002 FIFA World Cup. The game was watched by a crowd of 36,125, a tournament record. The 2007 event was also the first to feature 24 teams instead of 16, and it was won by Nigeria – after Spain missed all three of their spot-kicks in a penalty shoot-out.

HIGH-FLYING EAGLETS

In 2013, remarkably, the teams that finished first, second and third in Group F, ended the tournament in that order. Nigeria's Golden Eaglets won in fine style, whilst Mexico and Sweden finished second and third respectively.

SCORING RECORD
GOOD AND BAD BOY BOJAN

Barcelona star **Bojan Krkić** quickly went from hero to villain in the closing moments of Spain's semi-final victory over Ghana in 2007 – he scored his team's winner with four minutes of extra time remaining but was then sent off for a second yellow-card offence just before the final whistle. He was then suspended for the final, which Spain lost on penalties to Nigeria.

5

Nigeria have won more U-17 titles than any other country, five.

KRKIĆ

9

The first player to win both the Golden Ball and the Golden Boot at the FIFA U-17 World Cup was French striker Florent Sinama-Pongolle. His nine goals in 2001 set a tournament record for one player. His tally included two hat-tricks in the opening round.

HOST HISTORY
INDIAN OUTREACH

International football broke through another barrier when India played host to the world game for the first time by staging the FIFA U-17 World Cup in 2017. Indian fans proved once and for all that their heart beats for football just as much as it does for cricket and hockey, with a record 1.3 million fans attending the matches in New Delhi, Goa, Guwahati, Kochi, Mumbai and Kolkata, which staged the final where England defeated Spain 5-2. This exceeded the 1.2m fans in China PR in 1985 and was more than double the attendance at the 2015 finals in Chile. FIFA tournament boss Jaime Yarza hailed it as a "fantastic tournament", while Indian officials immediately announced their intention to bid for the U-20 tournament.

TOURNAMENT TOP SCORERS:

1 **Victor Osimhen,** (NIG, 2015) – 10

2 **Florent Sinama-Pongolle,** (FRA, 2001) – 9
= **Souleymane Koulibaly,** (CIV, 2011) – 9

4 **Marcel Witeczek,** (FRG, 1985) – 8
= **Rhian Brewster,** (ENG, 2017) –8

6 **David,** (ESP, 1997) – 7
= **Ishmael Addo,** (GHA, 1999) – 7
= **Macauley Chrisantus,** (NIG, 2007) – 7
= **Valmir Berisha,** (SWE, 2013) – 7

10 **Sontje Hansen ,** (NED, 2019) – 6

1991

The 1991 tournament was originally scheduled to take place in Ecuador, but a cholera outbreak meant it was switched to Italy instead – although it was played in much smaller venues than those that had been used for the previous year's senior FIFA World Cup.

SCORING RECORD
HOSTS MAKE HISTORY

Mexico became the first host country to lift the FIFA U-17 World Cup on home soil when they beat Uruguay 2-0 in the final at the Azteca Stadium in Mexico City in July 2011. The Golden Ball for the tournament's best player went to Mexican winger **Julio Gómez**, whose brace against Germany in the semi-final included a spectacular bicycle kick for the last-minute winner – although he played only ten minutes of the final, as a substitute, after picking up an injury in the previous game.

GÓMEZ

191

FIFA CLUB WORLD CUP

The world club prize has been contested in various formats since 1960, when Real Madrid defeated Peñarol. An expanded tournament is currently planned to succeed the current seven-team tournament.

INTERCONTINENTAL TITLE WINNERS BY COUNTRY:

1 11 – Spain
2 10 – Brazil
3 9 – Argentina
= 9 – Italy
5 6 – Uruguay

3
Spanish boss Pep Guardiola has won the tournament in its current guise three times: twice with Barcelona, in 2009 and 2011, and once with Bayern Munich, in 2013.

4-0
The most one-sided FIFA Club World Cup final was played in 2011, when Barcelona defeated Santos of Brazil 4-0.

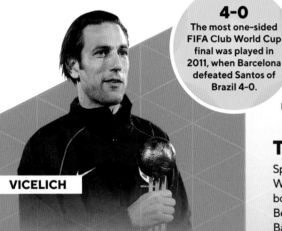

VICELICH

CLUB LEGEND
VETERAN IVAN

Auckland City were one of the surprises of the FIFA Club World Cup in 2014, spearheaded by 38-year-old **Ivan Vicelich** who won the Bronze Ball for the third best player of the tournament. Only Real Madrid's Sergio Ramos and Cristiano Ronaldo finished ahead of him. The New Zealanders finished third, the highest finish for a club from Oceania, after beating Cruz Azul on penalties following a 1-1 draw in the third-place play-off.

TOURNAMENT TRIVIA
THE REIGN OF SPAIN

Spain has dominated the FIFA Club World Cup since the world governing body's remodelling of the event. Between them, Real Madrid and Barcelona have won seven crowns. Barcelona launched the era of Spanish supremacy in 2009 by defeating Estudiantes de La Plata of Argentina 2-1 after extra time through goals from Pedro and Lionel Messi. They won again in 2011 before **Cristiano Ronaldo**'s Real Madrid triumphed three times in four years in 2014, 2016 and 2017. Real won yet again in 2018 after Ronaldo's departure for Juventus. Los Merengues currently hold a record seven all-format crowns.

RONALDO

FIRMINO

TOURNAMENT TRIVIA
LIVERPOOL AT LAST

Liverpool finally scaled the international pinnacle in 2019 when the *Reds*, under manager Jürgen Klopp, defeated Brazil's Flamengo 1-0 in Doha, Qatar. Previously, the English side had fallen at the final hurdle in the competition's different guises in 1981, 1984 and 2005. In 2019, however, Brazil's **Roberto Firmino** was the scorer of the extra-time goal that ended the hopes of his fellow countrymen. Liverpool thus became the first English side to win an unprecedented treble of Champions League, European Super Cup and Club World Cup in the same year.

OVERALL FIFA CLUB WORLD CUP CHAMPIONS (2000-2019):

1 4 – **Real Madrid** (Spain)

2 3 – **Barcelona** (Spain)

3 2 – **Corinthians** (Brazil)

4 1 – **Liverpool** (England)
= 1 – **São Paolo** (Brazil)
= 1 – **Internacional** (Brazil)
= 1 – **AC Milan** (Italy)
= 1 – **Manchester United** (England)
= 1 – **Internazionale** (Italy)
= 1 – **Bayern Munich** (Germany)

7 With seven goals to his name since 2008, Cristiano Ronaldo is the top goalscorer in FIFA Club World Cup history.

TOURNAMENT TRIVIA
LONG-DISTANCE, LONG-RUNNING RIVALRY

The precursor to the modern FIFA Club World Cup was the Intercontinental Cup, also known informally as the World Club Cup or the European/South American Cup, which pitted the champions of Europe and South America against each other. Representatives of UEFA and CONMEBOL contested the event from 1960 to 2004, but now all continental confederations send at least one club to an expanded Club World Cup organised by the world governing body. The first final, in 1960, was between Spain's Real Madrid and Uruguay's Peñarol. After a goalless draw in the rain in Montevideo, Real triumphed 5-1 at their own stadium in Madrid – including three goals in the first eight minutes by Ferenc Puskás (two) and Alfredo di Stéfano.

5 Toni Kroos has won the FIFA Club World Cup five times since 2013: a record.

TOURNAMENT TRIVIA
AFRICA AND ASIA CHALLENGE

In 2010, for the first time in the event's history, a club not from Europe or South America contested the final. African champions TP Mazembe from DR Congo defeated Internacional of Brazil 2-0 in the semi-finals before losing 3-0 to Italy's Internazionale. Mazembe achieved their surprise progress despite missing star striker and captain Trésor Mputu through suspension. In Morocco in 2013, home favourites Raja Casablanca became the second African club to reach the final before losing 2-0 to Bayern Munich. A third non-European club followed that up in Japan in 2016 when **Kashima Antlers** took Real Madrid to extra time before losing 4-2.

6 Barcelona's triumph in 2009 made them the first club to lift six different major trophies in one calendar year: the FIFA Club World Cup, the UEFA Champions League, the UEFA European Super Cup, and a Spanish hat-trick of *La Liga*, *Copa del Rey* and Super Cup.

MEN'S OLYMPIC FOOTBALL

First played at the 1900 Olympic Games in Paris, and although not recognised by FIFA as an official tournament until London 1908, the Men's Olympic Football Tournament became an under-23 tournament in Atlanta in 1996, with each team permitted up to three overage players.

13

Denmark's Sophus Nielsen is the top scorer in Olympic history with 13 goals to his name: 11 in 1908 and two in 2012.

23/27

Eastern European countries dominated Olympic football from 1948 to 1980, a period in which professional players were officially banned from taking part. Teams comprising so-called "state amateurs" from the Eastern Bloc took 23 of the 27 medals available during those years.

TOURNAMENT TRIVIA
CZECH OUT

The climax of the Antwerp 1920 Olympic Games tournament is the only time a major international football final has been abandoned. Czechoslovakia's players walked off the pitch minutes before half–time, in protest at the decisions made by 65-year-old English referee John Lewis – including the dismissal of Czech player Karel Steiner. Belgium, who were 2-0 up at the time, were awarded the victory, before Spain beat the Netherlands 3-1 in a play-off for silver.

PERALTA

TOURNAMENT TRIVIA
LONDON CALLING

Mexico were the unexpected winners when, in 2012, Wembley Stadium became the first venue to stage two Men's Olympic Football Tournament finals. The old stadium hosted the showpiece game when England's capital held the Olympics in 1948 and London is also now the only city to stage three separate summer Olympics, although the football final back in 1908 was played at White City. In 2012, **Oribe Peralta** scored both goals as Mexico defeated Brazil 2-1 in the final at the renovated Wembley. A late reply by Hulk was little consolation for the highly fancied South Americans, even though Leandro Damião did end as the tournament's six-goal top scorer.

NATIONAL LEGEND
BARCELONA-BOUND

Future Barcelona team-mates Samuel Eto'o and Xavi scored penalties for opposing sides in 2000 when Cameroon and Spain contested the first Olympic final to be settled by a shoot-out. Future FIFA World Cup or UEFA European Championship winners to have played at the Summer Olympics include Italy's Fabio Cannavaro, Gianluigi Buffon and Alessandro Nesta and Brazil's Roberto Carlos, Rivaldo and Ronaldo (Atlanta, 1996); Italy's Gianluca Zambrotta and Spain's Xavi, Carles Puyol and Joan Capdevila (Sydney, 2000); and Italy's Daniele De Rossi, Andrea Pirlo and Alberto Gilardino, and Portugal's Cristiano Ronaldo and Bruno Alves (Athens, 2004).

NATIONAL LEGEND
NEYMAR'S CROWNING GLORY

Football is usually just another event at the Olympic Games but, in 2016, it took centre stage in football-mad Rio de Janeiro. Brazil's bid to make amends for three final defeats by winning gold for the first time succeeded as they defeated Germany in the final. Two years earlier, in Belo Horizonte, Brazil had been routed 7-1 by the Germans in the World Cup so Brazilian nerves were understandably even more fraught. The 2016 gold medal game was played at the Maracanã stadium, and it was left to Brazil's superstar skipper **Neymar** to make history – and he duly beat Timo Horn from the spot to seal Brazil's first Olympic football gold medal.

3

Hungary are the most successful Olympic football team with three wins. Great Britain have also won three gold medals but those are their only medals, whereas Hungary also finished second and third in 1972 and 1960 respectively.

NEYMAR

14 SECONDS

Neymar holds the record for the fastest goal in a men's Olympic football match: he netted after 14 seconds in the semi-final against Honduras in 2016.

2

Two Olympic finals have been decided by penalty shoot-outs, including the 2016 gold medal match.

TOURNAMENT TRIVIA
AFRICAN AMBITION

Ghana became the first African country to win an Olympic football medal when they picked up bronze in 1992, but Nigeria went even better four years later by claiming the continent's first Olympic football gold medal thanks to **Emmanuel Amunike**'s stoppage-time winner against Argentina. Nigeria's triumph came as a huge surprise to many – especially as their rival teams included future world stars such as Brazil's Ronaldo and Roberto Carlos, Argentina's Hernán Crespo and Roberto Ayala, Italy's Fabio Cannavaro and Gianluigi Buffon, and France's Robert Pires and Patrick Vieira.

AMUNIKE

FIFA BEACH SOCCER WORLD CUP

The Beach Soccer World Championship was launched in 1995 and brought into the FIFA World Cup family in 2005. Since 2009, it has been staged every two years. The current champions are Portugal and the next edition is due to be held in Russia in 2021.

NATIONAL LEGEND
MAGIC ALEX

Alessandro Altobelli is still the only to score in both a FIFA World Cup final and a Beach World Cup. Altobelli struck Italy's third goal in their 3-1 victory over West Germany in the 1982 FIFA World Cup in Spain, and after abandoning grass for sand, he finished as the 1995 Beach Soccer World Championship's joint-top scorer with Zico on 12 goals. The next year, Altobelli was top scorer in his own right with 14. He notched a total of 30 World Cup goals on sand, all in the pre-FIFA era.

JORGINHO

NATIONAL LEGEND
TOP OF THE WORLD

Jorginho made history as the first player to win both the FIFA World Cup and the Beach Soccer World Cup. He helped Brazil to glory against Italy in Pasadena in 1994 but then went on to add the beach soccer prize to his career honours list in 1999 and 2004. He was voted player of the tournament on both occasions, having also been named in FIFA's All-Star squad for the senior tournament on grass in 1994.

2008
One of the most famous names in football made it onto the scoresheet in the FIFA Beach Soccer World Cup final in 2008: Diego Maradona. But this was not Argentina's 1986 World Cup-winning captain but his son Diego Maradona Jr, playing for Italy.

TOURNAMENT TRIVIA
BOSSING THE BEACH

Brazil have the most beach soccer world titles to their name – 14 – including a run of triumphs at the first six tournaments. They are the only team to have competed at all 20 finals tournaments to date and will top the rankings for many years to come ahead of second-placed Portugal (three titles), followed by Russia (two) and France (one). Portugal, Uruguay and Spain have all finished as runners-up on three occasions.

TOURNAMENT TOP SCORERS:

1. **Madjer,** (POR, 2006) – 21
2. **Gabriele Gori,** (ITA, 2017) – 17
3. **Dejan Stankovic,** (SUI, 2009) – 16
   = **Gabriele Gori,** (ITA, 2019) – 16
5. **Nemém,** (BRA, 2003) – 15
6. **Alessandro Altobelli,** (ITA, 1996) – 14
   = **Júnior,** (BRA, 1998) – 14
   = **André,** (BRA, 2011) – 14
9. **Júnior,** (BRA, 2000) – 13
   = **Madjer,** (POR, 2008) – 13

NATIONAL LEGEND
MADJER FOR IT

Angolan-born Portuguese star **Madjer** set a record for goals scored in one tournament in 2006 when he put the ball in the net 21 times. He finished as sole or joint-top scorer in six tournaments and played a key role in all of Portugal's three victories in 2001, 2015 and 2019. His seven goals in one game, against Uruguay in 2009, broke his own record of six against Cameroon in 2006. Madjer retired after the 2019 triumph having notched no fewer than 140 World Cup goals – 65 more than his second-placed fellow countryman Alan (75).

286

The 2006 and 2019 tournaments, in Brazil and Paraguay respectively, were the most prolific in terms of goals, with the 16 teams recording 286 each time.

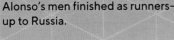

NATIONAL LEGEND
ALL-ROUNDER ALONSO

Joaquín Alonso enjoyed a stellar career on both grass and sand. He won 18 caps for Spain's full national team, scoring once between 1978 and 1988, and was selected for both the 1980 Olympic Games and the 1982 FIFA World Cup on home soil. The midfielder spent most of his professional career with Sporting Gijón then, after retiring, coached his country on the beach. In 2013, Alonso's men finished as runners-up to Russia.

MADJER

TOURNAMENT TRIVIA
FRENCH SELECTION

The 2008 tournament, on the southern coastal beaches of Marseille in France, was the first to take place outside of Brazil. The second was in the United Arab Emirates in 2009 and the third in Ravenna, Italy, in 2011. This was the first under a new system seeing the tournament staged every two years instead of annually. Subsequent hosts, as the competition became a truly worldwide event, have been Tahiti, Portugal, the Bahamas and Paraguay.

12

The tournament's spiritual home is Rio de Janeiro. The Brazilian city has hosted the event a record 12 times, most recently in 2007. The tournament has also been hosted in seven other countries.

1

Tahiti became the first Oceanian country to reach the final of a FIFA tournament in 2015, when they lost 5-3 to hosts Portugal.

SHISHIN

TOURNAMENT TRIVIA
RUSSIAN INVASION

The FIFA Beach Soccer World Cup final in 2011 was the highest-scoring showdown in the competition's history as reigning champions Brazil lost 12-8 to a country not usually associated with balmy climatic conditions – Russia. The Russians went into the tournament as reigning European champions, however, and clinched their first world title with the help of a hat-trick in the final from **Dmitry Shishin** and the performances of player of the tournament Ilya Leonov. Brazil's André had the consolation of winning the Golden Scorer award for his 14 goals.

FIFA eWORLD CUP

The FIFA eWorld Cup, the world's largest football video game tournament, was originally launched in 2004 as the FIFA Interactive World Cup in coordination with EA Sports before being renamed in 2018. Contestants battle through worldwide qualifying events on the latest version of the *FIFA* video game. The winner ends the ten-month season with the trophy, a cash prize and an invitation to The Best FIFA Football awards gala.

TOURNAMENT TRIVIA
E-MPIRE BUILDERS

The EA Sports *FIFA Global Series* is a competitive ecosystem in which players compete weekly to earn ranking points at marquee live events. The three major FIFA tournaments are: FUT Champions Cup, FIFA eClub World Cup and FIFA eNations Cup. The top 128 in the Global Series Rankings are whittled down via playoffs to the 32 who contest the FIFA eWorld Cup.

TOURNAMENT TRIVIA
CASHING UP

The explosion in popularity of eSports has been demonstrated by the rise in eWorld Cup prize money. The prize pool of USD 20,000 in 2004 had multiplied to USD 3m across the Global Series by 2019. Challengers for the eWorld Cup were chasing a top prize of USD 250,000, with USD 100,000 for the runner-up. The skills tests included adapting each year to the newly upgraded *FIFA* game – just as professional players must adjust to changes in the Laws concerning offside, handball, VAR, etc.

ESPORTS STAR
FIT OF PIQUÉ

In 2012, Real Madrid fan **Alfonso Ramos** became the first two-time FIFA Interactive World Cup champion. He also enjoyed another victory in a game played at the subsequent FIFA gala, this time with Barcelona centre-back **Gerard Piqué** at the controls as his opponent. Piqué predictably played as Barcelona against Alfonso's Real, and he not only lost 1-0 but saw the computer-game "Gerard Piqué" sent off. Ramos – nicknamed "Vamos Ramos" – celebrated both his 2012 triumphs with a dance inspired by Brazil striker Neymar. After retiring as a player, Ramos became coach of the Spanish eFootball national team.

RAMOS

FIFA INTERACTIVE WORLD CUP 2012
CHAMPION
Alfonso Ramos (Spain)
Dubai, 23 MAY 2012

PIQUÉ

LET'S GO CLUBBING

The visibility and commercial potential of eSports has persuaded plenty of traditional clubs to dip their toes in the electronic waters across a variety of platforms. Major teams with officially contracted *FIFA* players include clubs such as Barcelona, Ajax, Borussia Mönchengladbach, Bayer Leverkusen, Manchester City and West Ham United. Players who started out as armchair amateurs now travel the world as eSports professionals.

ESPORTS STAR
MO's THE MAN

Mohammed "MoAuba" Harkous, the 2019 champion, was surprised by his reception at The Best FIFA Football Awards gala, where he rubbed shoulders with the likes of Cristiano Ronaldo and Lionel Messi. He found himself being asked for advice on how to improve video game skills by award winners such as France superstar Kylian Mbappé. Mo later said: "It was amazing because I considered myself a fan but they were asking me for tips." The first tournament Mo won as a teenager cost him a EUR 20 entry fee and his prize was a PlayStation console.

47 MILLION

The 2019 eWorld Cup Grand Final was streamed in six languages for the first time – Arabic, Chinese, English, German, Portuguese and Spanish – and broadcast to more than 75 territories around the world. The three-day tournament generated more than 47 million views across a multiplicity of online platforms.

HARKOUS

FIFA EWORLD CUP ROLL OF HONOUR:

Year	Venue	Final
2004	Zurich	Thiago Carrico de Azevedo (BRA) bt Matija Biljeskovic (SRB) 2-1
2005	London	Chris Bullard (ENG) bt Gabor Mokos (HUN) 5-2
2006	Amsterdam	Andries Smit (NED) bt Wolfgang Meier (AUT) 6-4
2008	Berlin	Alfonso Ramos (ESP) bt Michael Ribeiro (USA) 3-1
2009	Barcelona	Bruce Grannec (FRA) bt Ruben Morales Zerecero (MEX) 3-1
2010	Barcelona	Nenad Stojkovic (SRB) bt Ayhan Altundag (GER) 2-1
2011	Los Angeles	Francisco Cruz (POR) bt Javier Munoz (COL) 4-1
2012	Dubai	Alfonso Ramos (ESP) bt Bruce Grannec (FRA) 0-0 (4-3 on penalties)
2013	Madrid	Bruce Grannec (FRA) Andrei Torres Vivero (MEX) 1-0
2014	Rio de Janeiro	August Rosenmeier [Agge] (DEN) bt David Bytheway [Davebtw] (ENG) 3-1
2015	Munich	Abdulaziz Alshehri [Mr D0ne] (KSA) Julien Dassonville (FRA) 3-0
2016	New York	Mohamad Al-Bacha [Bacha] (DEN) bt Sean Allen [Dragonn] (ENG) 2-2, 3-3 (5-5 agg., Al-Bacha on away goals)
2017	London	Spencer Ealing [Gorilla] (ENG) bt Kai Wollin [Deto] (GER) 3-3, 4-0 (7-3 agg.)
2018	London	Mosaad Aldossary [Msdossary] (KSA) bt Stefano Pinna (BEL) 2-0, 2-0 (4-0 agg.)
2019	London	Mohammed Harkous [MoAuba] (GER) bt Mosaad Aldossary [Msdossary] (KSA) 1-1, 2-1 (3-2 agg.)

WOMEN'S FOOTBALL

More than 30 million women now play football across the globe. The women's game has made great strides professionally in recent years, with the FIFA Women's World Cup 2019 proving a landmark event for the sport.

Such progress is long overdue considering the time wasted along the way. Although women's football was recorded in England more than a century ago, The Football Association banned it in 1921.

That led to the creation of an independent women's association with a cup competition of its own. Women's football developed simultaneously elsewhere and the surge of interest ultimately led, in the early 1980s, to the first formal European Championships and, in 1988, to a FIFA invitational tournament in Chinese Taipei.

FIFA launched an inaugural world championship in 1991, which was won by the USA to establish their claim to primacy in the game. The Americans duly hosted the next FIFA Women's World Cup in 1995, which saw a record crowd of 90,185 celebrate their shoot-out victory over China PR in the final in Pasadena. They underlined their No.1 status by winning the first women's football gold medal at the Olympic Games in 1996, before taking silver in 2000 and gold again in 2004, 2008 and 2012.

Women's football, once considered a fleeting sporting fashion, is here to stay.

United States captain Megan Rapinoe lifts the FIFA Women's World Cup trophy aloft following her side's victory over the Netherlands in 2019.

FIFA WOMEN'S WORLD CUP™

The first FIFA Women's World Cup finals were held in China PR in 1991, and the tournament has since grown astronomically. It expanded to 24 teams in 2015, and will be even bigger in 2023 when 32 teams will compete for glory.

FIFA WOMEN'S WORLD CUP FINAL RESULTS

1991 USA 2-1 Norway (China PR)

1995 Norway 2-0 Germany (Sweden)

1999 USA 0-0 China PR (USA) – USA won 5-4 on penalties

2003 Germany 2-1 Sweden (USA)

2007 Germany 2-0 Brazil (China PR)

2011 Japan 2-2 USA (Germany) – Japan won 3-1 on penalties

2015 USA 5-2 Japan (Canada)

2019 USA 2-0 Netherlands (France)

90,185
The highest-ever attendance for a FIFA Women's World Cup match remains the 90,185 fans who packed into the Rose Bowl to see the USA defeat China PR to win the 1999 tournament on home turf.

TOURNAMENT TRIVIA
SPANISH REBELLION

Spain's first-ever FIFA Women's World Cup finals appearance quickly turned sour after they won only one point from their three group games in Canada in 2015 and were eliminated. On returning home, the players blamed veteran coach Ignacio Quereda, citing insufficient preparation for the cooler climate, a lack of warm-up friendlies and poor analysis of opponents. They concluded: "We need a change. We have conveyed this to the coach and his staff."

ALL-TIME TOP SCORERS:

1 Marta, (BRA) – 17

2 Birgit Prinz, (GER) – 14
= Abby Wambach, (USA) – 14

4 Michelle Akers, (USA) – 12

5 Cristiane, (BRA) – 11
= Sun Wen, (CHN) – 11
= Bettina Wiegmann, (GER) – 11

STAR PLAYER
A TREBLE FOR CRISTIANE

In 2019, veteran Brazil striker **Cristiane** became the oldest player to score a FIFA Women's World Cup hat-trick when her hat-trick handed debutants Jamaica a 3-0 loss in a Group C tie in Grenoble. Aged 34 years and 25 days, Cristiane headed her first goal, scored a second from close range and rounded off her display with a free kick. Her feat even beat the men's FIFA World Cup record held by Cristiano Ronaldo, who was 33 years and 130 days old when he scored a hat-trick in Portugal's 3-3 draw with Spain in Russia in 2018. The Brazilian women eventually fell in the round of 16, losing 2-1 to hosts France after extra time.

CRISTIANE

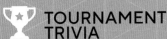

TOURNAMENT TRIVIA
HAVELANGE'S DREAM COMES TRUE

The FIFA Women's World Cup was the brainchild of former FIFA President João Havelange. The tournament began as an experimental competition in 1991 and has expanded in size and importance ever since. The success of the 1999 finals in the United States was a turning point for the tournament, which now attracts huge crowds and worldwide TV coverage. The USA and Norway – countries in which football (or soccer) is one of the most popular girls' sports – dominated the early competitions. The USA have the most impressive record overall with four titles, in 1991, 1999, 2015 and 2019. Germany, however, were the first to go back-to-back, in 2003 and 2007.

TOURNAMENT TRIVIA
MAKING AMERICA GREAT

The United States are the undisputed powerhouse of international women's football. Their 2-0 victory over European champions the Netherlands in the FIFA Women's World Cup 2019 final in Lyon sealed their record-extending fourth title after victories in 1991, 1999 and 2015. British-born Jill Ellis thus became the first coach to win back-to-back FIFA Women's World Cups. In addition, the USA have won Olympic women's football gold four times, in 1996, 2004, 2008 and 2012. No fewer than ten of their greatest stars have made more than 200 national team appearances, including Kristine Lilly (354), Christie Rampone (311), Carli Lloyd (288) and Mia Hamm (276). Seven players can boast more than 100 goals, with the list headed by Abby Wambach (184). Wambach was voted FIFA Women's World Player of the Year in 2012, and both Hamm and Lloyd have twice been named the best player in the world.

STAR PLAYER
MAGNIFICENT MEGAN

It is fair to say that United States captain **Megan Rapinoe** dominated the FIFA Women's World Cup 2019. Rapinoe, a 34-year-old from Redding, California, opened the scoring in the United States' 2-0 victory over Netherlands in the final, was voted player of the match and won the adidas Golden Ball as the tournament's best player. Rapinoe's penalty against the Dutch was her 50th goal in 158 appearances over 13 years for the USA. She has also made a name for her-self off the pitch. Rapinoe is an advocate for numerous LGBT organisations, and she famously knelt during the national anthem at an international match in support of American Football star Colin Kaepernick and his anti-racism protests.

RAPINOE

TERRIFIC TECH
VAR TO THE RESCUE

Stéphanie Frappart became the first referee to use video assistance in awarding a penalty at a major tournament in the FIFA Women's World Cup 2019 final. The 35-year-old French referee checked the touchline screen after Dutch defender Stefanie van der Gragt fouled American Alex Morgan early in the second half in Lyon. Megan Rapinoe duly converted the penalty. VAR made its tournament debut in France, and it was a constant feature throughout the finals, right from the opening match when hosts France beat Korea Republic 4-0. France, featuring seven players from European club champions Lyon, had a further "goal" by Griedge Mbock Bathy ruled out after a video review.

FRAPPART

TOURNAMENT TRIVIA
WHAT'S IN A NUMBER?

The number 13 proved unlucky for Thailand when they lost by that tournament record margin – without reply – to the United States in France in 2019. The goals were shared around six players, with Alex Morgan becoming only the second individual to score five times in one FIFA Women's World Cup match. The previous five-star forward had been fellow American Michelle Akers against Chinese Taipei in 1991. Morgan's single-match tally helped the Americans take their first steps towards a tournament record total of 26 goals.

7

Seven of the USA's FIFA Women's World Cup-winning team of 1991 were also in the squad who triumphed in 1999: Mia Hamm, Michelle Akers, Kristine Lilly, Julie Foudy, Joy Fawcett, Carla Overbeck and Brandi Chastain.

TOP TEAM SCORERS:

1 **USA,** 26 (2019)

2 **USA,** 25 (1991)
= **Germany,** 25 (2003)

4 **Norway,** 23 (1995)

5 **Germany,** 21 (2007)

250

The lowest attendance for a match at the finals came on 8 June 1995, when only 250 spectators watched the 3-3 draw between Canada and Nigeria in Helsingborg.

TOURNAMENT TRIVIA
CHINA PR ARE EVER PRESENT

The first game in the FIFA Women's World Cup finals saw hosts China PR defeat Norway 4-0 in front of 65,000 fans in Guangzhou on 16 November 1991. Together, China PR and Norway are among eight nations to have competed in all eight tournaments – along with Brazil, Germany, Japan, Nigeria, Sweden and the United States. Following the 2019 tournament, 36 nations have made at least one appearance at the FIFA Women's World Cup. Chile, Jamaica, Scotland and South Africa are the most recent debutants, with each making their bow in France.

STAR PLAYER
GOAL MACHINE MARTA

Marta Vieira da Silva of Brazil has cemented her status as one of the greatest female players of all time with her goalscoring achievements in the FIFA Women's World Cup. Her total of 17 goals is three more than both Birgit Prinz (Germany) and Abby Wambach (United States). In 2007, Marta was awarded both the Golden Ball for best player and the Golden Boot for finishing as the seven-goal top scorer. She has also been hailed a record six times by FIFA as the world's No1 female player, and she extended her World Cup tally in the 2019 finals with penalties against Australia and Italy. She and team-mate Cristiane are the only two players to have scored goals in five successive finals tournaments.

MARTA

TOURNAMENT TRIVIA
UNBEATEN CHINESE GO HOME EMPTY-HANDED

In 1999, China PR became the only team to go through the finals without losing a match, yet they still went home empty-handed. The Chinese won all of their group games, 2-1 against Sweden, 7-0 against Ghana, and 3-1 against Australia. They then beat Russia 2-0 in the quarter-finals and Norway 5-0 in the semi-finals but lost to the USA on penalties in the final after a 0-0 draw. In 2011, Japan became the first team to lift the trophy despite losing a match in the first round – as had eventual runners-up the USA.

1,353,506

The FIFA Women's World Cup 2015 still holds the total attendance record for a women's tournament.

SCREENING SUCCESS

The 2019 finals in France drew one billion viewers worldwide to programming by more than 200 broadcasters. TV records were set in many countries, including host nation France and eventual champions the United States, as well as Germany and China PR. A record 60.37 million people watched Brazil's second-round defeat by the French, making it the most watched women's football match of all time. England's semi-final defeat by the United States attracted a peak viewing audience of 11.7 million in the UK, a domestic record for women's football.

TOURNAMENT TRIVIA
A RECORD DEFENCE

In 2007, Germany became the first team to make a successful defence of the FIFA Women's World Cup. They also set another record by going through the tournament – six games and 540 minutes – without conceding a single goal. As a result, their goalkeeper Nadine Angerer overhauled Italy keeper Walter Zenga's record of 517 minutes unbeaten in the 1990 men's finals. The last player to score against the Germans had been Sweden's **Hanna Ljungberg** in the 41st minute of the 2003 final. Their run eventually ended when Christine Sinclair of Canada scored after 82 minutes of Germany's opening game in 2011.

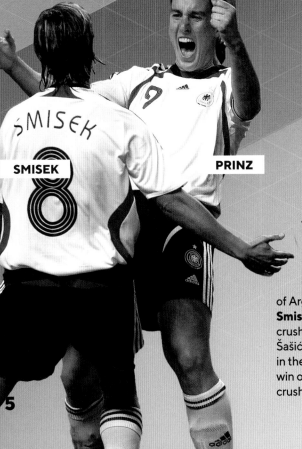

LJUNGBERG

SMISEK

PRINZ

7

Brazilian midfielder Formiga set a record in 2019 by appearing at her seventh FIFA Women's World Cup – more than any other player. She had first appeared as a 17-year-old at the 1995 tournament in Sweden.

STAR PLAYER
WHITE-HOT ELLEN

Ellen White shared top-scoring honours in the FIFA Women's World Cup 2019 when she scored six goals as England finished fourth. However, she did not collect the adidas Golden Boot because Americans Megan Rapinoe and Alex Morgan had both contributed more assists. White, the 30-year-old Manchester City striker, had also been a member of the England team who reached the last four in Canada in 2015.

SCORING RECORD
GERMANS AT THE DOUBLE

Germany are the only team to have twice hit double figures in a FIFA Women's World Cup game. The first time came in an 11-0 thrashing of Argentina in Shanghai in the 2007 finals, when **Birgit Prinz** and **Sandra Smisek** both scored hat-tricks. Then, in Canada in 2015, the Germans crushed Côte d'Ivoire 10-0 in the first round with trebles for strikers Célia Šašić and Anja Mittag. It is Norway, however, who hold the record for scoring in the most consecutive games – 15. They began their sequence with a 4-0 win over New Zealand on 19 November 1991 and saw it come to an end in a crushing 5-0 defeat by the Chinese in the semi-finals of USA 1999.

UEFA WOMEN'S EUROPEAN CHAMPIONSHIP

17 The youngest player a UEFA Women's Euro 2017 was Russia's 17-y old midfielder Viktori Shkoda from the sout city of Krasnodar whil the oldest was the 37-year-old Norwegia goalkeeper Ingrid Hjelmseth.

TAYLOR

Organised women's football has taken vast steps since it was banned in England in 1921. Its modern resurgence continued in 2017, with the Dutch victorious as hosts in the UEFA Women's European Championship.

SCORING RECORD
TAYLOR MAKES HISTORY FOR ENGLAND

England centre-forward **Jodie Taylor** enjoyed a sensational campaign at the 2017 finals of the UEFA Women's European Championship. She started with a hat-trick in a 6-0 defeat of Scotland and followed up against Spain and in the quarter-final defeat of France to become the first England player to finish as the tournament's top scorer. Taylor's treble was the first at the finals in two decades. Her five-goal haul for the Lionesses was one short of the record set by Germany's Inka Grings in 2009. Taylor, who had played for 12 clubs in five countries before exploding at UEFA EURO 2017, was only the third player ever to score a hat-trick in the women's EURO.

TOURNAMENT TRIVIA
ORANGE FEVER LIGHTS UP EUROPE

Hosts Netherlands celebrated victory in UEFA Women's EURO 2017 by defeating Denmark 4-2 to the delight of a capacity, orange-bedecked crowd in Enschede. Some 13 members of the 23-strong Dutch squad brought to the party their experience of playing with foreign clubs – notably goalkeeper Sari van Veenendaal and centre-forward **Vivianne Miedema** (both Arsenal), midfielder Jackie Groenen (Frankfurt) and the tournament's finest player in Barcelona left-winger Lieke Martens. Miedema scored once in each of Netherlands' knockout victories over Sweden and England then two in the final triumph over Denmark.

MIEDEMA

2 Inka Grings of Germany was top scorer of two tournaments running, in 2005 and 2009.

STAR PLAYER
NADIM'S LONG ROAD TO STARDOM

Forward **Nadia Nadim** grabbed the spotlight from even experienced team-mate Pernille Harder in 2017 as Denmark reached the UEFA Women's EURO final for the first time after five previous semi-final exits. Nadim, her mother and sisters had fled a war-torn Afghanistan in 2000 when she was only 11. They sought refugee status in Denmark, where Nadim began playing football for Aalborg. Her talent prompted the Danish federation to obtain a special regulatory exemption from FIFA so she could play for her adopted country. Her starring role at UEFA Women's EURO 2017, where she opened the scoring against the Netherlands in the final, prompted a transfer to Manchester City in the FA Women's Super League.

NADIM

1-0

At the UEFA Women's European Championship in 2017, Netherlands won all three group games without conceding a goal, ahead of the Danes, whom they beat 1-0 first time around.

TOURNAMENT TRIVIA
END OF AN ERA FOR THE GERMANS

Germany's 2-1 defeat by Denmark in the quarter-final of UEFA EURO 2017 ended an astonishing run of success featuring six successive titles won since 1995. Their exit was a bad start to a new job for head coach Steffi Jones, who had succeeded title-winning specialist Silvia Neid in 2016. Neid appeared an impossible act to match. She had been a European champion three times as a player and twice as coach as well as being voted FIFA Women's Coach of the Year on three occasions.

BIGGEST ATTENDANCES:

1 **41,301 – Germany 1-0 Norway,** (Stockholm, 2013 final)

2 **29,092 – England 3-2 Finland** (Manchester, 2005 group)

3 **28,182 – Netherlands 4-2 Denmark** (Enschede, 2017 final)

4 **27,093 – Netherlands 3-0 England** (Enschede, 2017 semi-final)

5 **25,694 – England 0-1 Sweden** (Blackburn, 2005 group)

61

The German women's Bundesliga provided the most players (61) at UEFA EURO 2017 followed by the English club game (41). Wolfsburg were the top club in being represented by 14 players.

TOURNAMENT TRIVIA
STEP UP FOR STEINHAUS

One of the most high-profile personalities at UEFA EURO 2017 was not a player but **Bibiana Steinhaus**, the German referee. Steinhaus, a police commander from Hanover, learned shortly before the finals that she had become the first woman official promoted to referee matches in the men's Bundesliga. This was 10 years after she had become the first female referee in German professional football in the lower divisions. Highlights in the women's game included the final of the FIFA World Cup 2011 and then the gold medal match at the London 2012 Olympic Games. Six weeks before UEFA EURO 2017, she refereed the UEFA Women's Champions League Final between Lyon and Paris Saint-Germain.

STEINHAUS

165M
Away from the stadia the total television audience for the UEFA Women's EURO 2017 final hit 165 million. The final was screened in 80 countries.

WOMEN'S OLYMPIC FOOTBALL

WOMEN'S OLYMPIC FOOTBALL TOP SCORERS

1   **Christine Sinclair** (CAN, 2012) – 6

2   **Cristiane** (BRA, 2004) – 5
= **Birgit Prinz** (GER, 2004) – 5
= **Cristiane** (BRA, 2008) – 5
= **Melanie Behringer** (GER, 2016) – 5

6   **Ann Kristin Aarønes** (NOR, 1996) – 4
= **Linda Medalen** (NOR, 1996) – 4
= **Pretinha** (BRA, 1996) – 4
= **Sun Wen** (CHN, 2000) – 4

Women's Olympic football has also been dominated by the USA since its introduction to the Games at Atlanta 1996. Team USA won four of the first six tournaments, while they also reached the final in 2000 and the quarter-finals in 2016.

NEID

TOURNAMENT TRIVIA
SILVIA'S GOLDEN GOODBYE

Germany put the icing on their cake in 2016 by beating Sweden 2–1 to claim gold in Rio de Janeiro. After two FIFA Women's World Cup and eight UEFA European Championship victories, this was their first Olympic success and a perfect climax to coach **Silvia Neid**'s career in her last match after 11 years in charge. She described winning gold as "a new summit for German women's football".

8

Germany hold the record for the most goals scored in a single Olympic finals match. The Germans beat China PR 8–0 in 2004, with five different players on the scoresheet, including a four-goal haul for Birgit Prinz.

NATIONAL LEGEND
MAGNIFICENT MARTA

Brazil superstar **Marta** finished with an Olympic silver medal in both 2004 and 2008 but missed out on home soil in 2016 when the *Canarinha* lost the bronze medal match against Canada. She would have found some consolation in becoming one of only four female players to have scored ten or more goals in Olympic football, alongside team-mate Cristiane, Canada's Christine Sinclair and Birgit Prinz of Germany. Prinz scored four of her goals in one game, an 8–0 defeat of China PR in 2004.

MARTA

STAR PLAYER
SUPER SINCLAIR

Captain **Christine Sinclair** led by example as Canada won a second successive bronze medal at the Rio de Janeiro Games in 2016, scoring their crucial second goal in the 2-1 victory over hosts Brazil in São Paulo. She also struck the post once in each half. Sinclair's goal was a remarkable 165th in her 250th international. She was also the six-goal leading scorer at London 2012.

SINCLAIR

TOURNAMENT TRIVIA
PIA AT THE PEAK

Pia Sundhage knows both sides of the Olympic women's football coin. The former international midfielder coached the United States to success in 2008 and 2012 and then returned to her native Sweden and led her own national team to silver at Rio 2016. Sundhage, who played for Sweden at the breakthrough 1996 Olympic Games in Atlanta, was voted the FIFA World Coach of the Year for Women's Football in 2012.

2.5

The number of matches played in the Women's Olympic Football Tournament rose from 16 to 20 in 2004 – but the goals per game ratio has fallen significantly since the first contest in 1996. In Atlanta, the women's competition produced an average of 3.3 goals per game, but this dropped to 2.5 in 2016.

TOURNAMENT TRIVIA
THE POWER OF THREE

Brazil's Cristiane Rozeira de Souza Silva was the first female player to score two hat-tricks in Olympic football. Her first treble came in a 7-0 victory over hosts Greece in 2004, and she followed that up by scoring all of Brazil's goals in a 14-minute spell in a 3-1 defeat of Nigeria in Beijing four years later. She and Brazil won silver in both tournaments. Cristiane, who spent her club career in France, Germany, Sweden, the USA, Russia and Korea Republic, led Brazil's attack in an impressive four Olympic Games and five FIFA Women's World Cups.

80,203

At London 2012, a tournament record 80,203 fans witnessed the USA defeat Japan in the final at Wembley. This remains the largest attendance for any women's football match in England.

WOMEN'S OLYMPIC FOOTBALL MEDALS:

1 **USA** (G:4, S:1, B:0)

2 **Germany** (G:1, S:0, B:3)

3 **Norway** (G:1, S:0, B:1)

4 **Brazil** (G:0, S:2, B:0)

5 **China PR** (G:0, S:1, B:0)
= Japan (G:0, S:1, B:0)
= Sweden (G:0, S:1, B:0)

8 **Canada** (G:0, S:0, B:2)

LLOYD

TOURNAMENT TRIVIA
BANK ON LLOYD

American **Carli Lloyd** is undoubtedly one of the greatest players in Olympic women's history. In 2008, she struck the winning goal for the USA against Brazil in the final in Beijing and then, four years later in London, claimed a decisive double in their 2-1 victory over Japan at Wembley.

2012
In 2012, Olympic hosts Great Britain fielded a team for the first time. Although they finished top of their first-round group with a perfect three wins from three, without conceding a goal, they were beaten 2-0 by Canada in the quarter-finals and missed out on a medal.

4
The USA have dominated the Olympics since women's football was introduced at the 1996 Games in Atlanta. They have won four gold medals and they also secured silver in 2000.

OTHER WOMEN'S TOURNAMENTS

The irresistible demand for greater opportunities for women on the international stage sparked the creation of both the FIFA U-20 and U-17 Women's World Cups. The lower staging requirements have helped the tournaments break down hosting barriers and emerge as some of the most exciting youth events in world sport.

LEROUX

🏆 TOURNAMENT TRIVIA
FRAPPART IN CHARGE

French official Stéphanie Frappart refereed the 2018 U-20 final in which Japan beat Spain 3-1 in Vannes, Brittany. One year later, she was appointed to referee the senior FIFA Women's World Cup final in Lyon in which the USA beat European champions Netherlands 2-0. A few weeks later, she became the first woman to oversee a major UEFA men's club match, the UEFA Super Cup, with Liverpool defeating Chelsea in a penalty shoot-out.

3

Only one player has scored a hat-trick in the final of the FIFA U-20 Women's World Cup: Kim Song-hui of Korea DPR in her side's 5-0 win over China PR in 2006.

FRAPPART

FIFA U-20 WOMEN'S WORLD CUP TOP SCORERS

1 Christine Sinclair (CAN, 2002) – 10
= Alexandra Popp (GER, 2010) – 10

3 Brittany Timko (CAN, 2004) – 7
= Kim Un-hwa (PRK, 2012) – 7
= Asisat Oshoala (NIG, 2014) – 7

6 Patricia Guijarro (ESP, 2018) – 6

7 Ma Xiaoxu (CHN, 2006) – 5
= Sydney Leroux (USA, 2008) – 5
= Mami Ueno (JPN, 2016) – 5

🏅 STAR PLAYER
SUPER SINCLAIR

In 2002, Christine Sinclair of Canada became the first player to score ten goals in a single FIFA U-20 Women's World Cup. Her feat would be matched by Germany's Alexandra Popp eight years later. Sinclair was also the first player to score five times in one game, Canada's 6-2 quarter-final win over England in 2002. She later went on to become leading scorer at the Women's Olympic Football Tournament at London 2012.

TOURNAMENT TRIVIA
NIGERIAN BREAKTHROUGH

In 2014, Asisat Oshoala became the first African player to collect the Golden Ball for best player as well as the Golden Boot for leading scorer at the U-20 Women's World Cup in Canada. She and her Nigerian team-mates had to make do with the runners-up slot, however, after going down to Germany after extra time in the final. Oshoala's seven goals included four in Nigeria's 6-2 semi-final victory over Korea DPR.

113

In 2016, Papua New Guinea staged a FIFA tournament for the first time after original hosts South Africa withdrew. A total of 113 goals made this the equal highest-scoring tournament in the competition's history alongside Chile 2008.

FIFA U-17 WOMEN'S WORLD CUP TOP SCORERS

1	**Yeo Min-ji** (KOR, 2010) – 8
	= **Ra Un-sim** (PRK, 2012) – 8
	= **Lorena Navarro** (ESP, 2016) – 8
4	**Mukarama Abdulai** (GHA, 2018) – 7
5	**Dzsenifer Marozsán** (GER, 2008) – 6
	= **Deyna Castellanos** (VEN, 2014) – 6
	= **Gabriela García** (VEN, 2014) – 6

STAR PLAYER
DARING DEYNA

Venezuela's **Deyna Castellanos** shot to global fame at the 2016 finals after images of her audacious goal from the halfway line went viral. Castellanos struck four minutes into stoppage time to secure a 2-1 victory over Cameroon.

CASTELLANOS

TOURNAMENT TRIVIA
JORDANIAN LEGACY

The FIFA U-17 Women's World Cup 2016 in Jordan made history as it was the first FIFA women's tournament to be hosted in a Muslim country in the Middle East. Matches were played in the capital Amman as well as in Irbid and Al Zarqa. The tournament left a valuable legacy as the upgraded facilities enabled Jordan to host the Women's Asian Cup in 2018.

2

The FIFA U-17 and U-20 Women's World Cups are held every two years, in contrast to the four-yearly senior contest.

KOREAN JOY
Two years after Korea DPR won the inaugural FIFA U-17 Women's World Cup, southern neighbours Korea Republic lifted the trophy the next time round. The event's second final, in Trinidad & Tobago, was the first to go to penalties, with the South Koreans beating Japan 5-4 after a 3-3 draw.

TOURNAMENT TRIVIA
SIMPLY THE BEST

Yeo Min-ji of Korea DPR in 2010 and Griedge Mbock Bathy of France in 2012 each enjoyed double success. Both were named as the best player of their respective tournament after their teams won the cup. In 2012, France beat the North Koreans in the final. Goalkeeper Romane Bruneau was the French heroine after saving two spot-kicks in the penalty shoot-out. France took the title 7-6 after a 1-1 draw.

ABDULAI

FIFA AWARDS

Every year, world football swaps match kit for black-tie formality to hail a range of achievements and achievers from the previous year. In 2019, FIFA took the show to Milan.

The stunning the Teatro alla Scala was the perfect stage for FIFA to hail international football's major achievers in 2019. FIFA originally launched its World Player awards in 1990. Between 2010 and 2015, FIFA linked up with *France Football* to organize one single awards ceremony around the Ballon d'Or, an award launched back in the mid-1950s.

In 2016, the awards were uncoupled and FIFA decided to step out with a new title, with the FIFA awards rebranded as The Best. In 2019, the gala – hosted by Ruud Gullit and Ilaria D'Amico – saw Lionel Messi claim the men's FIFA prize for the sixth time in ten years, the 32-year-old Argentina and Barcelona superstar taking the honours ahead of Netherlands and Liverpool defender Virgil van Dijk and Cristiano Ronaldo, now playing his club football in Italy with Juventus.

The Best Women's Player was Megan Rapinoe, captain and leader of the United States team that retained the FIFA Women's World Cup in France. Second and third in the voting were Rapinoe's USA team-mate Alex Morgan and England's Lucy Bronze.

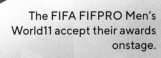

The FIFA FIFPRO Men's World11 accept their awards onstage.

THE BEST FIFA MEN'S PLAYER

FIFA's award for the outstanding men's player over the previous 12 months is established as one of the greatest individual honours in the international game.

2019 WINNER
LIONEL MESSI

Lionel Messi's status as one of the greatest players in football history was underlined by his sixth and latest award in 2019. The Barcelona icon finished ahead of Liverpool's Virgil van Dijk and Juventus' Cristiano Ronaldo after another year of goals and records. This was a second award of the night for Messi, who also featured in the FIFA FIFPRO Men's World11. Messi and five-time winner Ronaldo have dominated the award since 2008, with their command interrupted only in the 2018 World Cup year by Croatia captain and playmaker Luka Modrić.

Messi struck more league goals than anyone else in mainstream European club football in the 2018-19 season, scoring 36 times as he led the Catalan club to their 26th Spanish title. Messi also delivered a league-best 15 assists on his way to being hailed as *La Liga*'s leading marksman for the sixth time in his career and a third time in succession.

A chipped goal against Real Betis also earned Messi a place among the contenders for the FIFA Puskás Award for a season in which he helped Barcelona reach the semi-finals of the UEFA Champions League and the final of the *Copa del Rey*. Messi was also the Champions League's 12-goal top scorer.

PREVIOUS WINNERS :

2018	**Luka Modrić** (Croatia)
2017	**Cristiano Ronaldo** (Portugal)
2016	**Cristiano Ronaldo** (Portugal)
2015	**Lionel Messi** (Argentina)
2014	**Cristiano Ronaldo** (Portugal)

1991

The year the award was first presented, to Germany's Lothar Matthäus.

1

Zinédine Zidane is the only man to have won the top FIFA award as both player and coach.

8

Brazilian players have won the award on eight occasions – more than any other nation.

Liberia's **George Weah** is the only African player to win the award to date.

Votes for the award are divided equally between media representatives, national team coaches, national team captains, and the general public.

WEAH

THE BEST FIFA WOMEN'S PLAYER

This award acknowledges the ever-increasing popularity and success of the women's game, as was illustrated by the record global ratings achieved by the FIFA Women's World Cup in France in 2019.

2019 WINNER
MEGAN RAPINOE

USA captain Megan Rapinoe was hailed as the best women's player of 2019, ahead of team-mate Alex Morgan and England's Lucy Bronze, after her Golden Ball-winning performances in the Americans' triumphant FIFA Women's World Cup campaign. The 34-year-old scored six times at the finals and also stood out for her high profile in the campaign for equality in sport.

Winger Rapinoe, from Reign FC in the National Women's Soccer League, added: "[Coach] Jill Ellis and the rest have put us in a great position. This was an incredible year for women's football. For those who just noticed, you are a bit late to the party. It truly was incredible to be part of the World Cup. The enthusiasm we had was amazing."

Rapinoe won her batte to regain her place in Ellis's World Cup plans after a serious cruciate ligament injury had been followed by the disappointment of a quarter-final exit for the United States at the 2016 Olympic Games. She has also balanced her career with an insistence on speaking up on social issues and against gender discrimination. In Milan, she said: "We have a unique opportunity in football, different to any other sport in the world, to use this beautiful game to change the world for better. That's my charge to everyone. I hope you take that to heart and just do something. Do anything."

PREVIOUS WINNERS :

2018	**Marta**	(Brazil)
2017	**Lieke Martens**	(Netherlands)
2016	**Carli Lloyd**	(USA)
2015	**Carli Lloyd**	(USA)
2014	**Nadine Kessler**	(Germany)

2001
The year that the inaugural Women's World Player of the Year award was given to Mia Hamm of the USA.

20
Marta's age when she became the youngest winner of the award in 2006.

Nadine Angerer is the only goalkeeper (male or female) to have won a FIFA Player of the Year award.

6
Brazilian legend Marta's six titles (including five in a row from 2006-10) are the most by any female player.

4
The number of winning individual players from the USA, more than any other nation.

ANGERER

OTHER FIFA AWARDS

Brilliance in football is measured mostly by achievements out on the pitch, but FIFA also recognises other outstanding contributions to the worldwide game over the past year. This ranges from the leadership and insight of coaches to respect for the principles of fair play.

KLOPP

2019 WINNERS:

The Best Men's Player: Lionel Messi (Argentina, Barcelona)

The Best Women's Player: Megan Rapinoe (USA, Reign FC)

The Best Men's Goalkeeper: Alisson Becker (Brazil, Liverpool)

The Best Men's Coach: Jürgen Klopp (Liverpool)

The Best Women's Coach: Jill Ellis (USA)

FIFA Puskás Award: Dániel Zsóri (Debrecen)

FIFA Fair Play Award: Marcelo Bielsa and Leeds United

FIFA Fan Award: Silvia Grecco

FIFA FIFPRO Men's World11: Alisson Becker (Brazil), **Matthijs de Ligt** (Netherlands), **Marcelo** (Brazil), **Sergio Ramos** (Spain), **Virgil van Dijk** (Netherlands), **Frenkie de Jong** (Netherlands), **Eden Hazard** (Belgium), **Luka Modrić** (Croatia), **Cristiano Ronaldo** (Portugal), **Kylian Mbappé** (France), **Lionel Messi** (Argentina)

FIFA FIFPRO Women's World11: Sari van Veenendaal (Netherlands), **Lucy Bronze** (England), **Nilla Fischer** (Sweden), **Kelley O'Hara** (USA), **Wendie Renard** (France), **Julie Ertz** (USA), **Amandine Henry** (France), **Rose Lavelle** (USA), **Marta** (Brazil), **Alex Morgan** (USA), **Megan Rapinoe** (USA).

The measure of **Jürgen Klopp**'s status as The Best FIFA Men's Coach was in achieving primacy ahead of two other outstanding Premier League bosses in Mauricio Pochettino and Pep Guardiola. One of Germany's finest football exports began his coaching career at Mainz 05 in 2001. Subsequently, his ambition took him to Borussia Dortmund and then to Liverpool, with whom he won the UEFA Champions League in 2019. Klopp said: "Nobody expected 20, ten, five, four years ago that I would be standing here. I have to say thank you to my outstanding club. As a coach, you can only be as good as your team."

Jill Ellis concluded her successful spell in charge of the USA by collecting the award for The Best FIFA Women's Coach. The English-born 53-year-old had led the Americans to a second consecutive Women's World Cup triumph in France. Ellis had been similarly rewarded for the USA's success in 2015. She said: "Winning this award twice is incredible. Without the players and all the staff, you don't achieve these things. It is truly a team award."

ELLIS

THE BEST
FIFA FOOTBALL AWARDS

GRECCO

Brazilian fan **Silvia Grecco** received the FIFA Fan Award for her narration to her blind son, Nickollas, of the match action of their favourite club Palmeiras. A Brazilian TV reporter spotted the mother and son following a game and footage went viral worldwide.

DELAVAL

COOPER

The FIFA Fair Play Award went to Marcelo Bielsa and Leeds United. The Argentinian coach, having seen his team take the lead against Aston Villa with a goal when a Villa player was down injured, instructed his team to allow their opponents to equalise straight from the restart. The award was accepted by Leeds' **Liam Cooper** and **Benoit Delaval**.

The Best FIFA Goalkeeper award was double-handed this year as FIFA balanced the men's prize with a woman's accolade. Brazilian **Alisson Becker** had been a key figure in Liverpool's UEFA Champions League success. Netherlands' Sari van Veenendaal was acclaimed as the best keeper at the FIFA Women's World Cup.

BECKER

PREVIOUS WINNERS:

2018

The Best Men's Coach: Didier Deschamps (France)

The Best Women's Coach: Reynald Pedro (Olympique Lyonnais)

The Best Goalkeeper: Thibaut Courtois (Belgium, Chelsea)

FIFA Puskás Award: Mohamed Salah (Liverpool)

FIFA Fair Play Award: Lennart Thy (VVV Venlo)

FIFA Fan Award: Peru supporters

2017

The Best Men's Coach: Zinédine Zidane (Real Madrid)

The Best Women's Coach: Sarina Wiegman (Netherlands)

FIFA Puskás Award: Olivier Giroud (France, Arsenal)

FIFA Fair Play Award: Francis Koné (FC Zbrojovka Brno)

FIFA Fan Award: Celtic supporters

2016

The Best Men's Coach: Claudio Ranieri (Leicester City)

The Best Women's Coach: Silvia Neid (Germany)

FIFA Puskás Award: Mohd Faiz Subri (Penang FA)

FIFA Fair Play Award: Atlético Nacional (Colombia)

FIFA Fan Award: Borussia Dortmund and Liverpool supporters

Outstanding career: Falcao [Alessandro Rosa Vieira] (Brazil, futsal)

2015

Coach of the Year (men): Luis Enrique (Barcelona)

Coach of the Year (women): Jill Ellis (USA)

FIFA Puskás Award: Wendell Lira (Goianesia)

FIFA Fair Play Award: all football organisations assisting refugees

2014

Coach of the Year (men): Joachim Löw (Germany)

Coach of the Year (women): Ralf Kellermann (VfL Wolfsburg)

FIFA Puskás Award: James Rodríguez (Colombia)

FIFA Presidential Award: Hiroshi Kagawa (Japanese journalist)

FIFA Fair Play Award: FIFA World Cup volunteers

FIFA/ COCA-COLA WORLD RANKINGS

The movement of nations throughout all levels of the FIFA/ Coca-Cola World Rankings reflects the compelling and constantly shifting battle to be the world's most dominant international team.

FIFA introduced a world ranking system in December 1992 to provide a monthly statistical analysis of the rise and fall of the fortunes of all the world game's national teams in men's football. Placings are computed on results in what are termed international "A" games and consider match results, goals scored, the strength of the opposition, regional balance and competition status. The women's world ranking, introduced in 2003, is published on a quarterly basis.

The rankings are important, not least because they have previously been used as a form guide by FIFA for draws for international competitions. A short break in publication accompanied the 2018 FIFA World Cup, when the system was refined to adjust anomalies concerning the assessment of friendly matches. This new iteration of FIFA's formula, named "SUM", relies on a system of addition and subtraction rather than averaging points over a given time period, as in previous versions.

Belgium's 'golden generation' have risen to the top of the FIFA/Coca-Cola World Ranking.

FIFA/COCA-COLA WORLD RANKING 2020

The worldwide COVID-19 pandemic brought national team competition to an abrupt halt in early 2020. Health and travel restrictions imposed by national governments meant the postponement of a full schedule of international fixtures, including qualifiers for the FIFA World Cup™ in Qatar in 2022, the play-offs and finals of UEFA EURO 2020, as well as the *Copa América*.

This meant that the FIFA/Coca-Cola World Ranking following the shutdown included only four friendly matches and that the standings were virtually identical to those in the previous edition. The one change – for the record – saw South Sudan move into joint-168th position with Bermuda after the latter dropped a ranking point following a 2–0 defeat in Jamaica on 11 March. The five other teams involved remained static: Panama (played twice – 81st), Uzbekistan (85th), Belarus (87th), Guatemala (130th) and Nicaragua (151st).

The FIFA/Coca-Cola World Ranking has charted the ebb and flow in the men's national team game for almost three decades since being devised and launched in December 1992. The fluctuating fortunes of countries at all levels are based on computer-based comparisons of match results, goals scored, the strength of the opposition, regional balance and competition status.

Belgium took over the top spot in the ranking in late 2018 and maintained their primacy in 2019 after winning all ten of their senior internationals, which also saw them among the first qualifiers for the UEFA European Championship 2020.

RANKING

Pos.	Country	Pts	(+/–)
1	Belgium	1765	0
2	France	1733	0
3	Brazil	1712	0
4	England	1661	0
5	Uruguay	1645	0
6	Croatia	1642	0
7	Portugal	1639	0
8	Spain	1636	0
9	Argentina	1623	0
10	Colombia	1622	0
11	Mexico	1621	0
12	Switzerland	1608	0
13	Italy	1607	0
14	Netherlands	1604	0
15	Germany	1602	0
16	Denmark	1598	0
17	Chile	1579	0
17	Sweden	1579	0
19	Poland	1559	0
20	Senegal	1555	0
21	Peru	1544	0
22	USA	1542	0
23	Wales	1540	0
24	Ukraine	1537	0
25	Venezuela	1517	0
26	Austria	1507	0
27	Tunisia	1506	0
28	Japan	1500	0
29	Turkey	1494	0
29	Serbia	1494	0
31	Nigeria	1493	0
32	Slovakia	1490	0
33	IR Iran	1489	0
34	Rep. Ireland	1486	0
35	Algeria	1482	0
36	N Ireland	1476	0
37	Romania	1475	0
38	Russia	1470	0
39	Iceland	1465	0
40	Korea Rep.	1464	0
41	Paraguay	1461	0
42	Australia	1457	0
43	Morocco	1456	0
44	Norway	1451	0
45	Czech Rep.	1446	0
46	Costa Rica	1439	0
46	Ghana	1439	0
48	Jamaica	1438	0
49	Bosnia and Herzegovina	1430	0
50	Scotland	1422	0
51	Egypt	1420	0

Rank	Country	Points	Chg
52	Hungary	1416	0
53	Cameroon	1413	0
54	Greece	1409	0
55	Qatar	1396	0
56	Mali	1389	0
56	Congo DR	1389	0
58	Finland	1386	0
59	Burkina Faso	1381	0
59	Bulgaria	1381	0
61	Côte d'Ivoire	1378	0
62	Honduras	1377	0
63	Ecuador	1368	0
64	Slovenia	1365	0
64	Montenegro	1365	0
66	Albania	1356	0
67	Saudi Arabia	1351	0
68	N Macedonia	1347	0
69	El Salvador	1346	0
70	Iraq	1344	0
71	United Arab Emirates	1334	0
71	South Africa	1334	0
73	Canada	1332	0
74	Guinea	1328	0
75	Bolivia	1324	0
76	China PR	1323	0
77	Uganda	1321	0
78	Cabo Verde	1318	0
79	Syria	1314	0
80	Curaçao	1313	0
81	Panama	1305	0
82	Oman	1303	0
83	Gabon	1297	0
84	Benin	1295	0
85	Uzbekistan	1286	0
86	Haiti	1285	0
87	Belarus	1283	0
88	Zambia	1279	0
89	Congo	1269	0
89	Lebanon	1269	0
91	Madagascar	1267	0
91	Georgia	1267	0
93	Israel	1260	0
94	Vietnam	1258	0
95	Cyprus	1251	0
96	Kyrgyz Republic	1240	0
97	Jordan	1238	0
98	Luxembourg	1236	0
99	Bahrain	1225	0
100	Mauritania	1223	0
101	Libya	1215	0
102	Armenia	1213	0
103	Palestine	1204	0
104	Estonia	1202	0
105	Trinidad and Tobago	1201	0
106	Mozambique	1200	0
107	Kenya	1199	0
108	India	1187	0
109	Central African Republic	1184	0
110	Faroe Islands	1181	0
111	Zimbabwe	1180	0
112	Niger	1179	0
113	Thailand	1178	0
114	Azerbaijan	1177	0
115	Kosovo	1174	0
116	Korea DPR	1170	0
117	Namibia	1160	0
118	Kazakhstan	1155	0
118	Sierra Leone	1155	0
118	Guinea-Bissau	1155	0
121	Tajikistan	1152	0
122	New Zealand	1149	0
123	Malawi	1141	0
124	Philippines	1136	0
124	Angola	1136	0
126	Antigua and Barbuda	1127	0
126	Togo	1127	0
128	Sudan	1112	0
129	Turkmenistan	1107	0
130	Guatemala	1104	0
131	Lithuania	1089	0
131	Rwanda	1089	0
133	Comoros	1088	0
134	Tanzania	1086	0
135	Andorra	1082	0
136	Myanmar	1081	0
137	Latvia	1079	0
138	Chinese Taipei	1078	0
139	Lesotho	1074	0
139	St Kitts and Nevis	1074	0
141	Suriname	1073	0
141	Solomon Islands	1073	0
143	Hong Kong	1072	0
144	Yemen	1071	0
145	Equatorial Guinea	1066	0
146	Ethiopia	1061	0
147	Kuwait	1060	0
148	Botswana	1055	0
149	Afghanistan	1052	0
149	Burundi	1052	0
151	Nicaragua	1051	0
152	Liberia	1047	0
153	Eswatini	1042	0
154	Malaysia	1040	0
155	Maldives	1038	0
156	New Caledonia	1035	0
157	Singapore	1020	0
158	Dominican Republic	1019	0
159	Gambia	1015	0
159	Grenada	1015	0
161	Tahiti	1014	0
162	Barbados	1009	0
163	Fiji	996	0
163	Vanuatu	996	0
165	Papua New Guinea	991	0
166	Guyana	988	0
167	St Vincent and the Grenadines	986	0
168	South Sudan	983	+1
168	Bermuda	983	0
170	Nepal	974	0
170	Belize	974	0
172	Mauritius	965	0
173	Indonesia	964	0
173	Cambodia	964	0
175	Moldova	959	0
176	St Lucia	953	0
177	Chad	943	0
178	Puerto Rico	941	0
179	Cuba	936	0
180	Liechtenstein	926	0
181	São Tomé and Príncipe	923	0
182	Macau	922	0
183	Montserrat	921	0
184	Malta	919	0
184	Djibouti	919	0
184	Dominica	919	0
187	Bangladesh	914	0
188	Laos	912	0
189	Bhutan	911	0
190	Mongolia	906	0
191	Brunei Darussalam	904	0
192	American Samoa	900	0
193	Cayman Islands	897	0
194	Samoa	894	0
195	Bahamas	880	0
196	Timor-Leste	879	0
196	Gibraltar	879	0
196	Somalia	879	0
199	Guam	873	0
200	Aruba	867	0
200	Pakistan	867	0
202	Seychelles	866	0
203	Tonga	862	0
203	Turks and Caicos Islands	862	0
205	Eritrea	856	0
206	Sri Lanka	853	0
207	US Virgin Islands	844	0
208	British Virgin Islands	842	0
209	San Marino	824	0
210	Anguilla	821	0

FIFA/COCA-COLA WOMEN'S WORLD RANKING 2020

The United States have been the dominant force in women's international football ever since winning the first FIFA Women's World Cup in 1991, and they led the ranking between their 2019 triumph in France and the moment international football was suspended because of the COVID-19 pandemic.

The ranking at that point featured a record 159 teams, underlining the steady rise in quality and development of the women's game around the world. The USA have been top for most of the 17 years since the FIFA/Coca-Cola Women's World Ranking was introduced in March 2003. A unique feature is that the ranking is founded on a base created in 1971 that saw the first national-team match – between France and the Netherlands – recognised by world football's governing body. Another difference by comparison with the men's ranking system is that the table is published only four times every year rather than monthly. This reflects the comparatively less intense schedule for women's national teams.

RANKING

Pos.	Country	Pts	(+/-)
1	United States	2181	0
3	Germany	2090	0
3	France	2036	+1
4	Netherlands	2032	−1
5	Sweden	2007	0
6	England	1999	0
7	Australia	1963	0
8	Brazil	1958	+1
8	Canada	1958	0
10	Korea DPR	1940	+1
11	Japan	1937	−1
13	Norway	1930	0
13	Spain	1915	0
14	Italy	1889	0
15	China PR	1867	0
16	Denmark	1851	0
17	Belgium	1819	0
18	Korea Republic	1818	+2
19	Iceland	1817	−1
20	Switzerland	1815	−1
21	Scotland	1804	+1
23	Austria	1792	−1
23	New Zealand	1757	0
24	Russia	1708	0
25	Colombia	1700	0
26	Ukraine	1692	+1
27	Mexico	1686	−1
28	Poland	1683	+2
29	Czech Republic	1678	−1
30	Finland	1671	−2
31	Republic of Ireland	1666	+1
33	Portugal	1659	−1
33	Argentina	1659	+2
34	Wales	1658	0
35	Vietnam	1657	−3
36	Costa Rica	1644	+1
37	Chile	1640	−1
38	Nigeria	1614	+1
39	Thailand	1596	−1
40	Chinese Taipei	1589	0

41	Serbia	1558	0		81	Morocco	1289	0		123	Nicaragua	1116	-2

Rank	Country	Rating	Change	Rank	Country	Rating	Change	Rank	Country	Rating	Change
41	Serbia	1558	0	81	Morocco	1289	0	123	Nicaragua	1116	-2
43	Uzbekistan	1543	0	83	Guam	1282	-2	123	Cyprus	1114	-6
43	Hungary	1537	+2	83	Mali	1276	-1	123	Mongolia	1114	-2
44	Romania	1535	-1	84	Bahrain	1274	-1	125	Kosovo	1104	-3
45	Myanmar	1511	-1	85	Algeria	1271	-1	126	Armenia	1103	0
46	Papua New Guinea	1504	0	86	Faroe Islands	1259	-1	127	Suriname	1093	-4
47	Slovakia	1501	0	87	Senegal	1247	0	128	Singapore	1089	-4
48	Paraguay	1490	0	88	Tonga	1240	-2	129	North Macedonia	1072	-4
49	Slovenia	1471	+1	88	Cuba	1240	-2	130	Gabon	1066	-4
50	Jamaica	1460	+1	90	Malaysia	1238	-2	131	St Kitts and Nevis	1050	-4
51	Cameroon	1455	-2	91	Bolivia	1236	-2	133	Tajikistan	1035	-4
53	Croatia	1453	0	93	Moldova	1228	-2	133	American Samoa	1030	-4
53	Belarus	1434	0	93	Latvia	1223	-2	134	Bangladesh	1008	-4
53	South Africa	1434	+2	94	Indonesia	1222	-2	135	Barbados	1002	-4
55	Northern Ireland	1432	+1	95	Estonia	1210	-1	136	Bermuda	987	-4
55	India	1432	+2	96	New Caledonia	1208	-3	137	Kenya	986	-4
57	Venezuela	1425	+1	97	United Arab Emirates	1201	-1	138	St Lucia	982	-4
58	Jordan	1419	+1	97	Montenegro	1201	-3	139	Tanzania	978	-4
59	Bosnia and Herzegovina	1411	+2	99	Nepal	1200	-2	140	Sri Lanka	968	-4
60	Ghana	1401	0	100	Zambia	1198	6	141	Lebanon	967	-4
60	Panama	1401	-7	101	Malta	1197	-2	143	Maldives	966	-4
63	Greece	1396	0	103	Tahiti	1196	-4	143	Namibia	956	-4
63	Côte d'Ivoire	1392	0	103	Cook Islands	1194	-3	144	Rwanda	899	-4
64	Haiti	1391	+4	104	Congo	1178	-3	145	Malawi	887	-4
65	Peru	1376	-1	105	Dominican Republic	1173	-3	146	Uganda	868	-4
66	Fiji	1373	-1	106	Puerto Rico	1172	-3	147	Lesotho	850	-4
67	Philippines	1369	0	107	Lithuania	1169	-2	148	Botswana	848	-4
67	Israel	1369	-1	107	Samoa	1169	-3	149	US Virgin Islands	843	-4
69	Turkey	1365	0	109	El Salvador	1164	-2	150	Belize	824	-4
70	IR Iran	1358	0	110	Congo DR	1159	-2	151	Eswatini	822	-4
71	Equatorial Guinea	1356	0	111	Zimbabwe	1151	-2	153	Mozambique	814	-4
73	Trinidad and Tobago	1354	0	111	Ethiopia	1151	-2	153	Antigua and Barbuda	787	-4
73	Uruguay	1346	0	113	Gambia	1143	0	154	Bhutan	769	-4
74	Hong Kong	1329	0	114	Solomon Islands	1140	-2	155	Andorra	749	-4
75	Albania	1325	+2	115	Georgia	1138	-4	156	Comoros	731	-4
76	Azerbaijan	1321	-1	116	Honduras	1136	-3	157	Aruba	724	-4
77	Kazakhstan	1318	-1	117	Vanuatu	1131	-3	158	Madagascar	691	-4
78	Tunisia	1304	0	117	Palestine	1131	-3	159	Mauritius	357	-4
79	Bulgaria	1303	-1	119	Luxembourg	1124	-3				
80	Guatemala	1290	-1	120	Kyrgyz Republic	1118	-2				
				121	Angola	1117	-2				

PICTURE CREDITS

The publishers would like to thank the following sources for their kind permission to reproduce the pictures in this book. The page numbers for each of the photographs are listed below, giving the page on which they appear in the book and any location indicator (C-centre, T-top, B-bottom, L-left, R-right).

Getty Images: 137T; /2010 Qatar 2022: 153TL; /AFP: 40BR, 48B, 73BL. 88BR, 101BR, 142BR, 174BL, 177T, 179BR; /AMA/Corbis: 52C; /ANP Sport: 51BL; /Suhaimi Abdullah: 116BL; /Luis Acosta/AFP: 95TL; /Burak Akbulut/Anadolu Agency: 75T; /Robin Alam/Icon Sportswire: 130B; /Allsport: 57L, 159TR, 173TR; /Vanderlei Almeida/AFP: 173BL, 196TR; /Vincent Amalvy/AFP: 103BR; /Anadolu Agency: 34B; /Odd Andersen/AFP: 25BR; /Mladen Antonov/AFP: 154TR; /The Asashi Shimbun: 16T; /Matthew Ashton/Corbis: 45BR, 65B, 87T, 133BR; /Matthew Ashton/AMA: 37TR, 126-127, 144BL, 147TR; /Marc Atkins: 200-201, 203TR; /Naomi Baker: 202B; /Gokhan Balci/Anadolu Agency: 105TR, 107TL; /Steve Bardens: 169R, 211TR; /Dennis Barnard/Fox Photos: 91L; /Lars Baron: 31TL, 46T, 53TR, 158-159, 192L, 208BR; /Robbie Jay Barratt/AMA: 14BR, 15C, 80, 147C, 169BL; /Farouk Batiche/AFP: 106B; /James Bayliss/AMA: 4BR; /Robyn Beck/AFP: 151TR; /Sandra Behne/Bongarts: 119L; /Benainous/Hounsfield/Gamma-Rapho: 17BR; /Bentley Archive/Popperfoto: 64R; /Martin Bernetti/AFP: 210T; /Bongarts: 28BL; /Shaun Botterill: 19TR, 19B, 47B, 149L, 157BL, 165TR; /Cris Bouroncle/AFP: 127BR, 189BR; /Gabriel Bouys/AFP: 32B, 108; /Chris Brunskill: 11R, 76TR, 90TR, 140T, 146BL, 170-171; /Clive Brunskill: 94T; /Simon Bruty: 99B; /Rodrigo Buendia/AFP: 88T; /David S Bustamante/Soccrates: 33TR, 71BR; /Giuseppe Cacace/AFP: 123BL, 181L; /David Cannon: 17L, 30T, 40TR, 61B; /Alex Caparros: 222; /Jean Catuffe: 48T, 49B; /Central Press: 63BL; /Central Press/Hulton Archive: 49TR; /Graham Chadwick: 61TC; /Matteo Ciambelli/NurPhoto: 44TR, 101T, 132TR; /Robert Cianflone: 67R, 69TL, 96T, 145TR; /Michal Cizek/AFP: 43BR; /Fabrice Coffrini/AFP: 116TR, 151C; /Chris Cole: 148R; /Phil Cole: 18BL, 43L; /Kevin C Cox: 141BR, 220; /Jonathan Daniel: 86TR; /Stephane de Sakutin/AFP: 154L; /Carl de Souza/AFP: 99T; /Adrian Dennis/AFP: 56TR, 82B, 144-145, 164L; /Khaled Desouki/AFP: 182R, 183L; /Disney/Central Press/Hulton Archive: 15BR; /Kevork Djansezian: 131TR; /Stephen Dunn: 109BR; /Johannes Eisele/AFP: 5BL, 40BL; /Paul Ellis/AFP: 20TR; /Elsa: 148BL, 204; /Darren England: 115BR; /Etzel Espinosa/Jam Media/LatinContent: 128B; /Jonathan Ferrey: 43TR; /Franck Fife/AFP: 98, 166B; /Julian Finney: 11BL, 157TL; /Stu Forster: 39BL, 41BR, 78TR, 88BL, 160TR; /Foto Olimpik/NurPhoto: 136; /Stuart Franklin: 95TR, 208R; /Sebastian Frej/MB Media: 218-219; /Romeo Gacad/AFP: 45TR; /Daniel Garcia/AFP: 96B, 146BC; /Paul Gilham: 111TR, 195T; /Patrick Gorski/Icon Sportswire: 131BL; /Rich Graessle/Icon Sportswire: 133BC; /Laurence Griffiths: 63R, 64BL, 113TR; /Alex Grimm: 55TR; /Jeff Gross: 133L; /Haraldur Gudjonsson/AFP: 137B; /Gianluigi Guercia/AFP: 185L; /Jack Guez/AFP: 55BC, 84-85; /Norman Hall/LatinContent: 177B; /Matthias Hangst: 6, 22TL, 152, 167C; /Matthias Hangst/Bongarts: 168TR; /Etsuo Hara: 100R, 193TL, 193BR; /Oliver Hardt/UEFA: 65R; /Ronny Hartmann/AFP: 74TR; /Alexander Hassenstein: 21R, 22B, 147BR, 198; /Richard Heathcote: 97B, 135R, 203L, 203BR; /Alexander Heimann/Bongarts: 132B; /Mike Hewitt: 90BL, 127TC; /Maja Hitij: 5TC, 207T, 207BR; /Simon Hofmann: 156, 212-213, 216BR, 217TL, 217B; /Boris Horvat/AFP: 29BL, 165B; /Harry How: 129C; /Arif Hudaverdi Yaman/Anadolu Agency: 74BL; /isifa: 69BR; /Dan Istitene: 25L; /Catherine Ivill: 16BL; /Karim Jaafar/AFP: 117L, 118B; /Yorick Jansens/AFP: 161TR; /Jose Jordan/AFP: 35L; /Jasper Juinen: 13TR, 33TL, 34TL, 35BR; /Sia Kambou/AFP: 110BL; /Sefa Karacan/Anadolu Agency: 32T; /Keystone: 17TC, 62R; /Keystone/Hulton Archive: 57BR; /Mike King: 146TR; /Glyn Kirk/AFP: 194B; /Attila Kisbenedek/AFP: 166TR; /Joe Klamar/AFP: 42BL; /Christof Koepsel/Bongarts: 100TL; /Mark Kolbe: 114TR, 115C; /Ozan Kose/AFP: 66B, 106TL; /Patrick Kovarik/AFP: 82TR; /Stanislav Krasilnikov/TASS: 62B; /Jan Kruger: 168BL; /David Leah/Mexsport: 128TR; /Christopher Lee: 69TR; /Fred Lee: 97T; /Eddy Lemaistre/Corbis: 26BL; /Bryn Lennon: 59BR; /Francisco Leong/AFP: 23C; /Matthew Lewis: 55L; /Christian Liewig/Corbis: 47C, 180, 183BR; /Alex Livesey: 4TR, 36BL, 45C, 50BL, 71T, 73C, 85R, 120, 150BL; /Marco Luzzani: 27B; /Marcio Machado/Eurasia Sport Images: 186-187; /Ian MacNicol: 14TL, 41TR, 58BR; /Pierre-Philippe Marcou/AFP: 35T, 109TL; /Nigel Marple: 125TR, 125BL; /Hunter Martin/LatinContent: 94BL; /Ronald Martinez: 205BL; /Clive Mason: 109TR, 142T, 160B; /Stephen McCarthy/Sportsfile: 58TR; /Eamonn McCormack: 199C; /Jamie McDonald: 42T, 59C, 70B, 72TR; /Anatoliy Medved/Icon Sportswire: 54C; /Marty Melville: 124B; /Buda Mendes: 190R; /Craig Mercer/CameraSport: 36R; /Aris Messinis/AFP: 164TR; /Aurelien Meunier: 131BR; /Maddie Meyer: 211BL; /Vincent Michel/Icon Sport: 210BR; /Jeff Mitchell: 191BR; /Jiro Mochizuki/Icon Sport: 103TR; /Brendan Moran/Sportsfile: 79B; /

Alex Morton: 188BR; /Dean Mouhtaropoulos: 10, 29T, 33B, 115TL, 197BL; /Peter Muhly/AFP: 59BL, 82TL; /Dan Mullan: 56BL, 141TL, 143BR; /Marwan Naamani/AFP: 123TR; /Hoang Dinh Nam/AFP: 130TR; /Francois Nel: 95BR, 112-113; /Mike Nelson/AFP: 127TR; /Alexander Nemenov/AFP: 134-135; /Fayez Nureldine/AFP: 123BR; /NurPhoto: 23TL; /Kiyoshi Ota: 117BR; /Werner Otto/ullstein bild: 163TL; /Jeff Pachoud/AFP: 162; /Minas Panagiotakis: 215BR; /Ulrik Pedersen/Action Plus: 12TR; /Valerio Pennicino: 100BL; /Frank Peters/Bongarts: 52BL; /Hannah Peters: 124TR; /Hrvoje Polan/AFP: 38BL; /Popperfoto: 13B, 18T, 20B, 38TR, 71BL, 91B, 92BL, 111C, 118TR, 122TR, 145TL, 163BR, 175BR, 176R, 209B; /Mike Powell: 153B; /Bruna Prado: 171C; /Savo Prelevic/AFP: 83C; /Craig Prentis: 129C; /Pressefoto Ulmer/ullstein bild: 83B, 167TR; /Adam Pretty: 93R; /Gary M Prior: 39TR; /Professional Sport/Popperfoto: 26TR; /Tullio Puglia: 214TR, 215TR, 216TR, 217L; /Ben Radford: 58L, 92T, 190BL, 214BR; /David Ramos: 41BL, 150TR; /Michael Regan: 77T, 79TR, 119T; /Kyle Rivas: 131TC; /Rolls Press/Popperfoto: 12B; /Clive Rose: 5L, 67L, 77BL, 143TL, 155TL; /Martin Rose: 17R, 21TL; /Martin Rose/Bongarts: 75BL; /Rouxel/AFP: 183R; /STR/AFP: 121TR; /Karim Sahib/AFP: 192BR; /Sampics/Corbis: 60TR; /Issouf Sanogo/AFP: 107BR, 110TR, 111BL; /Alexandre Schneider: 209T; /Rich Schultz: 95BL, 176B; /Antonio Scorza/AFP: 197C; /Abdelhak Senna/AFP: 184B, 185R; /Lefty Shivambu/Gallo Images: 181T, 182B; /Patrick Smith: 139TR; /Andreas Solaro/AFP: 25T; /Javier Soriano/AFP: 104, 139BL, 163TR; /Erwin Spek/Soccrates: 161L; /Cameron Spencer: 113B; /Jamie Squire: 105BR; /Michael Steele: 70TR; /Srdjan Stevanovic: 67T; /Boris Streubel: 21BL; /Henri Szwarc/Icon Sport: 68BL, 81L, 138T; /Mehdi Taamallah/NurPhoto: 149TR; /Pier Marco Tacca: 76B; /Bob Thomas: 24BR, 27TL, 51TR, 54R, 59TL, 61TR, 87B, 93L, 105BC, 119BR, 140BL, 147TL, 155R, 157R, 159BR, 195BL; /John Thys/AFP: 81B, 189L, 206BL; /Lucas Uebel: 92BR; /ullstein bild: 66TR; /VCG: 79L, 121BL; /VI Images: 5TL, 22R, 31B, 63T, 206R; /Robert van den Brugge/AFP: 37C; /Geert van Erven/Soccrates: 31BR; /Manan Vatsyayana/AFP: 129BR; /Eric Verhoeven/Soccrates: 29BR; /Claudio Villa: 83TR; /Visionhaus: 102-103, 178-179, 183T; /Hector Vivas: 135BR, 154BR; /Luke Walker: 199TL; /Ian Walton: 68TR, 184TR; /Lakruwan Wanniarachchi/AFP: 122B; /Koji Watanabe: 172B; /Charlotte Wilson/Offside: 37BL; /Antti Yrjonen/NurPhoto: 161BR; /Vittorio Zunino Celotto: 24T.

PA Images: 67BR, 174TR, 194TR; /Matthew Ashton: 30BL, 93TL; /Barry Coombs: 47TR; /DPA: 114BL, 138BL; /Paulo Duarte/AP: 57T; /Dominic Favre/AP: 72B; /Michel Gouverneur/Reporter: 191T; /Intime Sports/AP: 46BR; /Ross Kinnaird: 175TR; /Tony Marshall: 75R, 93TR, 189T; /Peter Robinson: 28T, 50R, 64T, 89B, 188T; /S&G and Barratts: 149BR; /SMG: 65L; /Scanpix Norway: 53TL; /Ariel Schalit/AP: 107C; /Sven Simon: 91TR; /Neal Simpson: 39BR, 60B, 73BR, 175BL; /Jon Super/AP: 205T; /Topham Picturepoint: 82R; /John Walton: 81TR, 89T.

Shutterstock: /360b: 179TC; /Anabela88: 171R; /BOLDG: 85BR; /Colorsport: 44BL, 78B; /FMStox: 11L; /Khvost: 113TC; /Panatphong: 159TC; /RaimaD: 179L; /Namig Rustamov: 11T; /Rvector: 179TR; /Marcelo Savao/EPA: 196BL; /Wikrom Kitsamritchai: 8-9; /Tond Van Graphcraft: 11C.

Wikimedia Commons: 53BL, 172TR.

Every effort has been made to acknowledge correctly and contact the source and/or copyright holder of each picture. Any unintentional errors or omissions will be corrected in future editions of this book.

ABOUT THE AUTHOR

Keir Radnedge has been covering football for more than 50 years. He has written countless books on the subject, from tournament guides to comprehensive encyclopedias, aimed at all ages. His journalism career included the Daily Mail for 20 years, as well as the Guardian and other national newspapers and magazines in the UK and abroad. He is a former editor of World Soccer, generally recognised as the premier English-language magazine on global football. In addition to his writing, Keir has been a regular foreign football analyst for all UK broadcasters. He scripted official films of the early World Cups and is chairman of the football commission of AIPS, the international sports journalists' association.

ACKNOWLEDGEMENTS

Special thanks to Aidan Radnedge for support and assistance and an incomparable insight into the most intriguing corners of the world game.